The Developmental Lens

The Developmental Lens

Published by IPBooks, Queens, NY
Online at: www.IPBooks.net

ISBN: 978-1-956864-27-4

The Developmental Lens

A New Paradigm for Psychodynamic Diagnosis and Treatment

by

Gwyneth Kerr Erwin, Ph.D., Psy.D.

International Psychoanalytic Books (IPBooks)

New York • http://www.IPBooks.net

Dedication

To my beloved, Bill

William O'Neil Erwin, Ph.D.
Husband, Father, Grandfather, Psychoanalyst, Friend

and

the family we created

Table of Contents

Preface

If you want to know "essence," go to "voice." A bedraggled, cliched word, until you have read this book. Dr. Gwyn Erwin not only has revitalized this word but instilled it with riveting theoretical girders elucidating its developmental origins. What is the "voice" about which Gwyn writes? Of what is it made? Does it really evolve with time? Look in the mirror and your voice-soul stares back. Chilling, comforting, foreign, familiar. This complexity underscores the importance of reading this book.

You might find it helpful to know that I am a fellow traveler. Gwyn and I are soul-siblings. We got birthed together, and years ago she found me my voice. Seriously, no exaggeration. It happened in the strangest way. I asked for her help with a book I was writing. My writing was filled with the clumsiest, least literary garbage. I tried and tried but couldn't do better. Lucky I had a day job as a psychiatrist.

One day the sky broke open. My unfailing guide, GKE, looked at me. Honest. That penetrating look in her eyes. "Steve, that's it. That's your voice." I love you, Gwyn, but you are truly crazy.

Crazy talk. No basis.

Still, she insisted.

My first recollection was that this thing she called "voice" was like a tattoo. It stuck to me—oddly, recalling this "voice-state of mind" was no trick. No need to obsessively repeat my formulation over and over and over as I need to do with most of my original ideas in order not to forget them. I couldn't escape it (my found "voice"). It was just there, given its origins, part of my "being."

So, here I am, with Gwyn's blessing, attempting to show how Gwyn helped me find my "voice." And, remarkable to me, my current Gwyn inspired book is my eighth.

In her wonderful book, all 300 plus pages of it, Gwyn explains where one's voice comes from, how it develops, and why it holds (no matter how hard you may work to get rid of or even modify it). She goes further and ties disruptions in the developmental process to trauma. For voice to develop, indelible memory traces accumulate to form internal templates. The precursors are implanted in one's psyche and disseminate. At once, voice haunts and slowly becomes the celebrated core of one's identity. One's salvation.

Gwyn's Seven Keystones carefully follow both physical and psychological development culminating in the development of a "self." Watch your grandchildren as they move from the "wa-wa" stage, where everything is stimulus and indecipherable, to fussing about toilet training, to sweet sixteen parties and marijuana. This is the big picture, but what is happening underneath? Gwyn knows and tells you in this book. And she is expert at identifying what may go wrong within each of her "keystone" categories. She uses "trauma" as a central organizing principal of these unwelcomed developments. Sand in the gears messing everything up. Development is no longer smooth.

This is why her "keystones" (imperfectly reiterated here in colloquial language) involving psychological and neurological maturation are so important. They provide technical guidance. Otherwise, distorted development is easily attributed to a bad teacher, a disabling illness, betrayal by one or more "best" friends. There is where inference about the cause of a child's problems backfires (all guess work, little validation). Briefly the "keystones" are established bedrocks of development. They include, states, memory, internal regulation potentially locked in through a process involving a mental mechanism called identification, emotional (affect) regulation (a potential problem for both adults and kids), secure attachment (aka good, reliable relationships), hemispheric development (neurological maturation that includes creativity and disciplined thinking). All these dimensions work together and complicate the assessment of a child's developmental status.

Now is the time for me to leave it to you as you read and Gwyn as she teaches. She is a master theoretician and writer, penning with sophistication and pizzazz that will keep you engrossed.

—Steven Frankel, MD, FACP, DFAPA

Introduction

A New Paradigm for Contemporary Psychodynamic Practice

I was a senior candidate in psychoanalytic training having arranged to bring a world-renowned, highly published analyst to our Institute for six months of advanced case consultations. Two months into our process, I had the opportunity to present my case, eager, but now cautious. As these weeks had unfolded, I found myself mentally questioning such an astute clinician: for all the boldness of his writing, he was a traditionalist. He was also arrogant and impatient. I was disappointed but was sure, it must be me.

Each of the four weeks as I presented, he spoke a language with which I was intimately familiar, but which felt 'off'. Finally, at the end of week three's session, I swallowed hard against the lump forming in my throat (oh, no, I was NOT going to become my six-year-old self with my father in the living room about to ask me a question for which I had no answer!), and asked him, "But what about her earliest history? And her young childhood? What about all we know now about the consequences of early trauma? And infant research?"

He laughed. "You western analysts, you don't know what you're talking about. Not like the Europeans. Infant research? Interesting, but irrelevant!"

Another didactic instructor was acclaimed as an expert in early ("primitive") states. He was sure of himself and insistent. He chastised my fellow candidate presenting with, "You are doing supportive psychotherapy! If you are not interpreting the negative infantile transference at every possible moment, you are not doing analysis!"

Other instructors were ego psychologists, object relationists, self-psychologists, interpersonal, intersubjective, or relational analysts. They had their vantage points, their theoretical perspectives. They formulated interpretations based on the transference taking place; they eschewed any deep exploration of their own countertransference, at least not in the patient's presence, nor even agreed on what defined it. Developmental theory was a review of developmental thoughts of previous theory-makers. But none of these instructors brought developmental relevance to what went on 'in the room': the psychodynamic relationship, the frame, boundaries and provisions, interpretation, intervention, insight and working through, promoting that insight in and of itself produced results, especially when it was the analyst's insight.

I wondered then, *Why can analysis take place only on the couch? What about the analyst's gaze? What about the patient seeing and being seen in that gaze?* (I knew what I had needed.) *What about the patient's voice?* (My voice choked routinely on the lump in my throat.) *Was the analyst's interpretative stance the only authority? What about partnership, collaboration? What about those earliest years?*

Harriet Strachstein was an innovator in her time: a New York analyst trained at the New School. I was 23 years old and doing everything I could to put one foot in front of the other, while maintaining a polished, high functioning presence in my world. Despite her innovations, we met four times a week, me, on the couch, with two group analysis sessions additionally. They terrified me. In our first individual session, she asked, "Why are you seeking analysis?"

I answered simply: "I have lived from crisis to crisis for as long as I can remember, none of them of my making until college, but all my responsibility to handle." Tears formed, and my mouth twisted; there was that damn lump gathering.

"How could you have lived from crisis to crisis?" she asked, raising her eyebrows. "You are so young."

Exactly.

Then she asked for my earliest memory, which I had always remembered, though I was no more than 14 months old at best. I could tell she doubted the story. I did not, I *knew* it was true; there was also too much to substantiate it, with far more to come, more that I only dared to glimpse. Telling my memory would be the last time we delved into my first three years of life. My six-year analysis was deemed a "success," focusing on the Oedipal forward, assuming a good enough first three years, just like Freud. In year four, Harriet said to me one day, "I want you to work with my brother, for about a year. Then you can come back." Her brother, a prominent and highly esteemed analyst, was Alexander Wolf, one of the primary proponents of group analysis in the United States. I cried, shaking my head back and forth, words barely able to squeak out of my mouth. What was there was a whispered protest, "*No! I can't!*"

The next Wednesday, being the good girl I was, I was in the waiting room of his Fifth Avenue home office, shivering, unable to get warm. His welcoming smile could not dispel the chill. I spent fifty painful minutes, trying without success to talk, the lump in my throat squeezing breaths out of me, tears streaming down my face. The second session on Thursday was the same. He waited and waited. Monday, after another impossible fifteen minutes, I managed a tortured whisper, "Dr. Wolf, you are really nice, but I can't do this. I need to go back to Harriet," pointing over my right shoulder.

"Just a minute, I'll be right back." He did come right back, with his overcoat. "C'mon. Let's go for a walk."

WHAT? This was not proper!!

I was silent as we stepped into and rode down in the elevator. I followed him, mute, as we crossed the street, in the *middle* of the street, darting around a taxi, sidestepping a bus, into Central Park. My imagination ran amuck:

murder, rape, death, nearly sure things in any improbable order. "Let's just walk, and if you want to say something I'll listen," he said. " If not, I might talk. I like to talk. We'll just notice things, together."

We did that for a year, five days a week, even in the rain, and heat, and snow. And I, without ever actually acting so was a metaphorical two-three- or six-year-old, running, or skipping, or strolling ahead, or to the side, and bringing to him (through conversation) my symbolic nuggets (bugs or flowers or rocks or crumbling leaves or snowflakes). In my inner world I held his hand, or looked up into his face, wondering, asking, hearing. I talked, and he listened. Sometimes, he talked, and I listened. I was with a dad/man/analyst who was immensely and protectively interested in me. Because of him, I began to find my voice. And I did not know how I would leave him, but at year's end, I went back to Harriet to "graduate" (the word "terminate" was unheard of!) two years later. And even though neither he nor she ever talked about anything that happened in the first three years of my life, each assuming the good enough stance, me not brave or confident enough to challenge the idea, my development began to change. Because of him and our analytic walks, a few years later, I would be able to marry the man I had one date with and married ten days later, forty-nine years ago.

But those first three years of my life and the roll of crises that came after them haunted me every day, and it would be sixteen years after my work with Harriet Strachstein and her brother, when I would find Dr. Jane Wagner, the analyst who knew the significance of early development that ultimately transformed my life and who partnered me into becoming fully me.

In the years since, I have conceptualized, designed, and taught most of the Developmental Classes at the southern California psychoanalytic training institute where I trained. I supervise candidates in training, who are eager, sometimes desperate, to know what to do when they are confronted routinely with the portrayal of the early needs of their patients. I work with individual patients of all ages, couples and families, adolescents and children, some once a week, some five times a week, and while I never cloak them in a developmental mantel, they lead me there, session after session after session.

I carry great respect for my colleagues. I also embody the many relevant aspects of a variety of theory making from those significant, sometimes brilliant, trailblazers who have come before me. I have found over years of training and research that they each struggled to understand *how the psyche develops*. I do, too.

There are three repetitive refrains that I hear, which disturb and sadden me. The first, a whimper, now almost a cliché, is that *psychoanalysis is dead (or that 10 sessions of CBT is the 'cure' that insurance will cover)*. This is said by those who do not understand the dynamic process or are unaware of the effective changes that have been achieved in contemporary psychoanalytic work, who wonder why it takes so long, and who are among those who join with the money brokers of our society, managed care and the insurance companies, to proclaim the magic is in a pill, or a cocktail of pills, or in various kinds of Brief Therapy. They hold the antiquated picture of a rather distant, at times perhaps bemused, but mostly somber visage, sitting behind a couch, a veritable "blank screen," posed in evenly hovering attention formulating interpretations, which are meant to be curative. A caricature, to be sure, but one that is potent. Current day therapists of every ilk, and the university graduate programs that train them, barely mention Freud, let alone his psychological descendants, but if they do, it is in statements of barely disguised irreverence and often a scoff! *You do psychoanalysis?*

The second refrain nips at the heels of the first: *What is psychoanalysis?* (for heaven's sake!) And psychoanalysts compete to answer: It is *not* what the relationists do (except to the relationists)! It is what only the classicists still do. No, the intersubjectivists! Certainly, the Europeans! Or is it the Brazilians? But not the Japanese, where provision, before the need is even felt, is the name of the game. Most agree, psychoanalysis *is* the work of the unconscious, the structure and the boundaries of the frame and the analytic relationship, the process of the fundamental rule, transference, with countertransference handled by the analyst's analysis, asymmetry and semantic language taking the lead in the talking cure. How many would say it is Developmental?

The third refrain barks at clinicians and a suffering patient population: *Psychoanalysis is not an effective treatment for trauma.* Sigmund Freud (1893/1955, with Josef Breuer) had it right one hundred and twenty-nine years ago:

> In traumatic neuroses the operative cause of the illness is not the trifling physical injury but the affect of fright—the psychical trauma.... Any experience which calls up distressing affects—such as those of fright, anxiety, shame or physical pain—may operate as a trauma of this kind.... It not infrequently happens that, instead of a single, major trauma, we find a number of partial traumas forming a group of provoking causes. These have only been able to exercise a traumatic effect by summation and they belong together in so far as they are in part components of a single story of suffering.... We must presume rather that the psychical trauma—or more precisely the memory of the trauma—acts like a foreign body which long after its entry must continue to be regarded as an agent that is still at work (p. 6).

Daniel Siegel (1999) said much the same thing:

> The emotional suffering, the stress-induced damage to cognitive functioning, the internal chaos of intrusive implicit memories, and the potential interpersonal violence created as a result of trauma produce ripple effects of devastation across the boundaries of time and human

> lives (p. 60).... Lack of resolution of traumatic events or loss from the past directly affects [current] emotional experience (p. 111).

Psychoanalysis and psychodynamic psychotherapy, as *thought* to be practiced, appears to many like a very long road through these internal minefields, and the therapeutic relationship as at some remove. But early psychoanalysis was offered mainly for traumatic sequelae, unfortunately called hysterical neurosis, while contemporary psychodynamic work has its practitioners who work with trauma in fresh and highly effective ways.

What I define as unresolved trauma is experience that was originally intense, had duration, and was repeated, without intervention. Such trauma is not only of events (although it can be), but cumulative and relational, occurring over years, usually in insidious ways. While many individuals function at a high level of success and accomplishment, such trauma inhabits them, forcing them to operate in these exhausting minefields, with the slightest whiff today provoking the same intensity as the originating experiences, often beyond understanding as to why they are having such powerful reactions to seemingly insignificant prompts. These stalwart individuals may seek out various treatments, or they may simply trudge on, coping with the fallout by themselves.

Am I just a rebel who disagrees with these negative refrains? Am I so disillusioned that I throw out analytic theory and practice? Not at all. In fact, I could claim myself as an object relationist, who finds true the power of the inner world, and as an interpersonalist or intersubjectivist (and who does know the difference), who experiences the relevance and veracity of a two-or-three-person psychology, yet who also experiences (impossible, many would say!) that the other has his or her own mind, and I have mine. I am relational, yet spend fruitful time with patients in silence, slowly, carefully following their leads. What I am *not* is an analyst who thinks that interpretation (mine especially) is the only avenue that leads to cure. Instead, I discover and re-discover that it is the patient's interpretations (gathered together over weeks or months or years) that lead to shared insight, and of even greater importance that such deep and alive understanding is then used in the brave and active service of working through—healing and change.

The Developmental Lens has at its heart a three-fold purpose: one, to offer a new developmental paradigm that I have conceptualized as the Seven Keystones of Healthy Development; two, to demonstrate how and what compromises healthy development as the result of environmental gaps, failures, and unresolved trauma, whether acute or cumulative and relational; and three, to provide innovative and creative ways of working with repair and healing for transformed development. Early trauma haunts our patients, as well as the years that piled on after that, and they yearn for freedom from the consequences of their unresolved trauma. They want to live, fully and now, before it is too late. The *Developmental Lens* partners them, and their therapists, in finding the way.

Ultimately, what I *am*, without using it as a template I impose on patients, or on other clinicians, is a contemporary Developmental Psychoanalyst: someone who has found a profound appreciation for the developmental forces, healthy and traumatic, which play out within our patients. These forces have beginnings and continuations in the profound repercussions that insert themselves into our patients' everyday psyches and lives. I, and they, lean into the stories they ache to tell to find the intricate narrative threads that are still weaving their influences today. But more, people come to us in their suffering to heal, to change, and to continue to develop. That is why I practice psychoanalysis. That is why I am writing this book.

Part One

Through the Developmental Looking Glass

Model I The Seven Keystones of Healthy Development

Healthy Development of the Essential Self

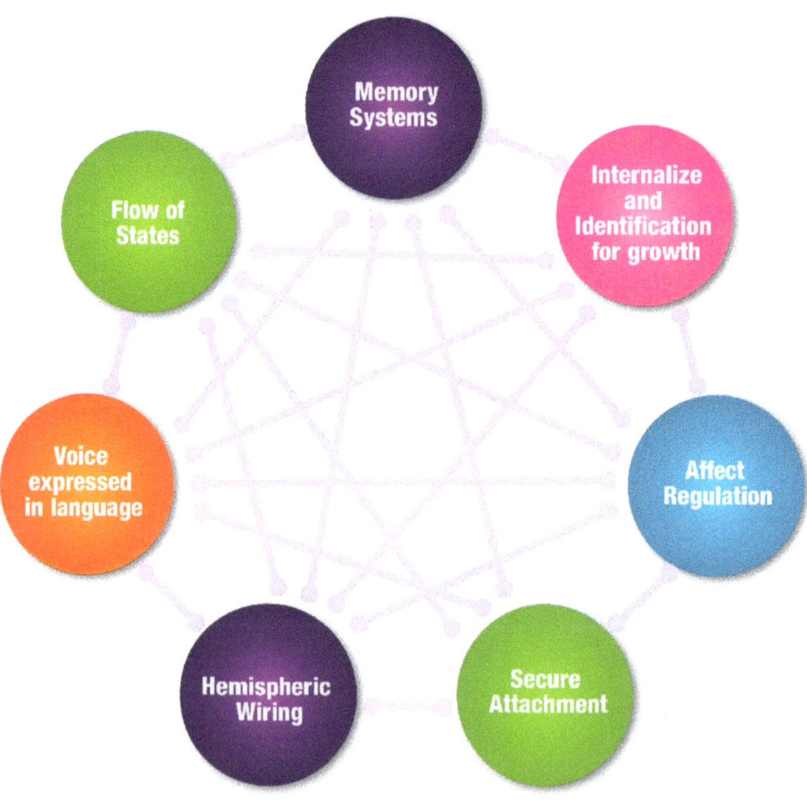

MODEL I - the Essential Self ©Gwyneth Kerr Erwin, 2001

The Seven Keystones

To grasp the complexity and significance of what comprises development, I use the analogy of a juggler who rotates flexible poles to keep the plates on their tips spinning in synchrony, fast enough not to topple off, but not so fast as to sail off into the air and shatter upon the ground below. Theoretically, I conceptualized and designed a new "Model of Healthy Development" (Erwin, 2000, 2005) of our burgeoning selves, development that is achieved through the successful integration of seven foundational and interdependent keystones. Each keystone influences the others, so just as when the juggler loses the necessary balanced motion causing one or more plates to topple or fall, a deficit in one area of our development affects the development in the others. This model captures both the linearity of each aspect as it 'comes on board' and the dynamic interrelationship between them.

We could argue that in this linearity of The Model of Healthy Development, there is a beginning keystone and an order to those following. As I originally conceived and worked to design this Model, I changed my mind any number of times as to which comes 'first.' I finally chose STATES because, in my thinking, it spoke best of the developing infant's earliest (even in utero), and most foundational lived experience. I then determined the order of the others based on how a baby's experience unfolds, physiologically, neurologically, mentally, and emotionally. But the non-linear, dynamic nature of these keystones needs as close attention because of the intimate influence each has upon the other. As we comprehend the weighty nature of these keystones, we can first glimpse how each one is pivotal to the healthful growth of our *essential selves,* as well as of our *sense of self,* and then understand the impact of trauma upon every one of them.

CHAPTER ONE

Our Essential Selves

An evolving life swims in an amniotic sea, her needs for nourishment and warmth and growth met without even having to be felt. Her experience is in the ever-present, no past, no future, just being. Still, she is impacted by the outside world. Loud sounds make her tremble and her heart beat faster. After the seventh month in utero when her fetus' eyes open, she can notice the "reddish shimmer" of light that passes through the mother's abdominal wall. At this point, weighing only about a pound, she begins gaining weight at a rate of nearly half a pound a week. *Every single minute*, two hundred and fifty thousand nerve cells are being created, further developing her brain. By forty weeks, she is filling the space; no more somersaults, just elbows and knees and tiny fists nudging the uterine walls (for the preceding, see Nilsson, 1990).

Something new is happening. At first, it is a tightening, some sense of pressure, then release. Hours later, the tightening becomes a series of squeezes; movement is slow, but intensifying. Her environment is pressing harder against her, the contractions interspersed with only minutes of rest. Stress hormones, adrenaline and noradrenaline, are secreted, their amount never to be equaled again in external life, offsetting her oxygen deficiency during contractions with adrenaline shock and preparing her for breathing through her lungs.

Then, a gush. The sea parts, whooshing away. A hard push. A thrust. Her universe shrinks; the space is so small. Force propels her down. Someone's skilled hands cradle and draw her head forward and out. A twist, a turn.

Another twist. One shoulder is free. Then the other. In an instant, her body wriggles out, and her chest expands. She gasps in air and, with singular presence, lets out a cry, an emergency cry intended to expel any fluids from her lungs and allow her to suck in oxygen (see Ribble, 1943). That first cry signals the voice of her essential self: *I am. I feel. I need.*

In moments, her bloodstream is re-directed; the heart's hole in the partition between the atria becomes sealed. Her eyes blink against the light. She cannot comprehend the doctor's announcement, "It's a healthy girl!" She does not feel the cut of the cord—her lifeline till now to her mother—after its pink blush fades to white, and it is clamped. She does not know yet that it is her father who stands over her, his mouth ovaling at the sight of her wriggling and squirming, nor can she know that her mother's soft crying of relief and joy are for her.

She is wiped and wrapped, then the one who stood over her seems to float her through space. She does not know that he cannot remember ever seeing anything as small and fragile as she. That he cannot imagine ever feeling anything but love for her, ever getting angry, ever hurting her, ever telling her she is anything but beautiful and strong and wondrous.

In the first moments after birth, as her efforts are exerted toward learning to breathe, something so nearly like her own skin brushes her cheek. Arms fold around her, her first response to this touch being respiratory (see Ribble, 1943). Now her mouth purses and makes suckling motions. It opens all by itself, searching; her head wobbles. There is something, someone she needs as much as life itself, something she had. *Where is it?* Her nose scrunches up as her lips form around the precious object, the muscles of her mouth and throat working hard. It slips away. She bleats, as if to say, *Where did it go? How can I get it back?*

A crooning voice weaves through the air to her, "It's right here." The object appears again, like magic. Her mouth grabs hold, sucks harder. *It is mine.* She does not know that her mother's tears have become bubbles of cooing, nor of the sweep of awe that has caught her father. But there is something so familiar, something she belongs to. Her tiny eyelids flutter and close, as she swims in a waking dream. She has been born for thirty minutes. She recognizes the scent of the one who holds her, hears the voice she already knows, even though she does not understand the words, nor even that there are such things as words to be spoken: "Danielle," her mother whispers. "Her name is Danielle."

Like Danielle, when we are born, each of us already has a particular temperament, the *nature* part of us: we may be placid and readily calmed; we may be hyper-sensitive and quickly over-aroused; we may be active and curious; we may be hypo-sensitive and need to be wooed; we may be easily distressed and difficult to soothe (see Greenspan, 1995). Those who care for us have a significant dual function to provide, what Martin James (1960), called 'a protective barrier', within a nourishing and sheltering environment, the *nurture* part of us. One aspect of this function is for caregivers to '*bring in*': to track and attune to what we, as infants, need at any particular moment and to find ways of providing this care, to soothe and calm, as well as to interest us. The other aspect of this function is for our caregivers to '*keep out*' what could be overwhelming to our young nervous systems, to know what could be impinging or noxious. "The mother, especially, through her devoted attunement, will intuitively learn to anticipate and divert almost all stimulation reaching her baby or ration it so that it is enough but not too much… [acting] as an auxiliary ego and sav[ing] the baby from both under-and-over-stimulation and from premature development of its own resources" (p. 290). Optimally, this nurturance and protection fits our individual temperaments, supporting the development of our intrinsic beings, not forcing us through intrusions or neglect to make such fundamental accommodations that we begin to lose our core essential self.

As infants, to survive *and* thrive, we must learn at an amazing pace, adapting to a multitude of sensations, as well as the urges and impulses of *needs* we never before have had to manage. We are not the same creatures 'on land' as we were in our amniotic sea. We are disorganized, unable to control much of anything about ourselves, and utterly dependent. We learn about physical and emotional nourishment from what and how we are fed: are we held close in someone's caring arms, rocked and whispered to, or are we left in a bed or carrier, a bottle propped precariously in our mouths? We learn through the smells of our environment: the fragrance of our own and our parents' bodies being lovingly attended to, or the sour smell of their neglect. Long before comprehending a single word, we learn about the safety or the danger of our immediate worlds through the soothing or jarring sounds around us: the murmuring voices offering comfort or the shouting voices that frighten. We learn through our primary sense organ, our skin, from the ways we are touched and handled. Our need for close bodily contact is so compelling that without it we become withdrawn or depressed. And we learn through our images of sight, especially by means of that special gaze between our primary caregivers and ourselves, the purest expression of relating. That look of abiding affection and interest draws our attention. Our enlivened and returned gaze creates pleasure and deep emotions in our parents. As they communicate their delight back to us through the gleam in their eyes that is *for* us alone, our sense of value is enhanced (see Greenspan, 1997a).

Throughout our pivotal early years, our parent(s) are key to our learning to self-regulate. Our enthusiastic explorations as toddlers are necessary in helping us differentiate ourselves as individuals, but we do not yet have the development in brain or body to recognize danger or keep ourselves safe, let alone consider appropriate social behavior. Our parent's ability to engage us as *valued* little beings when they fully enjoy our burgeoning selves or repair the inevitable breaches between us that cautionary signals or disapprovals cause will help us eventually learn how to explore *and* be safe, how to interact in collaborative ways, how to take emotional stands *and* learn when to compromise, as well as to self-regulate our negative physiological and emotional affect *and* augment our positive states.

So begins the lifelong process of our development.

CHAPTER TWO

Keystone One—States of Being

States comprise the vital inner landscape in which we live. As we have just seen, they are formed beginning in utero and continue to be shaped, clustered, bridged, or dissociated throughout our lives. Everything we experience is state dependent, meaning that whatever states we are in that have intensity, duration, and repetition impact everything that comes after. Frank Putnam (1997), one of the leading theorists and researchers about states, defined a state as "a condition of being" (p. 151). While Putnam's fuller description of states was nuanced, he was always referring to "...the concept of a discrete state of consciousness as a specific and unique configuration of a set of psychological, physiological, and behavioral variables... [this] concept of 'state' is encountered at all levels of brain-mind analysis" (p. 152-153). Daniel Siegel's (1999/2011) definition expanded our understanding, as he suggested that, "A state of mind can be proposed to be a pattern of activation of recruitment systems within the brain responsible for (1) perceptual bias, (2) emotional tone and regulation, (3) memory processes, (4) mental models, and (5) behavioral response patterns.... One can discover the elements of an individual's state of mind by focusing on the elements of her perceptions, feelings, thoughts, memories, attitudes, beliefs, and desires—and how these may be influencing her behavior and interactions with others" (p. 211).

I have expanded this understanding of states as a *unique blend* of what I determined to be eight aspects of lived experience (Erwin, 2014):

- Attachments patterns
- Memory
- Physiological Sensation
- Emotion
- Belief systems
- Perceptual Bias
- Voice and Language
- Behavior

A State is NOT any one of these aspects INDIVIDUALLY but a gathering together of all eight of these aspects, which in their aggregate profoundly affects cognitive functioning:

- A State is NOT ONLY how we attach to people and experience, but our attachment experiences heavily govern our States.
- A State is NOT ONLY what we remember or experience as living memory but is organized around those early, embedded memory systems.
- A State is NOT ONLY what we feel in our bodies, but our physical sensations are determinant factors in our States.
- A State is NOT ONLY emotional affect or mood but contains emotional affect or mood.
- A State is NOT ONLY what we believe but incorporates our beliefs (see mental representations).
- A State is NOT ONLY the perceptions that we bring to new experience but is influenced deeply by perceptions carved out by our historical experiences.
- A State is NOT ONLY our personal voice and the words we use to express that voice, but our personal voice and language are altered depending upon the State that we are in.

- A State is NOT ONLY determinant of our behavior, but our behavior emerges from the blend of all these factors.

A State is a powerful way of being and although we are born with only five states

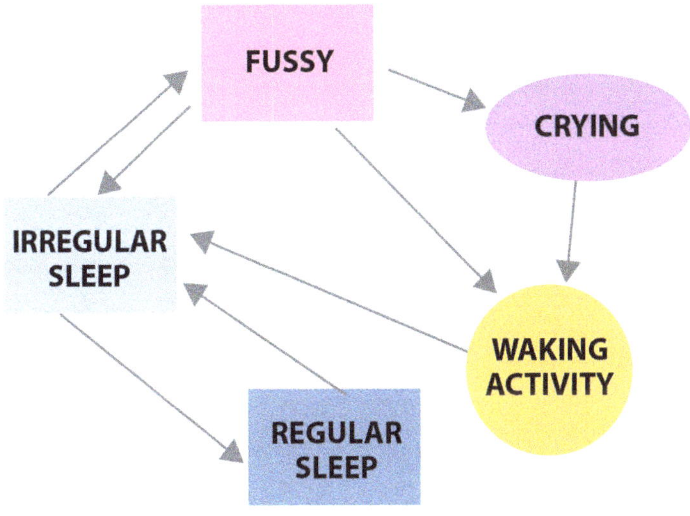

FIGURE A | BIRTH

(see Putnam, 1997, p. 151), we have many thousands of states by the time we are 18 months old: what Putnam called State Architecture, or Personality (p. 152).

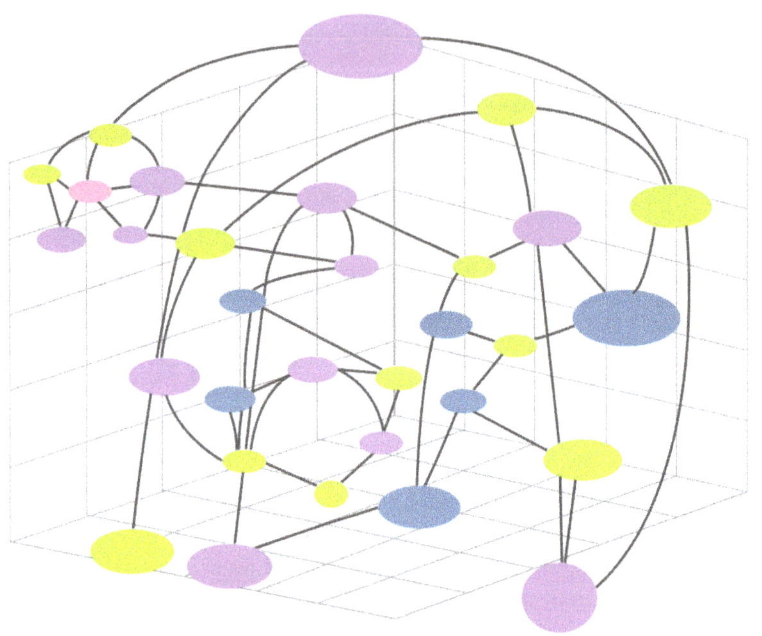

FIGURE B | 18 MONTHS

State Clusters

States do something very interesting: our mind forms them into clusters according to their 1) intensity, 2) duration, and 3) frequency. When a particular State has a great deal of energy (intensity) in it (positive or negative), and when it lasts a noticeable amount of time (duration), a new neuronal pathway fires in the brain. When it repeats (frequency), it is wired in the brain causing the brain in future experience to 'fire' in the same way as that original neuronal pathway when the neuronal pathway is provoked by a matching trigger. As time marches on, and particularly significant to trauma and Posttraumatic Stress Disorder (PTSD), and Complex Posttraumatic Stress Disorder (CPTSD, the same neuronal reaction can be elicited by even a "whiff" of the originating experience. When other States become associated with a specific state through likened experience, or by how other states respond to that experience, our brain then forms them into a cluster.

As an illustration, think of a solar system (your brain): in it, some stars are singular, others form constellations. A star is a "luminous sphere of plasma held together by its own gravity"… "while a… galaxy is an interstellar medium of gas and dust and dark matter… that is a massive, gravitationally bound system" (Wikipedia, 2006, p. 1). Similarly, in our brains, our States can gather into clusters, like stars. Some States are formed into a dense cluster, other clusters have just a few states, and some States are more singular or split off (what we call dissociated).

As we will see in Models II and III, the more environmental deficits or chronic trauma a child experiences, the less 'bridging' there is between states that help the brain communicate productively. The more a child's mind is confined to repetitive, destructive experience, the less emotional repertoire s/he has, and the more narrowly focused available brain energy becomes, making learning, problem-solving, and creativity difficult, if not impossible.

State Transitions

Moving or "switching" (Putnam, 1997, p. 156) from state to state or cluster to cluster is called a State Transition, and this activity usually unfolds according to what has been programmed neuronally in our brains.

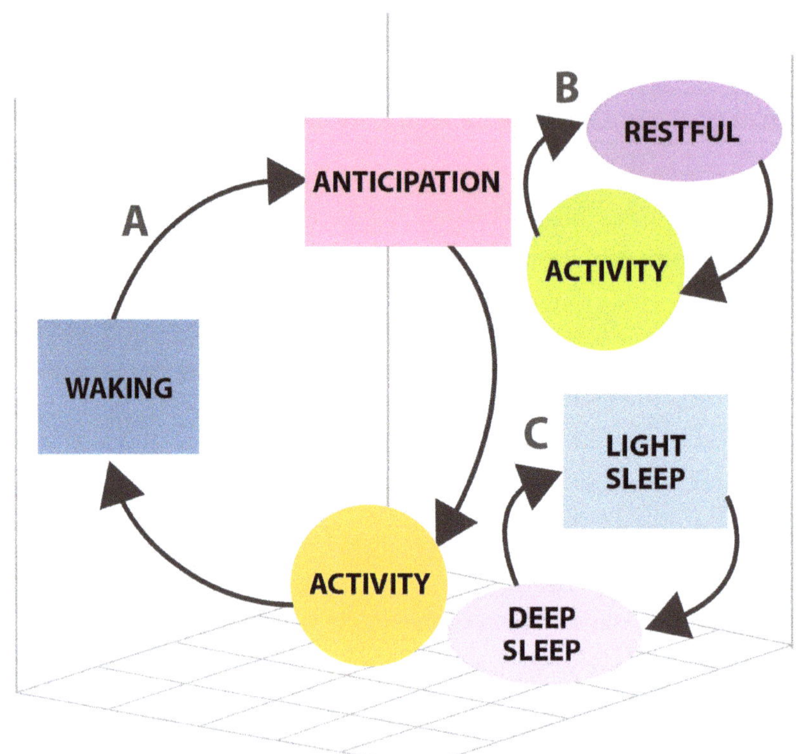

FIGURE C | SWITCHING

The ability to transition states smoothly is dependent on the bridging established in the brain, so the lack of a bridge makes moving from one cluster of states to another a challenging journey. Without such bridging, the traumatized individual becomes 'stuck', unable purposefully to shift into a different state with any kind of ease. The person may feel as though s/he has suddenly shown up in Albany, New York and does not know how to get back to Los Angeles. While this is always true of traumatic states, it can be true of Creative ones too, either because our experience of living in those Creative States was not made accessible environmentally or has been viscerally discouraged or prohibited. Additionally, we also may have had to use our imagination not for creative pursuits but for precocious problem-solving we were not yet ready for developmentally or for anticipating the next traumatic experience.

Because of their dynamic and lasting influence, one of the most significant things to understand about states is that they are 'use dependent' that is, "neurons that fire together, wire together" (Hebb's axiom, 1949, p. 70, see also Post & Weiss, 1997). Use dependency means that everything we experience, learn, and do is state dependent. Whether we are talking about learning, emotional regulation, attachment, implicit and explicit memory, brain development, knowledge, personal voice and language development, and physiological response, each is *use or state dependent* to varying degrees, both for their encoding and for their retrieval.

States are formed as the result of the impact of experience, but they also serve as *defenses* against the repetition of feared experience (see S. Freud, 1896/1955, A. Freud, 1936/1966, and Hopper, 1991). We can see that states are an essential ingredient in 'resistance': "as a dialectic between preservation and change—a basic need to preserve the continuity of self-experience in the process of growth by minimizing the threat of potential traumatization" (Bromberg, 1995, p. 174). This resistance is a state-defensive response to the danger feared in the "exposure of the private self" (Modell, 1991, p. 732).

Even the so-called 'negative' states we see in treatment are necessary when they provide a signal function for self-protection, for productive action, or for mourning. But engrained states become debilitating when they *prevent* the individual from acting in ways that are in his or her best interest, or *prevent* the resolution of problems, or when they influence *in distorted ways* how we perceive and what we expect from relational interactions, or when they are dysregulating, leaving us unable to self-soothe. These disabling states are retrieved through the triggering of what I call *implicit memory banks* (Erwin,

2000, 2005), and dictate, in spite of what we might choose for ourselves, how we behave, especially in self-destructive or self-diminishing ways. When we enter these engrained states, we live within them, not as a memory of the past, but as the reality of our current time experience.

Dissociation is a vital topic that will be more fully discussed especially as to its clinical relevance later in this book (see Chapter Thirteen), but for our purposes here, just as bridging makes possible the inter-and-cross-hemispheric communication needed to maximize brain function and knowledge, that is, *association*. Conversely, when a single state or a cluster of states has been psychologically and neuronally split off from access to other states or clusters of states an individual cannot purposefully access a desired state or cluster, that is, *dissociation*.

In healthy development, states are necessary for the "going-on-being" (Winnicott, 1949/9175, p. 145) of the individual. In my view, psychological health is the coherency of the essential self as it flows among diverse affective, physiological, mental, and behavioral states of being across time and within state space (Erwin, 2001, see also Putnam, 1997, p. 161). One of the greatest challenges in therapy is accessing fractured states in ways that are not re-traumatizing and that build bridges between them. The therapeutic goal is to be able to 'visit' traumatized states for the purpose of understanding and processing their meanings and functions, without having to 'live' in them any longer or being 'sideswiped' by them. Just as the qualities of our states contributes mightily to healthy development, clinically, our patients' states determine the course of treatment to a large extent, whether they act as an impediment within the therapeutic endeavor or become a rich resource for eventual healing.

Our states impact every other keystone of our development.

CHAPTER THREE

Keystone Two—Memory Systems

Most of us think of memory as recall, exclusively. But recall or Explicit Memory (Declarative Memory) only begins to function about the 3rd year of life, continuing to do so throughout our life spans. On the other hand, Implicit Memory (Procedural Memory), which begins in the last few months in utero and functions throughout our life spans is a far more powerful system. This crucial memory system is formed by, among other attributes, the encoding and subsequent retrieval of lived experience, 'recorded' and 'relived' in the same procedural steps as the originating experience. Pivotal for developmental skills, such as walking, for instance, it is at the heart of happy experience, like love and positive attunement and optimal responsiveness. As significantly, Implicit Memory holds the power of our traumatic experience, causing us to be triggered intensely in current time by even 'a whiff' of the traumatic past.

Explicit (declarative) memory functioning within the individual begins in the same time frame as left hemispheric 'wiring'. Representing the encoding and retrieval of factual (semantic) and autobiographical (episodic) based knowledge and experience, explicit memory becomes invaluable for learning, continuity, and planning, since it is made up of conscious cognitive learning, requiring focal attention for encoding. Cortical processing selects events and information to form a part of permanent storage, or long-term memory, allowing the remainder of information or events to reside briefly in short-term memory or to be released. Explicit memory includes the 'recall' of the past as well as our autobiographical sense of self and of time but is a memory system that is altered by the subsequent influence of people and context and experience.

Rita Carter (1998) showed that the brain "works by linkages [bridging] ... [with] 100 trillion connections joining billions of neurons and each junction hav[ing] the potential to be part of a memory" (p. 175), so we can see the tremendous power and influence of memory upon the individual. With this information, we are then able to understand the profound impact of trauma, especially when it remains unresolved. Although unnamed as such, I think that this is what Winnicott (1974) discovered in his concept of the fear of breakdown: "Fear of breakdown is *the fear of a breakdown that has already been experienced.* It is a fear of original agony" (p. 104). Erik Hesse and Mary Main (2000) wrote that such a fear of breakdown represented "... fear of anticipated breakdown in the future [that] could actually be the effect of repeated 'breakdowns' in behavior, attention, and affect regulation suffered in the distant past" (p. 1119).

As an abbreviated way of demonstrating each type of memory system, I created the following Comparison Chart (Erwin, 2001). In the left column, the many attributes of Implicit Memory are spelled out; in the right column, those of Explicit Memory. But we can also compare one column to the other to highlight the considerable differences in the formation and functions between each type of memory system.

MEMORY COMPARISON CHART

IMPLICIT MEMORY	EXPLICIT MEMORY
Present at birth and functions throughout the lifespan	Functions from 3 years of age throughout the lifespan
The encoding and retrieval of lived experience	The encoding and retrieval of factual (semantic) and autobiographical (episodic) information and experience
Does *not* require conscious attention for encoding or retrieval	Requires focal attention for encoding
Encoded and retrieved in the *procedural steps* of the originating experience	Cortical processing selects events to form a part of permanent storage
To *encode*, mind needs intensity, duration, and repetition, to be *triggered* only needs a whiff of original experience	To learn, mind needs conscious repetition and practice
When triggered, the past becomes current time experience	Recall of the past
Accurate and stable over time	Alters over time as influenced by further experience, people, context
Use and state dependent	Cognitive learning
No subjective sense of recalling self or time	Sense of recall includes the self and time frame
Made up of emotional, sensory, perceptual, and body experience, in emotional language	Made up of facts, mind operations, verbal behavioral (linear, semantic) language
Establishes mental models, and therefore, "perceptual bias"	Establishes order, sequence, spatial locations time, and dimensional sense of self,
Amygdala is the mediating limbic structure, which is *activated* during traumatic encoding and retrieval	Hippocampus is the mediating limbic structure, which is *suppressed* during traumatic encoding and retrieval
When cocooned in the right hemisphere, implicit memory cannot be used for learning, only for reliving	Must be integrated with implicit memory so that implicit memory can become usable for learning

References: Schore, A. (2003a). Affect dysregulation and disorders of the self. New York: W. W. Norton & Company. and Siegel, D. J. (1999). The developing mind: Toward a neurobiology of interpersonal experience. New York: The Guilford Press.

We now have the psychoneurobiological understanding to explain how such implicit memory relivings take place in the brain. Learning to talk, walk, eventually run, skip, and jump, as well as relate to others, are all constructed by the activity of implicit memory. But trauma, whether acute, cumulative, or vicarious, is also 'use-and-state dependent' and thus implicit memory bound.

In healthy development, these two memory systems work in concert. In the first three years when implicit memory is dominant, the day to day lived experiences of the infant-baby-young child are internalized through the natural process of living. This activity represents the encoding aspect of implicit memory. Then, as the usual requirements of life occur or the young child has the desire to get from here to there, for instance, s/he does not have to think deliberately about how to walk: implicit memory is retrieved energizing the child to take necessary and desired steps. As the child enters the third year, explicit memory comes on board so that purposeful and repetitive learning can take place: the child learns how to color or to ride a tricycle. Throughout life, our primary memory systems then continue this crucial dual function, encoding and retrieving implicit memory and learning through the functions of explicit memory, all in ongoing support of living with vitality and effectiveness.

CHAPTER FOUR

Keystone Three—Internalization and Identification

How do we become the person we started out to be? At birth, already ripe with our intrauterine life, we bring with us what I call an 'essential' self, an inner identity that is unique, whole, and indispensable (Erwin, 2005, also see Freud, 1900/1955, Fairbairn, 1952, Winnicott, 1955-6/1975, and others). Growing that self, the unique and indispensable I, requires the life nurturing, heart and mind centered care from those with whom we have emotional ties. Our essential selfhood will be shaped into a developing 'sense of self' depending upon the impact of the positive and negative influences of our significant relationships (Winnicott, 1960b/1965, Putnam, 1997, and Damasio, 1999): *a who in the process of how.*

Internalization

Internalization (Meissner, 1976, 1979) is the *process* by which *who we started out to be* is built up, from infancy throughout the lifespan. This transformational process utilizes external relationships, interactions, and forms of affect regulation for the purpose of building the *structure* of the internal world, thus setting the tone for the *experience* of the inner world (see Meissner, 1971). By implication, internalization is the integration of structural co-created elements with that part of the psyche that is seen as most central to its inner identity—the ego. Internalization occurs through several developmentally based processes: incorporation, primary identifications, secondary identifications, and what I have identified as traumatic identifications (see Chapter Twelve).

- **Incorporation**

In the earliest months of life, incorporation is the first means by which the infant takes the mother or other primary caregiver into its "inner psychic organization" (Meissner, 1971, p. 287), a parallel process to the physical one of oral ingestion through feeding. As a mechanism of internalization, incorporation in the oral phase means that, "The union is such that the external object is completely assumed into the inner world of the subject" (p. 287). What this means dynamically is that the infant is not even aware of taking in the other or of building up the self; it is a happening.

- **Identification**

The internalization process of incorporation we have just examined is the 'on-the-road-to' precursor of both **primary** and reinforcing **secondary** identification processes (see Meissner, 1970, 1971, 1972). Developmentally, what follows incorporation are primary identifications with mommy, daddy, siblings, and other fundamental relationships. As we identify with and internalize the influential features of these significant others, we are structurally changed in ways that build up our sense of self (see Blum, 1986).

In Freud's "Three Essays" (1905/1955), he shifted his long unfolding views of identification from being a hysterical phenomenon to a developmental one with the conclusion that primary identifications support the growth of the ego. By Freud's definition (1900/1955), ego (Ich) meant the self, and so he viewed these pivotal identifications as not only early life opportunities but lifelong possibilities (Freud, 1921/1955): first, "identification is the original form of emotional tie with an object;" second, "in a regressive way it becomes a substitute for a libidinal object-tie"... and third, "it may arise with any new perception of a common quality shared with some other [significant] person.... The more important this common quality is, the more successful may this partial identification become, and it may thus represent the beginning of a new tie" (p. 107-108, see also Freud's development of identification theory 1897/1955-1923/1955).

How do incorporation and identification compare? In incorporation, the 'other' is absorbed without the infant's conscious awareness, and in that sense, the 'other' is lost as a separate other, becoming instead an integral part of the infant. In primary identification, the infant internalizes the mother, father, or primary caregiver in ways that grow the infant's very selfhood (the ego). For example, as the parent(s) repeatedly offer affective attunement to the infant's efforts of crying or cooing, etc., the infant experiences being valued by the parents and internalizes that as a primary source of identification of finding itself valuable. Or, as the parents delight in the infant such delight becomes a foundational identification for the infant as being worthy of joy. Over time, as the parents teach and learn with the growing child, the child identifies with the capacity for curiosity, understanding, and knowledge. And, of course, as the child is loved, s/he identifies with being a loving person. These primary identifications, of which there are countless examples in addition to the ones cited, build upon the temperament, personality, and qualities of being that the child inherently brings with him or herself, as well as both enhancing what already exists and adding new aspects to their evolving, developing selfhood.

Secondary identifications build upon our primary identifications, either validating and augmenting them or conversely contradicting and perhaps diminishing them through introjects. Just as with primary identifications, these secondary identifications occur throughout our lives. As life unfolds, siblings, grandparents, aunts and uncles and cousins, friends, and teachers offer new avenues of identifications. Later, spouses, partners, mentors, even their own children, add to the sense of self with the uniform catalyst always coming from emotional object ties.

CHAPTER FIVE

Keystone Four—Affect and Its Regulation

What about feelings? Affect, the powerful heart of the individual, and its effective regulation, the equally important avenue of attunement, communication, and rupture and repair between humans, is the fourth keystone in my Model of Healthy Development.

Affect

Antonio Damasio (2021) captured our attention regarding affect with his statement,

> "*… everything we feel corresponds to states of our interior.… what we 'really' feel* in the proper sense of the term, is how … parts or the whole of our own organism are faring, moment by moment.… Feelings owe their existence to the fact that the nervous system has direct contact with our insides and vice versa. The nervous system literally touches the organism's interior, everywhere in that interior, *and* it is 'touched' in return" (p. 45).

Much earlier, Charles Darwin (1872/1965) postulated that each of what he called *categorical affects* (happiness, sadness, fear, anger, disgust, surprise, interest, and shame and their combinations) had an innate expression on the face and evolved in order to produce signals or cues implicitly understood by other members of society for the purpose of survival of the species. Further, each categorical affect had two dimensions: *activation*, the intensity of the affect, and *hedonic tone*, the degree of pleasure or unpleasure of the affect. Many years later, Silvan Tompkins (1962) formalized what is called modern affect theory. Based on a group of observable facial responses in infants, he delineated what he called 'innate affects', each present from birth and visible on the faces of newborns. Of these, the *positive* affects are *interest* or *excitement*, *enjoyment* or *joy*, and *surprise* or *startle*. The *negative* affects consist of *distress* or *anguish*, *fear* or *terror*, *shame* or *humiliation*, *dissmell 1*, *disgust 2*, and *anger* or *rage*. Tompkins (1978) held that, "The affect system is therefore the primary motivational system because without its amplification, nothing else matters, and with its amplification, anything else *can* matter. It thus combines *urgency* and *generality*. It lends its power to memory, to perception, to thought, to action no less than to drives" (p. 202).

Affect is indivisible from concurrent physiological experience, and thus has a psychoneurobiological basis. In psychoanalysis, affect has long been considered to play a central role, in both theory-making and clinical application. As early as 1937, Marjorie Brierley wrote, "... no analyst fails to pay attention to his patient's feelings... with few exceptions, [patients] one and all complain of some disorder of feeling and tend to estimate their own progress by changes in their feelings and in their ability to cope with them" (p. 257). Decades later, Virginia Demos (1986) focused her research on the "motivational function of affect for the developing infant" (p. 40), assuming, following Tompkins, that:

> the crying neonate neither knows why she is crying nor that there is anything that can be done about it. The cry in this initial experience represents an innate affective response to a continuous level of nonoptimal stimulation.... Over time, the neonate will begin to

> organize her crying experiences by gradually, within the limits of her cognitive capacities, associating the crying with a variety of causes and with a variety of outcomes, and by beginning to organize her behavior accordingly (p. 40).

In contrast to these categorical, or discrete, affects, Daniel Stern (1985) described a more visceral type of affect (1985), what he called "vitality affect" (p. 54-60). Vitality affects consist of the alive internal landscape in which we live and are "captured by dynamic, kinetic terms" (p. 54) such as, 'sailing,' or 'falling through space', for instance. We may experience a sense of 'defeat' or 'triumph' or 'exhaustion' or 'inspiration' as parts of our inner environment. Stern considered this type of affective experience more elusive than concrete, but significant because "we are never without their presence, whether or not we are conscious of them, while 'regular' [categorical] affects come and go" (p. 54).... "There are a thousand smiles, a thousand getting-out-of-the-chairs, a thousand variations of performance of any and all behaviors and each one presents a different vitality affect" (p. 56). The entire range of vitality affects plays a central role within therapeutic approaches, both in theory-making and in the clinical endeavor.

Edward Tronick (1989) observed infants and adults as "participants in an affective communication system" (p. 112). As such, he recognized that infants have multiple goals at any one time and "process information about their current state in relation to their goal. They evaluate whether they are succeeding or failing and then use that evaluation to guide actions aimed at accomplishing their goal or redirecting their efforts to other goals" (p. 113).

Affective Attunement

Such affective experience within the self and in the interactions between self and other necessitates affective attunement (see Schore, 1994, Siegel, 1999) as a guide for affect regulation. Affect attunement refers to the capacity of the caregiver to be accurately aware of the infant's internal states to bring them into external expression to foster or mitigate them within the interactions between mother and infant. Daniel Siegel (1999) offered two related terms to affective attunement: alignment and resonance. "In alignment, one person [the caregiver] allows his or her state to be influenced by the state of the other [the baby].... Resonance involves more than the alignment of states; it also includes the ways in which the interaction affects the individuals in other aspects of their minds" (p. 280).

The parents' ability to remain affectively attuned despite even momentary lapses due to fatigue, confusion, or the newness of an infant, leads to affect regulation. Any pervasive lack of affective attunement will inevitably lead to the infant's affect *dys*regulation.

Affect Regulation

Throughout this book I discuss the coherency of the essential self. This coherency provides the bedrock of the regulation of the affective system within the individual, which includes its mental, emotional, physiological, and behavioral components across and within a flow of self-states. From the first moments after birth when doctors, nurses, and parents are working with and cradling newborns, their ministrations are directed at the physiological, nervous system, and emotional regulation that is life giving: attempts to clear the lungs, assisting the infant's early breathing, skin to skin touch that is essential for various kinds of regulation, helping her or him to latch on for nursing, regulating blood pressure, blood sugar, swaddling for temperature, holding for the experience of safety, crooning tenderly with voice, modulating light, movement, all for the regulation of this new on-land being who is fundamentally disorganized, dependent, and needing the deepest connection to caring and regulating others. As the infant becomes a bit sturdier as a baby, the parents' responses to the baby's reaches assists in the primary identification process, and as the baby internalizes such care, it eventually becomes its own tool for self-regulation.

In our human development, mastering three object relation milestones are essential for our affect regulation and our overall well-being. The first, at approximately 8-15 months is *object constancy*: in this, the baby learns that even if the parent is not momentarily physically present that s/he still exists and is going to return because the baby is of value. Object constancy creates the fundamental bond of assurance that infuses the affect regulation of calm and interest with its effectiveness. Between 15 months and approximately 2 ½-3 years, if development is proceeding in a healthy way, the young child acquires *object permanence*: even when the parent temporarily disappoints or makes a mistake with the child, the child does not feel the parent as all bad but is able to still feel the good in the parent even when s/he is angry or hurt in the moment. Repair follows rupture. During the mastering of these milestones, a third object relation achievement is in the making, culminating between the ages of 3-4 years of age: *object usage*. We find in object usage that the child has successfully internalized and identified with the parent(s) to such a degree that even without the immediate presence or engagement of the parent, the child is still able to make use of the parent internally.

A discussion of affect regulation cannot be considered whole without being aware of the critical contribution of vagal tone upon any individual's ability to regulate and express affect. Stephen W. Porges' et al (1994) work concerning vagal tone (the vagus is the 10th cranial nerve, originating in the medulla) suggested, "Vagal tone control increases developmentally as the nervous system matures . . . and has direct and inverse relationships with three variables:

> "(1) reactivity, (2) self-regulation, and (3) expression of emotion" (p. 118, 119). The results of his research showed that "vagal tone is highly correlated with autonomic activity, the relationship between vagal tone and expressivity appears to be dependent on development, [but] independent of development stage, vagal tone is correlated with self-regulation" (p. 125).

Allan Schore (2003a) pointed out the essential principle of affect regulation: "Affect regulation is not just the reduction of affective intensity, the dampening of negative emotion; it also involves an amplification, an intensification of positive emotion, a condition necessary for more complex self-organization" (p. 143-44, see also Porges, 1994). Schore further discussed the far reaching and necessary benefits of affect regulation, demonstrating that the orbitofrontal cortex facilitates affect regulation of arousal by utilizing an emotional 'clutch' that disengages the sympathetic 'accelerator' and activates the parasympathetic 'brakes'. The parasympathetic system is later deactivated with realignment, and the proper adjusted or regulated level of arousal is established through reactivation of the sympathetic system. In other words, the brakes are applied with the disconnection; the repair process allows the child's energies to be redirected, and then the accelerator is applied again with resumption of the emotional connection during the repair process" (p. 145, see also Siegel, 1999, p. 281). This "balance between the accelerator and the brakes . . . is the essence of affect regulation" (p. 281).

One of my primary developmental mentors, Psychoanalyst and Psychiatrist Stanley Greenspan (1997a), delineated six functional emotional milestones in development through his research and clinical work with children over many decades:

1). 0 – 3 months
interest in the world [arousal] while developing the ability to be calm [regulation]

2). 0 – 5 months
falling in love with being alive – early attachment and simple sense of self

3). 4 – 10 months
becoming an intentional two-way communicator

4). 10 – 18 months
learning to interact to solve problems, have and express simple emotional ideas, with a complex sense of self developing

5). 18 – 24 months+
functional use of language, imaginative sense of play, further complexity of self, representational thinking

6). 24 – 48 months
building bridges between ideas, emotional thinking, concentrating on tasks, sequencing ideas with bridging to action

In each of these, any immediate interpersonal situation, positive or negative, can have lasting results if the effects become internally represented, meaning that the infant/baby/young child may have mastery, partial mastery, or deficits in any of these areas, subsequently impacting the next milestone and continuing to play out within later development, well into and throughout adulthood. In all the research I have studied, my own personal therapeutic experience, and in my therapeutic practice, I have learned that affect regulation is one of the areas of greatest struggle for patients, requiring a substantial amount of time and effort and patience in putting in place new ways of regulation for the patient, often for the first time in their lives.

CHAPTER SIX

Keystone Five—Attachment

How do we attach as children?

Do we attach similarly as adults?

John Bowlby's (1951) primary conclusion that, "the infant and young child should experience a warm, intimate, and continuous relationship with his mother [or permanent mother substitute] in which both find satisfaction and enjoyment" (p. 13) laid the cornerstone for attachment theory-making. Today, attachment is universally described as proximity-seeking behavior on the part of the child in its necessary quest to find safety, comfort, and protection with his or her significant adult caregiver. As the child and parent establish their *secure* interpersonal relationship, the infant/child's immature brain uses the adult's mature regulating functions to organize its own processes, to experience amplification of its positive emotional states and modulation of its negative states (also see Siegel, 1999, Schore, 2003a). Such successfully repeated interactional experiences then become encoded in implicit memory of the young child's brain, serving as templates and expectations for future relating. Attachment provides the core foundation from which the child's body/affective mind develops.

Bowlby (1958) demonstrated that while in the animal kingdom an animal runs *from* something frightening or dangerous to some *place of safety* (a den, burrow, etc.), the human child runs *to* some*one*. When that someone is an attachment figure who should be a haven of safety but instead is an inept, dismissing, or dangerous source of fright for the child, the child is caught in the simultaneous impulse to approach and flee from the same person. Bowlby thus not only delineated the secure base but proposed that separation anxiety (1959) was due to these adverse experiences for which the child feels responsible, and thus expected subsequent separation anxiety can actually be inappropriately low or absent, giving the impression of the child's maturity, which is instead a mark of pseudo-independence. Bowlby also created two categories for insecure attachment, *anxious ambivalent*, the tendency to be anxious and clingy when needs are not met, and *avoidant*, the tendency toward blockage of deep relationships, the result of being rebuffed in efforts for comfort or protection.

Through her laboratory procedure known as The Strange Situation, Mary Ainsworth et al (1978) expanded Bowlby's classification system into Secure Attachment, Insecure/Ambivalent (or resistant) Attachment, and Insecure/ Avoidant Attachment. Mary Main (2000, with Solomon, Cassidy, Hesse, and others) added pivotal dimensions to attachment theory-making with her fourth classification of Insecure/Disorganized/Disoriented Attachment, and through the AAI (the Adult Attachment Interview), which is a reliably 100% predictor of future attachment patterns between parent and child. Karlen Lyons-Ruth (2001) established two subtypes to this fourth classification: #1 is Disorganized Approach, and #2 is Disorganized Avoidant. Jeremy Holmes (2001), as one of many contemporary clinicians for whom attachment theory has become central, has captured the efficacy and necessity of attachment theory with his evocative analogy, that of the *psychological* immune system:

> Affects and their disorders are central to many psychological illnesses and each can be seen in terms of attachment. The psychological immune system is mediated via affect. Our feelings alert us to whether we or our loved ones are safe or in danger (p. 1-2).... Trauma overwhelms and disrupts the psychological immune system altogether (p. 3).... To the extent that it is not available outside, a secure base

has to be constructed within the self. Psychotherapy is needed to facilitate that precarious process" (p. 5).

While attachment research is prolific and reliable, I bring a fresh understanding of the attachment process as it contributes to our development as a whole. Once again, we can see in my Model of Healthy development, the intricate play and interdependence between the seven keystones. The formation of secure attachment is achieved as the baby's positive states are encoded in implicit memory, with internalizations and identifications for ego (self) growth becoming part of the baby's internal architecture, combining with affect regulation through the parents' affective attunement. What is established is the development of critical wiring of neuronal pathways in the functions of the right and left hemispheres with personal voice and elaborative language beginning to unfold. The networking between these seven keystones is profound as it supports the fullness of the young human as s/he develops.

Mental Representations

Another essential element for us to consider when connecting attachment to healthy development is that of mental representation. Sidney Blatt and Kenneth Levy (2003) in their thoroughly researched and pivotal paper, "Attachment Theory, Psychoanalysis, Personality Development, and Psychopathology" show that mental representations are the "enduring cognitive-affective psychological structures that provide templates for processing and organizing information so that new experiences are assimilated to existing mental structures. These cognitive-affective schemas guide an individual's behavior, particularly in interpersonal relationships" (p. 120).

Blatt and Levy also drew the connection to object relations theory when they wrote, "Mental representations in *object relations theory* are generally analogous to the *internal working models (IWMs)* discussed in attachment theory. Both attachment theory and object relations theory posit that mental representations or IWMs of self and others emerge from the early relationships with caregivers and then act as heuristic [a person discovering or learning something for him/herself] guides for subsequent interpersonal relationships influencing expectations, feelings, and general patterns of behavior.... In healthy development [*with secure attachment*], the cognitive and affective components of these mental representations (and IWMs) of self and other evolve epigenetically, from lower to higher levels of representation, so that new representational modes are increasingly accurate, articulated, and conceptually complex" (p. 121).

Perceptual bias is another phrase that can be used synonymously to help patients understand the mental representations or IWMs from which they operate. They may not feel an emotional connection to the language of mental representations, but they readily grasp experientially the power of their own perceptual biases. They can easily identify with painful or failed times in their lives that set up belief systems that new experience was likely to resemble and repeat the old. So, too, does perceptual bias come out of our attachments: how we attach to our primary caregivers, especially when our attachment experiences repeat without intervention, is predictive of our perceptual bias and ultimately of our future attachment relationships.

This brings us to a pressing question to answer. What attachments systems do our patients bring with them into the consulting room? Building secure attachment between therapist and patient will become indispensable for healing. The first requirement, of course, is that the therapist has resolved her or his own attachment challenges, or at least, can manage attachment *dys*regulation occurring in transference or countertransference situations. Research has shown that a secure attachment can take up to five years to establish between someone who has an insecure attachment with someone (parent, teacher, mentor, therapist, loved one) who is securely attached.

Most of our patients have had both acute and cumulative attachment disappointments or injuries throughout their lives, so any sense of a secure base may have to be built from the ground up and in the face of previously broken trust. As we will see in later chapters, there are significant challenges along this rocky road, but there are also creative solutions as well.

CHAPTER SEVEN

Keystone Six—Hemispheric Development

Brain development and functioning is a topic of both depth and breadth, in an ever-expanding quantity of new discoveries and detailed information. Fundamentally, this three-pound yet intricately complex organ holds the structures and forces that characterize us as humans. The brain is the sum of its parts, yet each part carries specific attributes:

- the hindbrain, comprised of the brain stem, spinal cord, and cerebellum has dominion over our body's core operations, like how our heart rate functions and how we breathe, as well as organizing our movements;
- the midbrain has to do with voluntary and involuntary activity;
- the forebrain, which takes up the most real estate of the brain is also the most sophisticated and developed; it houses the cerebrum, the more modern-day development of the brain, and the inner brain;
- the cerebrum is where our thinking, imagination, memories, our "mind and its functions" occur. The surface of the cerebellum and the cerebrum is covered by indispensable layers of tissue known as the cortex, with infolds (sulcus) and bulges (gyrus), which is where the majority of the brain's processing occurs. The cerebrum is divided into two hemispheres, made up of many modules, each module having its own specialization. All of the modules are "interconnected by criss-crossing ropes of axons" (Carter, 1998, p. 16), bands that are covered in myelin sheaths, which act as insulation for the brain's electrical

impulses, in order that the electrical firing flows quickly and to its intended receptor. Every one of these modules is duplicated in each hemisphere, except for the pineal gland, which is at the base of the brain.

The hemispheres have four lobes:

1) The occipital lobes are at the back and responsible for visual processing and connecting that with memory images
2) The temporal lobes are on the lower side around the ears and responsible for sound, speech comprehension (left side only), and some memory
3) The parietal lobes are on the top and responsible for movement, calculation, and recognition, and
4) The frontal lobes are on top, in front, and responsible for thinking, conceptualizing, planning, and the appreciation of emotion.

Conducting the electrical activity of the brain are the neurons, or cells, which carry the electrical firing from one cell to another across a tiny space called the *synapse* (where each axon of the neuron carries away from the cell nucleus, and each dendrite of the next neuron receives the incoming information). Neurotransmitters are secreted by the axons and "are released into the space when the cell is suitably fired up. These chemicals trigger the neighboring cell to fire, too, and the resultant chain effect produces simultaneous activity in *millions* of connected cells" (Carter, 1998, p. 14, italics added).

The corpus callosum, just beneath the cerebral cortex, is what joins the two hemispheres together and acts as a communication link for the transmission of information between them. Beneath the corpus callosum lies the limbic system (the mammalian brain), an unconscious system, but one which has crucial and on-going influence on our experience, because it is where our emotions, especially fear, are registered and generated, as well as most of our impulses, appetites, and desires. The limbic system is "densely connected to the conscious cortex above it and constantly feeds information upwards" (Carter, 1998, p. 16). Within the limbic system are four modules each with their own unique functions:

- the Thalamus takes incoming information and relays it to the part of the brain that is necessary for processing it
- the Hypothalamus (with the pituitary gland) adapts the body to the environment
- the Hippocampus is responsible for the laying down of long-term memory
- the Amygdala both registers and generates fear

Finally, the brainstem, or reptilian brain, evolving over more than 500 million years, is made up of nerves from the body by means of the spinal column and is responsible for regulating both alertness and the 'vegetative' functions of the body – breathing, heartbeat, and blood pressure – and then transmitting this somatic information to the brain for response and processing.

What is particularly relevant to this sixth keystone of healthy development is the research provided by Daniel Siegel (1999) and Allan Schore (1994, 2003a) among others (see R. Koutlak, 1996, J. Ledoux, 1996, R. Carter, 1998), which demonstrates the sequence in which the brain hemispheres develop, along with the wiring of the autonomic nervous system and the functioning of the limbic system.

- **Right Hemispheric Development and the Sympathetic Branch of the Autonomic Nervous System**

What is first needed for healthy hemispheric development in an infant is "the psychobiologically attuned caregiver interactively regulat[ing] the infant's positive and negative states, thereby co-constructing a growth-facilitating environment for the *experience-dependent maturation of a control system in the infant's right brain*" (Schore, 2003b, p. 179, italics added, see Carter, 1998, Kotulak, 1996, LeDoux, 1996).

This facilitating environment has multiple opportunities for growth and 'mapping'. This staggering amount of cell production and linking is well underway in utero followed by specific opportunities after birth when the brain overproduces cells by the billions to provide the optimal possibility of mapping them for development and performance. As the result of positive relational experiences during such pivotal times these trillions of cells form connections initially in the right hemispheres of our brains. Between the ages of 10-12 months this first post-birth brain cells surge occurs, wiring the excitatory or sympathetic branch of our autonomic nervous system (see Schore, 1997). This branch enables our baby selves to respond to sensory stimulation from within the environment and within our own bodies, and to experience sensory arousal with pleasure, in other words to be curious, have wonder, delight in discovery, that is, metaphorically to say "yes" to being alive. All formation of memory is primarily the encoding of lived experience, implicit (procedural) memory, not requiring conscious awareness for its encoding or eventual retrieval. Simultaneously, as we incorporate our parents' endearments, and provisions, we become regulated by them. In this way, our excitement does not flood us, but with increasing regulation, we will use this excitement throughout our lives for our future development of interest in the world's offerings and inspiration. Overtime, as we have repeated internalization experiences of precious regulation, we learn to self-calm. This 'wiring' also gives us emotional range, planting the seeds for future social and intimate relationships.

The *Sympathetic* Branch of the Autonomic Nervous System

- Induces excitation
- Activates arousal in bodily states
- Increases heart rate, respiration, sweating, and alertness
- Decreases digestion

However, if we do not have caregivers who provide such delight in us and their regulation of our excitement, the over-production of brain cells does not get mapped fully and what is not mapped is pruned away and lost forever.

- **Right Hemispheric Development and the Parasympathetic Branch of the Autonomic Nervous System**

In our second year of life, as the right hemisphere of the brain advances in its development, a second cortico-limbic loop is laid down—the *inhibitory circuitry* or what is known as the parasympathetic branch of the autonomic nervous system. This loop will give us the capacity to wait, to respect boundaries, and limits, and to regulate our excitation from arousal (soothing), metaphorically accepting the "no"s in life. The development of early emotional language also takes place during this second year, communicated at first through sounds and gestures, then simple naming words.

> The *Parasympathetic* Branch of the Autonomic Nervous System
> - Induces excitation
> - Mediates arousal
> - Decreases heart rate, respiration, cools the body, and dampens down alertness
> - Increases digestion

Again, the parent or other primary caregiver serves as that resource for the wiring of this inhibitory circuitry. S/he helps focus our budding social skills, expands our capacity to control our impulses, and supports us as we slowly comprehend that there are consequences to our actions. Just as in the first months of life, when our parent's gaze, facial expressions, and vocal tone communicated delight in us, now their gaze, expressions, and tones put the brakes on our unbridled and impassioned impulses and behavior. We need the signal of caring disapprovals, warnings, re-directions, because they trigger the release of certain hormones to slow us down. But we might also feel deflated and have few means yet of regulating our disappointment, our shame, or our temporary fury—hence what will begin in those early months of our second year of life and culminate before its end, 'the terrible twos'.

The formation of memory is still implicit (procedural) memory, the encoding of lived experience, which does not require conscious awareness for its encoding or eventual retrieval. Again, at the end of the second year, there is an enormous overproduction of billions of brain cells, and whatever is not wired, or linked up into neuronal pathways, is pruned back and lost.

- **Left Hemispheric Development**

In the 3rd year of life, the wiring of the brain shifts in emphasis to the left hemisphere as the brain's neuronal branching becomes far denser overall, allowing the child to comprehend, use, and sequence semantics (words), accelerating emotional and mental languaging. Each hemisphere is becoming more specialized. Explicit, or declarative, memory becomes active, *requiring* conscious awareness, semantics, and a sense of autonoesis (autobiographical self in time experience) for encoding. From this third year of life throughout the lifespan, both implicit (procedural) and explicit (declarative) memory function for encoding and retrieval.

- **Hemispheric Communication**

Only beginning in the 4th year of life does communication occur across the mid-line of and between the two hemispheres. This "Freudian brain," as Allan Schore (1997) called it, in one of many growth spurts since intrauterine life, supports the creation and comprehension of emotional, cognitive, and creative ideas, and connections among words and meanings. The autobiographical sense of self across time and space is now in full development.

Perception

We need to draw attention to the larger picture of how a baby or young child's brain, with all of its interacting intricacies, constructs overall perception. Louis Sander (2002) captured this process when he described "the brain first deconstructs its sensory input into the bits and pieces that make up the perception. It places each sensory component of the input into a category—line, color, depth, contour, movement—which the brain then processes, each category in a different brain area. The map of this widely distributed process is then brought back together to construct the whole of the percept, including relevant affective, or emotional, categories . . . and from these, the meaning of the percept is constructed for the perceiver. . . . As part of this process, the infant's repertoire of actual behavioral strategies governing how to 'be with' significant 'others'—mother, father, and the like—within the idiosyncrasies of its particular caregiving system is being constructed" (p. 27). Having taken a look at the basic structure and functions of the brain in healthy development we can begin to comprehend the impact of each Keystone upon the others.

CHAPTER EIGHT

Keystone Seven—Personal Voice and Expressive Language

Personal Voice

What I call Personal Voice, the vocal and written expression of our unique, fundamental, and indispensable *essential* self, makes its initial appearance at birth with the baby's first cry. After years of my own strivings as a professional writer, editing and book 'doctoring' others' work for publication, and in teaching writing privately to professional writers and university graduate students, I found that central to all of these endeavors was the work of finding my own and their 'unique writer's voice'. As the notion of personal voice captured my interest in writing, I then explored its parallel in early human development and in the personal narratives and non-verbal and verbal aspects of voice in the fervent strivings of my patients. In adult development, this personal voice represents our ability to *think* representationally while feeling, without defensiveness, and then to *communicate* our thinking while feeling, as well as receiving such communication from the other in an *elaborative* dialogue of meaning making.

After this personal voice makes its initial appearance at birth's first cry, it is followed by gurgles, gestures, and tiny squeaks. Using these forms of communications, most babies, by three months of age, can express distress and pleasure, and begin to convey outward directed looks and gestures, both as response to various sensory stimulation and to initiate contact. The baby uses her communicative skills to *make things happen*. Roy Schafer (1980) pointed out, "In considering the psychology of the self, one wants to know who or what esteems or does not esteem the self. It seems that some sort of superself or superordinate self is implied, in which case one does implicitly get back to some central and unitary agency as a point of reference.... The self, then, is not what one *has* but what one *does*; and it is what one tells about what one does" (p. 91).

What supports the on-going development of this personal voice is the attuned responsiveness of the primary caregivers to their baby's expressions. In the first couple of years of life, it was necessary for the parent to attune to and decode through the child's earliest communications what provisions and protections to put in place—to 'speak' for the child. Until about the age of three, parents' resonating propositional 'naming' (see Whitmer, 2001) by the parents is essential. This propositional naming becomes the provision of soon enabling the growing child's "authorial self" (Wolf, 1990, p. 185), by encouraging and respecting the child to begin to think for itself, forming his or her own agenda, opinions, desires, needs and naming them. "I want a cookie!" at 9:00 am may be followed by a minor temper tantrum when the wish is not fulfilled, but the parents' nurturing of the child's propositional thinking and authorial voice by *proposing* that a morning apple could be tasty with a cookie provided for dessert after dinner supports the propositional thinking of the child.

We can see by this and thousands of other parenting examples that the child will not always be able to have what s/he wants, but such regard for the child's expression is vital to its individual growth of personal voice. Antonio Damasio (1999) has said, "I believe it is legitimate to take the phrase 'I know" and deduce from it the presence of a nonverbal image of knowing centered on a self that precedes and motivates that verbal phrase. The idea that self and consciousness would emerge after language and would be a direct construction of language is not likely to be correct.... If self and consciousness were born de novo from language, they would constitute the *sole* instance of words without an underlying concept" (p. 107-108, italics added). The elaboration of the child's communications through the parents' respect for the child's growing mind, perceptions, and affective experience is fundamentally influential in supporting the child's authorial self.

Expressive Language

Ultimately and ideally, personal voice communicates by using *affective, elaborative language* comprised of words that arise out of mental and emotional imagery, that is, multisensory 'pictures', which represent one's experience using six senses—sight, hearing, taste, touch, smell, and intuition—and which builds within communication with the other. We have seen that personal voice represents our ability to *think representationally while feeling* in our inner world, and to *communicate* that experience in articulated elaborated language in the outer world. Voice expressed in this 'emotional' language offers the symbolization in words of a wide spectrum of categorical and vitality affects within a flow of states, building non-verbal and verbal bridges between categories of experiences, while differentiating what is 'me' and 'not me'.

Narrative Making

Narrative making requires both left and right hemisphere involvement: the left being the interpreter, the understanding of cause-and-effect relationships, the right making sense of what is perceived, processing "the overall gist of a scene and creat[ing] a context-rich representational understanding... [but] coherent narratives are created through inter-hemispheric integration" (Siegel, 1999, p. 331). As we have seen, if all goes well in development, this narrative capacity emerges in children about the third year of life as they develop their own early propositional thinking and resultant authorial selves, which subsequently allow them to create stories about the events that influence them during the course of their daily lives. Thus, "children begin as biographers and emerge into autobiographers" (Siegel, 1999, p. 323, see also Wolf, 1990).

These Seven Keystones, as they are chronologically and dynamically building and realized through interpersonal relationships, comprise the ideal of healthy development. What arrives in our consulting rooms, however, is seldom if ever the narrative of such an ideal. Instead, we are met again and again with the wounding or traumatization of this development, calling upon us as therapists not only to have the knowledge of developmental keystones but to understand what has happened to each and all of them in our patients' experience. The Creative Process becomes the heart of the resolution of trauma, the attachment nature of the analytic relationship, and the narrative process in which analyst and patient engage to weave together for the first time the patient's lived experience.

As in the beginning of life, with the birth cry of personal voice, so, too, do we return to a rebirth in the analysis, which *breathes* respiratory life into that personal voice emerging through the wounding and unresolved trauma our patients carry. In the doing, as the elements of each of these seven foundational aspects of human development integrate and influence one another, the patient becomes able to hold his or her original wounding with the respect it deserves while moving toward healing and the resolved and transformed development of his or her essential self.

Part Two

What the Looking Glass Reveals

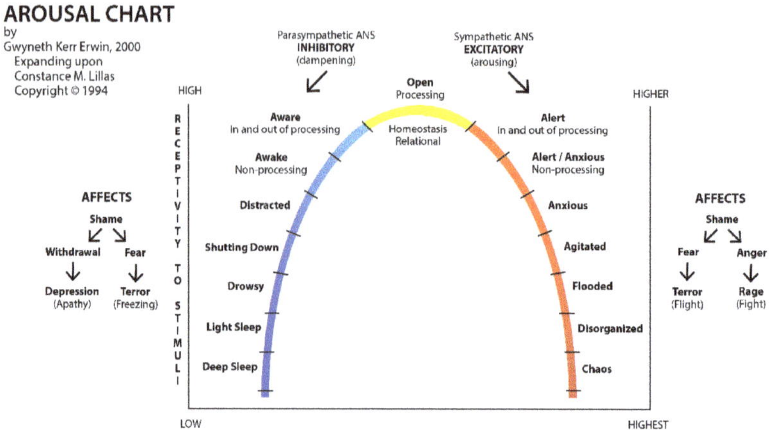

The Arousal Chart

Connie Lillas (1994) originally developed a bell curve Arousal Chart to show basic categories of response to arousal in the parasympathetic and sympathetic branches of the autonomic nervous system. As a candidate in her Infant Observation class many years ago, I was privileged to be allowed by her to expand upon her work, delineating the various increments of arousal response within the response continuum from its two ends of hypo and hyper arousal while integrating with the Arousal Chart the affective aspects present in the receptivity to stimuli.

Central to the primary thrust of this book is that the two cases into which I have chosen to delve demonstrate in nearly opposite ways the visceral need for us as treating clinicians to recognize and understand that development is not purely a series of 'stages' of the early years. Instead, development is made up of more than hundreds of thousands moment-by-moment threads that weave the fundamental fabric of our ongoing lives, especially when the filaments of unresolved developmental trauma lace into the consequences that follow us throughout decades to come.

The qualitative methodology in this book is illustrative, in part, for the purpose of illuminating the affect arousal continuum. The first case, Will, a middle-aged man seen three times a week for seven years, and twice, then once, a week for a year and a half, represents the *hypo*aroused response to trauma. The second case, Julia, a woman in her forties seen five times a week for seven years, and twice, then once, a week for a year and a half, represents the *hyper*aroused response to trauma.

Will and Julia epitomize this profound nature of unresolved trauma and its lasting consequences to which they had to adapt as they grew into adulthood, became educated, and created families of their own. We see how these two individuals, from the beginning moments of life, unconsciously incorporated trauma that remained unresolved due to their primary caregivers who perpetrated, ignored, minimized, or disavowed this original trauma. We see as well how Will and Julia's subsequent developmental twists and turns added layers to their unresolved trauma.

In their eventual treatment, Will and Julia's therapeutic experience with me narrates the careful building of our therapeutic alliance. This connection allowed for the revelation of their profound developmental betrayals, unmet early needs, in the here-and-now demands and trials for them and for me toward healing in the therapeutic endeavor. The challenges inherent in the reparative shifts that are necessary for such patients to trust in the full, authentic presence of the therapist, who must provide the necessary lifeblood of the holding environment, are weighty. The crucial insight and deep developmental knowledge that is essential for working through and ultimate healing is to be found in this new object relationship and its unbridled support for transforming development in all its complexities.

CHAPTER NINE

Will's Beginnings

Will was tall, lanky, and a bit stooped, with startling ocean-blue eyes. As he preceded me into my office for our first session, he ducked going through the doorway, hunching his shoulders, his arms hanging at his sides. His eyes now avoiding mine, he began to explain why he was there. His speech, much of the time, was halting, punctuated by many 'uhs' and 'ums', all failed attempts at filling in spaces where there were no words. He was a grown man but seemed a lost, uncertain boy.

In his forties, he sputtered that he loved his intense and hard-working wife, Samantha. She was exciting to him. The marriage, though, was nearing its breaking point, a clear motivation for Will seeking help because of his compromised ability to earn a consistent and reliable living while depending on his wife to be the primary breadwinner. They were parents of an eight-year-old girl and eleven-year-old twin boys. One of the boys seemed "difficult to reach," who imploded, taking his frustrations out on himself, unable to speak his feelings, but bright and talented as a painter, and passionate about soccer. Will described the other twin as "a regular kid." His daughter was "like her mother," and Will was intimidated by her.

Another clear motivation for Will wanting therapy was his inability to stay on task, even to remember details of life's everyday requirements. He was sure, or hoping, that he had ADD, something that medicine might fix. As he struggled to get out most of his words, I was touched by his attempts to express what he hoped and wished for as a young man and how derailed he became in college, the shame he felt, and the yearning, for what, he was no longer sure. I said, "It seems as though you had a dream that died, a long time ago." His face crumpled, his lips quivered, his mouth twisted, as he nodded in silence. But he did not know what that dream was.

Over the next months I learned in 'slow motion' and in patchwork, Will's story, his own and his and Samantha's together. He continued to talk in a halting, disjointed, and foggy manner, which vividly communicated to me the *hypo*aroused affective sense of what he meant when he spoke of being weak. Countertransferentially, I had the repeated experience, especially the slower and 'thicker' Will became, of an overwhelming grogginess in myself, as though I had been drugged. I came to find that these sensations lifted instantaneously when I could help Will *feel his feelings*. But when he felt them in any depth, his facial muscles trembled, his face crumpled again, and he wept, wordless. By each next session, he had 'undone' the power of his previous affective experience. He might question its "reality," he might "forget" what he had felt, he might "not know how to get it back," he might "contradict" what he did remember or question its relevance. And we would start all over again. Even though I found this avenue of helping him (and me!) 'wake up,' I had the on-going and disturbing sense that pivotal parts of his story were missing regardless of what he shared.

Over months, something of an eventual coherent narrative was stitched together by Will and me from many small remnants and threads of the loosely held historical and affective fabric he could offer at times. His mother was agoraphobic, who never learned to drive or ventured out unaccompanied, who was suspicious of others, and, at times, contentious. She hovered over and cocooned Will, the youngest child of four and the only boy, especially in his early school years when he wanted to stay home from school with tummy aches or because he was behind in his work. He remembered his parents as being very affectionate and not "uptight" about sexual matters. He remembered, too, that there was a great deal of conflict between his mother and the youngest of the three daughters, particularly in that daughter's adolescence. Whenever their yelling matches flared up, complete with slamming doors, Will escaped to another part of the house, hiding, watchful and listening, but shaken by their fights. This sister, though seven years older than Will, was the closest in age to him, and was a good friend to him as well as a sibling, taking him with her into her more "grown-up" world of adolescence, letting him hang out with her and her friends. He experienced a profound loss as she became more consumed by anger, confused by her later teenage pregnancy, and the subsequent change in their friendship status as she became a single mother while still living at home and going to college.

Will admired, but was somewhat awed by his father, a man he viewed as a "real man," in charge of his own company, supervising many employees, a man willing to take risks that usually paid off, and who was a robust outdoorsman. When at home, his father was involved with and devoted to Will, especially by bringing Will into *his* world, teaching him about car repair and crafting woodworking projects together. He could "fix," anything, and overtime, taught Will to do the same. Will seemed to exhibit a secure attachment to his father, but certainly missed him as he traveled a great deal, sometimes being gone for weeks at a time, leaving Will to attend to his fearful, overprotective, and smothering mother.

The "prince" in the family, Will was the only child with his own bedroom. His three sisters, who Will was alternately enticed by and oblivious to, dressed him up as a baby doll when he was very young. In his pre-adolescence, Will found himself imitating them, something he felt embarrassed by and shamed about at the time but was more accepting of as an adult. In his adolescence, whenever Will initiated any move to "go out in the world," his mother, rather than supporting his pursuits, pulled him back emotionally. Will became her "companion of sorts," which fueled his already well-established ambivalent attachment to her.

In the face of nuclear or extended-family conflict, Will's mother was at the heart of it, either in an argument or by cutting off relationships for herself, her husband, or her children with those by whom she felt affronted. The father, one of fourteen children in his family of origin, took the usual stance of becoming immersed in work and not stepping into the fray. Will became trapped in the bind of being unable to leave his mother to cope with her own moods and his terrors of the larger world, forfeiting the impetus of his young robust self that beckoned him to move outside his mother's protective cocoon.

Usually, Will sat at a diagonal away from me, glancing sideways from time to time, cocking his head. I considered his aversion as avoidance of direct contact, considering that a transferential ambivalent attachment was present from the start. Almost a year into our work, he asked one day, "What did you say?" but before I could respond, he said matter-of-factly, "I have a hearing loss."

For the first time, he told me, shaking his head and mumbling, "I should have told you before, I guess," the story of a near-fatal car accident. He was eight-years-old, sitting in the front seat of his aunt's car between his aunt and mother as his aunt drove them to visit the newborn baby of a family member. Out of nowhere, a pickup truck plowed into them headfirst. While all three of them were injured, Will was thrown so hard by the impact that he was impaled on the gearshift sticking out from the steering wheel post.

His next awareness was of being in the back seat, blaring sirens, then the blur of the hospital. His injuries, including internal hemorrhaging, were life-threatening. Both legs were broken so, despite surgery, his recovery required many months in casts and then prolonged physical therapy before being able to return to school. He told me how his father built him a large wraparound lap play board, so that he could draw or play or construct things while being immobile from the waist down, his casted legs sticking straight out in front of him, and how his mother doted on him, making this period a "cozy time."

Once Will returned to school, although he had recovered sufficiently well enough to participate, he was kept in the library for the remainder of the year by his mother's insistence as protection against possible injury on the playground. His feelings of fragility were growing. He also suffered his hearing loss in the accident, although it was still not clear to him how that came to be. This loss was not detected until sometime later, and he simply tried to adapt to it. The family story evolved so that the accident and its aftermath became interpreted as a badge of honor that he survived and from which he was considered recovered.

Often fighting against rising tears, Will talked with difficulty about the bullies on his various school playgrounds. He remained adamant that he himself had never been bullied, and he did not have any explicit memory about specific events where he witnessed someone else being bullied. But what was very alive in the room was the way he would stare off into space, and say, as though 'seeing' something, "You know how it is on playgrounds, there's always a bully, and I'm standing off to the side, watching, trying not to be noticed, because [shaking his head], I wouldn't be able to stand up to them. No, no [shaking his hands in a back-and-forth, waving away motion], I wouldn't be able to do anything about that!" As he talked about how immobilized he would be against intervening against a bully, the picture that he was witnessing in his own mind was so vivid that I realized this affective experience of what he called his "cowardice" was the implicit memory encoding of lived experience he could not recall: the cowardice he found in the "bullying" quality he feared in his mother, the vicarious trauma her anger had on him, fostering his sense of fragility.

By the time Will was in junior high, he was shy and a loner. At twelve, when he wanted to try out for several team sports, the family doctor told him he could never play contact sports due to the repercussions to his knees and legs from the accident. In the same time frame, Will's father, who Will held as bold and masculine in a rough-and-tumble way, nearly broke his neck in a surfing accident and accidentally shot himself on a hunting and fishing trip, causing him to give up his more vigorous life at the very time when Will was striving to move into a world of adventure with his father. Two years later, Will's favorite uncle, a scientist/explorer who mentored Will and was certainly a hero to and role model for Will, was killed on an expedition out of the country. The report was that he was hurled off a truck on the expedition, but the rumors suggested he was murdered. The exact nature of his death remained a mystery, but the impact upon Will was silently devastating, confirming his growing conviction that the world was unexpectedly dangerous, and it behooved him to play it safe, or not play at all.

Will had only one early explicit memory of himself, prior to his own brush with death in the car accident, when he was what he called "robust and bold." He thought he was probably four or five years old, maybe in kindergarten. In a swashbuckling move, he jumped off the roof of the family home's carport, only to break his arm. Undeterred apparently in the aftermath, he remembered using his casted arm as a "friendly" weapon, a different kind of sword he could wield as he played with his friends. But before long, the message that became underscored was that bold and robust moves led to trouble.

An excellent student in high school, Will dated only one girl, and she, in his senior year. After graduating, Will set his sights on architecture, his father's dream. In college, away from home for the first time, he quickly became overwhelmed and lost his way, feeling he could not measure up to the unexpected mathematical and engineering challenges of becoming an architect and by being away from home. He did not return to that college his second year, instead beginning a several years' process of finishing a few college classes at community college in fits and starts while living at home, and then finally at a local university, changing majors several times, trying English and philosophy. He moved into an apartment only when he bowed to his girlfriend's pleas and married her. Just out of high school herself, she suffered from longstanding insecurities and depression. Her clinginess and fears were soon unmanageable for Will. Despite Will consulting a psychiatrist and his young wife going into therapy and being on medication, they divorced within the year. While feeling liberated by the divorce, Will found again that bold and impulsive actions were as dangerous as the possible and "terrible" events that might likely occur "out of the blue" in everyday life.

Finally graduating from college as an art major, Will traveled cross country, considered backpacking in Europe but "chickened out," became sexually adventuresome and played the mild drug scene, both activities animating great anxiety and a mix of difficult feelings of excitement. Due to his hearing loss, he avoided having to serve in Vietnam, a prospect that filled him with terror. As relieved as he was, he felt quite guilty about his own ongoing "cowardice." He finally went to work for his father, when he could not realize how to shape a career "in art." He met his current wife and after an ten-year-long ambivalent relationship, when they wanted children and she became pregnant, they married.

Throughout the marriage to that point, Samantha worked in skilled administrative positions to fund the family, although both she and Will were originally art students, a creative area of life that drew them together. Their sons were cared for by Will's mother during their first three years of life when Samantha was at work until her daughter was born, overwhelming Will's mother, necessitating Will taking on work for his father from home. Samantha and Will were very involved parents, but with a new baby and one of the twin's challenges, serious enough to cause him to enter therapy and be enrolled in special schools for a number of years, Will's responsibilities increased, which both justified his failures in meeting work pressures and made him feel increasingly inept.

With the children now in grade school, Will "luxuriated" in a "cozy" and partially soothing morning routine. He woke early and immediately had to grapple with his inner demons, where in the shower, he would "survive" a torrent of internal superego attacks, ridiculing him, demeaning him, and frightening him. Already spent, he dressed, made lunches for the kids and Samantha, got "everyone up and going" while he prepared breakfast, then drove the kids to school as Samantha left for work. Most days, he went surfing for an hour, which somewhat restored him, picked up doughnuts and coffee, before returning home to disappear into the newspaper, reading every word, from back cover to front, until the thought dawned on him, he ought to do some work. Shortly after, lunchtime arrived and two hours later, it was time to pick up the kids, run a few errands, and begin dinner preparations before Samantha arrived home. Samantha was unaware of this routine, and while she appreciated the household and parenting contributions Will made, she was increasingly frustrated with his "inexplicable" lack of making money.

Moving from once a week to twice a week sessions, Will continued to talk in either energized spurts or in a slow, stammering drawl. Even though he could concentrate intensely in various activities, even to the degree that he lost all sense of time while so involved that he then forgot the next appointment or task, Will was still convinced that he suffered from ADD. While he was frustrated and embarrassed over his inability to manage work requirements in a timely and efficient way, Will did not stay with intense feelings of any kind for very long. In moments, he could move from an active, feeling state (sympathetic nervous system excitatory arousal) to "all of his energy draining out," to not feeling very much of anything at all (parasympathetic nervous system inhibitory dampening down). Out of immediate awareness of his states, categorical or vitality affects, Will spent a great deal of energy trying to live in a 'mild' zone, the spectrum of which was quite narrow, from being 'zoned out' on the parasympathetic side to 'feeling fine', barely, on the sympathetic side, that is, not feeling any categorical affects of intensity. In Stanley Greenspan's (1997a) regulatory disorder terms, Will was a mix of hypersensitive/fearful and hypoaroused/underreactive. Most sessions, I was, in Greenspan's terms, 'wooing' Will into contact and engagement with me, as he vacillated between his searching struggle for energy and words and his energized talking where there was little, if any, room for me even to offer any response.

After enacting his process of getting so involved in an activity that he forgot all else directly into the treatment by missing several appointments over weeks, we came to an agreement for a period of several months, that if ten minutes passed and he had not arrived, I would call him, and he would "zoom" up. At the same time, he was having a hard time keeping track of himself in the sessions, as well as in between sessions, so that most sessions had the feeling, to him and to me, of starting over from scratch. Yet, he was obviously intelligent, and had been an avid reader for years, so was highly knowledgeable about diverse subjects, philosophy, the political scene, literature, sports, and how to "fix" just about anything. He was the household hand's on daddy, car mechanic, home renovator, and multipurpose guy, who could spend extended periods of time in the sessions without any stammering or searching for words, 'teaching' me about a wide range of subjects, including such things as ocean currents or mitering a handcrafted fireplace mantel.

I learned through such 'teaching' how expert a surfer Will was, an activity he had pursued since puberty when he was told he could not play contact sports because of the repercussions of the car accident. The first time he shared with me his love for surfing and how he tracked the ocean, I was convinced he did not have ADD. His eyes cleared, then sparkled, his voice grew deeper, his muscles took on tone, his skin pinked, his mind was alert, and he became very engaged with me. At such times, when he rhapsodized about surfing or arrived at a session fresh from surfing, I could feel his robust self, although it would take only a small life disappointment or challenge to bring him back to feeling weak and impoverished.

I consulted with an expert on ADD, a man who had been involved with some pivotal research with jet pilots, some of whom washed out of their training although there was no obvious reason why this should be. Their research found that a certain number of candidates could not carry over their learning from the simulated environment to the actual flying environment, demonstrating problems with transitioning learning. Once the research group worked with these pilots on carrying their knowledge across transitions, the candidates not only did not wash out of the training program, they excelled at it. After a lengthy discussion, he and I came to the same conclusion: Will's problem seemed much more to do with the difficulty in carrying experiential knowledge [noesis] and awareness [autonoesis]) across transitions than with ADD.

As a result of this consultation, I began to focus on transitions with Will, transitions between concrete experiences in his everyday life and transitions between affective states in the sessions. I offered Will open ended sessions for a few months to help him locate within himself beginnings, endings, and transitions. He eagerly agreed. I re-arranged our appointment times when I could have an open hour following our scheduled session. The first such session lasted over two hours before Will came to his own ending point, actually feeling and being able to verbalize, "I think I'm done for today." In the next few sessions, he was aware of his end point after an hour and a half, and this pattern continued for another couple of months. After that, he reached a natural end-point after a fifty-minute hour, and he carried that internal time clock about the end of the sessions from then on.

At that point, when Will came in and sat down, he emptied his pockets, placing his keys, his checkbook, his cell phone, whatever else he might be carrying, on the floor near him. I could see him 'settling in', and although I never mentioned it, Will had found a 'place' for himself in this shared environment. With the shift in tracking time more effectively, and in his comfort in the analysis and within our analytic relationship, Will began to notice shifts and transitions in his life, even if he was not yet always able to make them easily or carry specific awareness across the transitions. He also brought to session a drawing journal he had purchased so that at moments of his own choosing, he could jot a few notes to "help him remember."

In concert with working on transitions, we naturally turned our attention to what happened in his work life. Will told me about the only regular full-time job he had, years before. Hired as a manager of the supply department of a construction store, he had a very difficult time keeping track of the various projects he oversaw, planning them, keeping them on target, tracking the employees for whom he was responsible. Will experienced spontaneous nosebleeds, severe headaches, and was finally fired, a result that had a demoralizing effect on him for years. After that, he returned to work on a self-employed basis with his father.

Will's marriage continued to be on shaky ground, though the fact that he was dedicated to his therapy gave Samantha some rays of hope. She accused Will of being passive, passive aggressive, even hostile, while Will clearly demonstrated that he was afraid of his wife. He avoided any communication to her that could lead to problems (and, thus, solutions), which meant him, or especially her, becoming "upset," or by cowering under her "tornado-like rages" for which there was no soothing her, only an escalation until the episode spent itself. At times, he might acknowledge the similarity to his mother's storms but would quickly protest to me how different Samantha was from his mother and how much he loved Samantha. Much of his adult life, Will drifted in a state in which he felt an abject failure. He woke up before dawn with a vicious 'tape' already playing in his head about all the things there were to worry about and how bad, inept, and failing he was. Will had never earned much more than about $20,000 in any single year. He repeatedly tried to set goals, being unable to implement them. His inability to stay on track to make a living, along with the semi-perpetual fog he was in, ignited his wife's attacks of frustration and fury. She also felt abandoned and scapegoated by Will being the "good, attentive" parent, and she the "bad," but responsible parent who carried the financial burden.

We turned our energies to trying to estimate how many hours a week Will actually worked, what he did or did not accomplish, and how much time he felt slipped through his fingers, always due to a state of fogginess or vagueness. He tried keeping logs, lists, tracking in a variety of ways, including in his drawing book, how he might be functioning in the work part of his days. To no avail. After one session I got an idea about how early this failure in tracking might have occurred in his life, so I purchased a box of colored blocks. In our next session, as he and I sat on the floor, he chose and laid out the different sized and colored blocks to represent the various aspects of his life: short and green for work time, long and blue for personal time, orange and mid-length for home time, yellow for family time, and so on. He arranged and re-arranged the blocks until they felt 'right' to him. Then we 'counted' the hours. He was astonished to realize that he was working only about ten hours a week.

Toward the middle of our second year, three pivotal events occurred for Will. First, his cousin to whom he was very close in age and in friendship dropped dead of a heart attack. They had been separated in early adolescence for a number of years because Will's mother had a breach with the father of this cousin, that father being Will's uncle, the adventurer/scientist who died on expedition. Upon the adult reunion in their twenties, of Will and his cousin, their friendship rekindled and remained steadfast. Will wanted desperately to go to the funeral, but Samantha was resentful of his being gone for several days and of spending the necessary travel expense. After our session, Will made the bold move of arranging to go to the funeral, despite Samantha's objections. He spent the plane trip composing a eulogy and found himself at the heart of family and friends, touching them with his presence, and for the first time in his life, could accept his more emotional nature, which revealed itself during the eulogy, as a possible sign of strength and courage.

Second, his wife entered analysis. A turbulent time ensued in their relationship culminating in an exchange of written communications between

Will and Samantha, hers a four-page single space 'storm' of frustration she had been carrying for years, feeling that she had been forced into being the wage earning drudge in ever more high end positions where she excelled but which she hated, having to abandon her art and dreams, while Will got to move about the world at his leisure. His was a brief and vague note of avoidance.

We spent weeks in the analysis going over her letter line by line, as Will struggled to sort out and face what was true of him and his dynamics and what of Samantha's emotional life might be related to her own history. Through this painful process, he came to see the truth in her complaints about him, especially his passivity and his passive-aggressiveness toward her. He also came to see how terrified she was of being abandoned, although she used her anger to defend against this fear and to organize herself. Will began to confront in only the most rudimentary way, how and why he was so afraid of her, finally making the links himself to the parallel between his mother's anger and retribution and the power he assigned to Samantha. Through their parallel therapeutic experiences and what appeared to be the ending of the marriage, they discovered that each was terribly afraid of losing the other. The marriage took a profound turn then, with a renewed commitment from each of them that they wanted to stay together and make their marriage work.

Third, during the summer, Will's mother died after many months of declining health. During her illness, Will had several opportunities with her to discuss elements of his childhood, helping him weave together his own narrative. Will's ability to be an integral part of his cousin's funeral stood him in good stead as he coped with his one sister who, along with her own daughter, was particularly difficult and antagonistic in the aftermath of their mother's death and disposition of personal belongings. Because of the family disruption, and his father's avoidant response to the disruption, there was no funeral or service of any kind, except a quiet family dinner without the one sister and niece. Will requested some of his mother's ashes, spending the next couple of years before deciding what kind of private ceremony and location he, his wife, and their children might have together to scatter the ashes.

Intermittently, Will felt a 'new' sense of strength beckoning within himself and had times of making and holding affective links, having more open communication with his wife, and beginning to act on some outer-directed goals in terms of work. One morning, when he was usually buckling under internal attacks in the shower, he had a new sense of me being "his light at the end of his tunnel." With this, his early morning 'tapes' began to subside. Whenever they did reoccur, although at a diminished level, he reported being able to "answer back to them."

During the fall, Will experienced some increasing success in his work life, and by the end of the year concluded three major projects. His income that year, and again the following year, was the most he had ever made in a single year and in one month he made as much as he had in some years. He was able to buy a 'new' used car, which he sorely needed, a computer system for his family, and put away the rest to cover his expenses for the coming few months. But within days of this heady success, I watched his energy, focus, and sense of self fade and, in just a few weeks, finally collapse. Over the coming months, as I witnessed him slide further and further into the quicksand of passivity in his life, filled with sadness and boundless inertia, I wondered how much of an essential self in Will still existed.

CHAPTER TEN

Julia's Beginnings

In Julia's voice mail message to me to set up an appointment, she mentioned that she had had my name and number for a year, and that she wanted to have a full analysis. When I returned her call, she reiterated these statements but modified the second to say she wanted to "move into" a full analysis.

At our first meeting, I was struck by her dark hair, long and flowing down to the middle of her back. As she spoke, she appeared calm, measured, and quite intelligent. She carried her petite self with economical grace. I was surprised when she told she was an emergency room nurse, since her delicate manner belied the kind of sturdiness I imagined would be required in such demanding work. To me, she felt 'young' in an eager kind of way, making sure I understood she was committed to an analysis, "four or five times a week, seven years."

Shifting in her chair after our initial exchanges, she said, "My problem is with men. That's why I'm here." She recounted a story about the man she recently dated but with whom she had broken up. After the break-up, he left a series of voice messages, clearly masturbating as he did so and using explicit language. She called him, demanding that he stop. A few days later, he called her as though his previous voice mail messages had never taken place. In their conversation, he acted "kind of whiney." In the face of his denial, she "jabbed him," something she said she often did with men inadvertently, not aware until later that she had found a way to hurt them. Her "jab" was that she told him she found it curious that he would leave these messages and masturbate during them when they both knew perfectly well that he was impotent. He retaliated by telling her that their relationship had been good practice for the relationship he was now having with another woman who looked like her, was bright like her, but "was better, much, much better."

She hung up and cried for over an hour—about how he had hurt her, how she had hurt him, about her recent divorce. She met with a friend the next day and related this story to her. The friend said in response that she really should go into analysis. Julia had considered analysis a year earlier when she ended her marriage. She was referred to me by an associate at her hospital, but postponed calling. This time, she called me the Friday afternoon she returned from lunch with her friend, and we met the following Monday.

She abruptly changed topic, talking in a rush of words, telling me about an incest survivor's group she attended a couple of years earlier. After she confronted her father for his inappropriate behavior with her, her family of origin disowned her. *My problem is with men,* she had said. During this recounting, Julia played with her hair, swooshing it up and over the back of the chair, stroking it, pulling on it, moving it to the side, sectioning it. The greater the intensity of feeling she experienced, the more she played with her hair, but intermittently, if she calmed a bit, she would stop. At one resting point, I said, "Tell me about your hair."

She shivered and went to hold it still, "Why, because it's still wet?"

"Not at all," I responded. "I just noticed that it seemed to soothe you, to play with it."

She became very teary and with another gush of words, said, "I was a hysterical baby. I cried all the time from the minute I was born. My mother told me I had a terrible temper in my first weeks of life, and when I was six-weeks-old she overdosed me on Phenobarbital. After that, she and my father used Phenobarbital all the time to keep me quiet. How did you know I did that with my hair?"

"I think you found a reliable and important way to take care of yourself."

I could see a few tears tickling down her cheek. She said she thought since her problem was with men, maybe she should have a male analyst, but that she was happy to be with me. She decided to start at twice a week, building into a "full analysis;" we established the fee and set the time for our next meeting.

At that session, she walked in, smiled, and headed straight for the couch, lying down with precise dignity. I was seated at one end, so when she leaned her head back onto the pillow, she scooped up her hair so it fell over the end of the couch and cascaded into my lap. She drew her arms in close to her sides and did not move. She talked about already wanting to idealize me, her fears of being disappointed, then apologized in advance if she happened to "zing" me. In a fluid manner, she told me more of her history. She had been conflicted about marrying her now ex-husband, Greg, her earlier dating life being comprised of young men who soon disappointed or "grossed" her out sexually. She had a close friendship with Greg, who felt more like a brother to her than anything else.

Their children, a daughter and a son, were the center of her life, and she worked in a shared shift arrangement so that she was at work only when the children were in school. She and Greg were actively involved in the children's upbringing on a daily basis, the children living with her while Greg, a patent attorney, lived in a home just blocks away, so that the children could go back and forth as they desired. As she spoke, I was aware of feeling as though a protective presence was "presenting" her to me, not a false self (Winnicott, 1960a) in the usual sense of the term, but more a hovering self, safeguarding that she was protected.

During the ensuing weeks as Julia talked, she made it clear that I was listening to stories that had never been witnessed to by anyone. Julia was the oldest of three children, one brother and a sister. Her deceased father was a physician of note, who had a penchant for cyclical mood swings, enjoyed violence and alcohol, but who was also known for being charismatic. The only mention of her mother was Julia's description of her as vacant and creepy. She ended this with, "I hate her."

She soon elaborated on being considered a hysterical baby with a terrible temper. By the mother's own report in a singsong, high-pitched little girl voice, she told Julia throughout her life, "You were an albatross around my neck." In the mother's recounting, the mother intended to nurse Julia in the hospital, trying to put on a good image as a young resident's wife, but to immediately bottle-feed her upon arriving home. That plan completely failed. Julia refused the bottle. Her refusal ushered in a battle where the mother struggled actively but unsuccessfully to wean her from the breast.

When Julia was six weeks of age, her mother took her to a pediatrician who diagnosed the baby as having "an immature nervous system," prescribing Phenobarbital as a soothing agent. The mother gave Julia the first dose in the parking lot of the doctor's office, repeatedly telling Julia throughout her growing up years what a relief it was to have her stop crying and doze off within moments. When the medication wore off, Julia's frantic attempts to nurse and refusal of the bottle continued, with her crying escalating. Just days after this visit to the doctor, her mother "accidentally" overdosed Julia with the Phenobarbital, sending her into a coma lasting *three days*. Significantly, the father, toward the end of his medical training, kept her home without seeking additional medical care, wondering aloud at times whether the baby had contracted polio. Toward the end of the third day of her listless, drugged state without food, she began moving, and her father exclaimed, "Look! She's working her jaw!"

After Julia emerged from the coma, her father regulated the dosage of Phenobarbital himself until she was three months old and "learned to stop crying." For Julia, there was no mother to whom she could attach as an attuned, caring, and providing other, helping her calm, organize, and find pleasure in her neonate states. There was only the mother who wanted to get away, even to the point of nearly annihilating her infant to relieve herself of "the albatross around her neck," to drug her baby into a state of non-need. In Julia's internal object world, the primary identification that should have been forming with a present, loving object of secure attachment, was instead the introjects of absence, hostility, neglect, and impinging trauma. Her mother told Julia that "miraculously," she learned to feed herself solid food by six months, following this self-feed just two months later with her first words, "Me do."

Julia's father apparently found some ways to soothe her as an infant. He demonstrated for the mother "how easy it was," by doing an "angel dance" with Julia, placing her on her tummy on his arms as he floated her around the room. I was aware that Julia was unconsciously instructing me how to feed her and soothe her, to be the analyst/mother who wanted to be devoted to her, to meet and regulate her states of distress, while also finding her a source of delight, who did not want to rid myself of her, but who could give her the support *and* the space in which to find calming and interest. Yet, did not that space need to provide a 'secure base', not a place in which only to 'float'?

In our work, Julia concentrated on her relationship with her father, including her conviction that there had been some incestuous experiences with him, though her memories about that were more like shards of sense impressions. When she was two, three, and four years old, her family lived in the southwest, as her father, taking a leave between medical residencies, became a flight surgeon in the Air Force. Her father was on call a good deal, but worked in flight only ten hours a month, so he was at home and involved with Julia most of the time, especially after her baby brother was born. This new baby had his own violent reaction to the mother, arching away from her, screaming most of his waking life.

Julia remembered the sound of ambulance sirens, flashing lights, her father being whisked away, coming home upset, saying how tired he was of having to "pick up body parts off the desert floor." She comforted him, even at age three and four, patting him, talking to him. He, in turn, made grilled sandwiches for her, played with her, read to her, taught her. He was full of life and enlivened her. At this time, living in the protection of the military base, Julia could ride around on her tricycle and "visit" the houses, barracks, and staff on the base. Everyone looked out for her, except her own mother, from whose depression, neglect, and oppression Julia sought to escape.

Julia always wept when she told me these stories. She also said something precious was lost for her at that time in the southwest. She recounted sense impressions of a man in her bedroom, in the middle of the night, near her shoulder—mental flashes of a penis, her feeling repulsed and disgusted. She worried aloud that there was a bottomless well of such feelings, that she would be "too much for me," and that she would be in "this kind of pain" all her life.

She followed these kinds of impressions by telling me her mother accused Julia from when she was quite young into her adolescence of "inciting" her father, then "forced" Julia into calming down the father. In those instances when Julia inevitably failed, she was blamed and castigated by her mother.

As a married adult, Julia, Greg, and their children went with her parents on what turned out to be a final family ski trip. Julia requested a separate suite for her family, but her parents refused. One evening, after dinner, Julia's father pinned Julia up against the wall, trying to kiss her. Greg intervened, and the young family returned home immediately.

Later, still shaken and having flash, implicit memory retrieved, vitality affect ridden, pictures of her father diapering her, and of how repulsed she was by her father during her adolescence, Julia insisted upon meeting with her parents. Two other influences prompted the meeting as well. Routinely, Julia's father was very hard on Julia's little boy, being critical and belittling, with Julia and Greg's concern increasing on the trip. That, combined with the events on the ski trip, prompted Julia and her husband not to leave her father alone with their little boy anymore. Although Julia's mother initially honored Julia's request, she soon violated their agreement. Concurrently, Julia's younger sister's daughter was undergoing an abrupt and noticeable change in behavior, with the three-year-old asking various family members to have "her pussy rubbed the way grandpa did it."

Alarmed, Julia discussed this with her sister and brother, the three of them deciding that Julia would call child protective services to see if someone would come to her sister's house and talk with them about what to do. Mistakenly, the police picked up her sister at work, took her away in handcuffs, and placed her daughter in protective services. While the mix-up was quickly sorted out and the child returned to her mother later the same day, members of the family took sides.

At a quickly assembled family meeting, Julia confronted her parents with her father's history of sexual and violent behavior and her mother's disavowals and lack of intervention. Julia's father was furious and vehemently denied all of the behaviors, including the ski trip incident, and within days disowned Julia for being the "child" who hurt the family, a role I came to learn she had been scapegoated into over and over. None of her family of origin had had any contact with Julia since, not even allowing her to attend her father's funeral a year and a half later. Following the experience on the ski trip, Julia's revulsion being exacerbated by the incidences surrounding her niece, and Julia's "exile," Julia became "grossed out" by sex in general, finding herself bursting into tears after sexual encounters with her husband. Within months, she and Greg separated.

In between relating these traumas to me, Julia told me of a dream. In the dream, she was a very young girl, leaving the city to protect its inhabitants, journeying into the world alone, burdened and forlorn. She was allowed to take only a wheelbarrow like cart that was nearly too big and unwieldy for her little girl self to push.

In a following session, Julia turned to more current issues, relating an experience that she felt reiterated behaviors of hers that increasingly concerned her. Another man she recently dated expressed his desire to have a family, along with his new worries about his excess weight after his physician issued him a health warning. Julia's spontaneous response was to say, "Well, you won't live long enough to have a family." He broke off the relationship with her with a note, telling her how stung he was by her "jab."

In processing her jab with me, she noticed that whenever a man offered her intimate information about himself, she felt obligated to tell him the 'truth'. In what felt to her like innocence, her responses came out in stinging remarks, leaving her surprised that what she said was perceived to be hurtful, not helpfully corrective. When the man became upset and retaliated, she felt misunderstood and betrayed. I asked her what the jabs might provide her, and after a few minutes, she thought they offered her emotional distance from intimacy. I felt compassion for, as well as concern about, the many ways she had developed to jockey for position with others in her efforts to stay safe, maintain control, keep distance from threatening intimacy and need, theirs and hers, while demonstrating her intellectual acuity, her rapid-fire ability to 'figure things out,' an ability used to preserve her psychic equilibrium.

I discovered more of the multiple layers of her unresolved trauma in the months ahead. Julia carried a small facial scar, the result of falling down a steep embankment when she was about two years old, to be found hours later only when she managed to climb back up. As an adult, the scar was undetectable until she cried or became embarrassed, when her face reddened. In her childhood, her father who was perceived as the responsive and enlivening parent, was viewed as highly skilled and fascinating by those who knew him socially and professionally. At home, he vacillated between violent outbursts and deep depression, where he would go to bed for months at a time except to get up to work before returning home to bed. It was not uncommon for him to fly into a rage and throw a television through a plate glass window or drop and shatter a prized possession of his wife's, or walk around the dining table drunk, pressing the point of a knife into family member's necks while exhorting them to be happy and sing. Julia's mother's response invariably was to admonish Julia "not to take him so seriously. Let it roll off, like water off a duck's back."

Julia described how she felt in her body every day of her life: as though a knife had been plunged into her back and she was made to live with it in there throughout her days. She was caught in a life of fierce emotional binds. Her mother seemed a phantom to Julia, menacing, yet emotionally blank, passive, who routinely handed off Julia to keep her father "in control."

While the mother was considered quite beautiful, a model originally and a "model-looking" mother, she was completely incapable of nurturing any of her children. Neither did she exhibit any interest in doing so, other than to dress them "properly," minimally feed them, and coerce them to behave in ways appropriate to the social life they lived in their elite community. Julia's mother appeared to be interested only in herself, in shopping, and in maintaining her social position. Julia was vocal in her hatred of her mother, while she yearned for a mother who would know her and love her, having found the only approximation of that in her lively but cruel father.

As a child of four and five years old, Julia became the little mother herself, interceding for and protecting her rambunctious and "difficult" younger brother and providing care to her new baby sister, a baby who was compliant, non-resistive, and undemanding. School became another saving avenue of success for Julia, which became the arena in which she shone. She was always an excellent student, popular with her classmates. Concurrently, Julia clearly remembered bath time when she was six years old and older with her father scrubbing her and her younger sister, "hard, up inside," her protests drawing only his scorn and the admonishment that the girls needed to be "very clean." She experienced a major bout of depression at age nine when she broke her arm and as a result felt her "flaws were showing."

Throughout the years, Julia became an excellent sailor, and as a young girl usually won or placed in sailing races. After one particularly important event, Julia's father took her second-place trophy and with great fanfare dropped it into the bay, his expression of disapproval and disappointment on show for all to see. In her early adolescence, her father forced her to work for him in his office during the summers, often to observe and assist him at procedures. Afterwards, Julia would need to serve as "audience" as her father regaled her with his feelings of disgust, especially toward female patients. Julia went through another major bout of depression when she was twenty years old and attending an exclusive eastern women's college, where she felt alone and miserable. Once she transferred to a western university, she recovered and excelled. She wanted to become a physician herself, but her father would not allow her the opportunity of eclipsing him so supported her only in going to nursing school.

At this point in the treatment, Julia experienced me mainly as the new good object. She and I established a strong connection and a solid working alliance. A few months into the treatment, Julia began leaving me one or two brief voice messages a day, short on-going moments to share. My voice mail responsiveness served a significant purpose for Julia of having someone in her life who for the first time truly cared about her and was attentive to her, with whom she could process her daily life. I never found her messages intrusive or burdensome; in fact, this telephone message contact proved invaluable in our work, giving her the experience of someone on whom she could really count, of my presence and interest in her.

Julia had another dream. This time as she struggled on the road to who knew where, trying valiantly to push her cart, there I was, by the side of the road, maybe sixteen or twenty years old to her little four-year-old self. She did not know me quite but saw that I was going to travel with her and help her by pushing the cart. We might even gather flowers together or find sweet berries to eat. Maybe, she might eventually be able to play at my feet. I was clearly the 'new object experience', someone who wanted to "meet" her, know her, soothe her, and travel with her. Understandably, Julia could not tolerate even a hint at any possible negative transference or transference interpretation, adamant that I was all for which she could have hoped. But I wondered how the various developmental transferences might emerge in the consulting room. I would soon find out.

Eleven months after our work began, Julia agreed to a dinner with a male aide at the hospital, someone who had pursued her insistently for weeks. So far, she managed to put him off, demurring because of her children, being older than he was, or telling him she was not ready to start dating. But now, trying to appease him, she finally gave in to his forceful requests. He got quite drunk at dinner, pressuring her to go home with him and have sex. She was able to get assistance from the host at the restaurant who called a cab to take her home.

The next day, he called Julia, apologizing profusely and asking for another chance. When she refused him, he begged her to meet with him, explaining his actions by how depressed he was, even thinking about suicide. She found his neediness compelling and agreed to go for a walk with him near the hospital. The walk extended into a lengthy conversation during which he shared with her the stories of violations perpetrated upon him in childhood. Julia, in turn, opened up to him about what appeared to be their similar woundings. The day was turning into late afternoon and as the sun was setting, and he became agitated, Julia began to feel panicky. Trying to extract herself from their now prolonged time together, she worked to soothe him, just as she had her father, hoping to convince him that they could talk again another time but telling him kindly that she needed to leave. Under the darkening sky, he pulled her down an embankment and raped her. Her impulse to scream for help was silenced by the flooding of fear and shame.

We were scheduled to meet the next day to transition into four times a week sessions. As she talked with me and sobbed that morning about what had happened, I listened with tears welling up in my eyes and fury toward this man pounding in my chest. Then, as I heard the elevation in her voice, her tremble of pleasure, my feelings were replaced with growing dread and horror as I watched her terror and shame convert into excitation. Moments later, when she got up to leave, she blinked once and whispered, "I'm in love with him."

CHAPTER ELEVEN

Gazing Together—What Patient and Therapist Glimpse

Anguished Questions

Who am I? What has happened to me? Why am I the way I am? Can I ever be what I want to be? For the adult with unresolved trauma, these are not philosophical or existential considerations. They require answers, answers that resonate with what such an individual has lost, accompanied by an old and early sense, almost recollection, of who s/he started out to be.

Patients, like Will and Julia, cause an urgency in me for each of them, one that also resonated with my own early traumatized self to know who I was, why I was here, and what was the purpose of my life. Over years of later exploring discussions with my husband, my analysts, close friends, various spiritual mentors, and eventually colleagues I found an evocative path offered by Neville Symington. Symington (1986) looked at psychoanalysis as "a method for investigating the truth" (p. 22). I agonized once more: *Truth?* I wondered. I knew there were true facts, like gravity, but truth? Symington continued, "Truth is real; it exists" (p. 17), but that truth cannot be possessed—only glimpsed. While real, Symington pointed out, "Truth does not exist though as some external idea, as Plato thought, but as a reality that exists *in between*: in between two persons seeking it, in between psychoanalysis, sociology, psychology, economics and religion" (p. 17). For himself, he found that, "When I see the truth some change occurs in me. I can never be the same again. Something in my personality has altered ... this means that the individual is always in relation to truth and is in a state of *potentia*" (p. 17) ... [and] is grasped in dialogue with another.... Truth emerges between the analyst and the patient, and in the moment of understanding there is a change in both" (p. 19).

What is the 'Truth' of the Self?

As we turn our attention to these urgent questions, we cannot escape that at their heart rests uneasily the concept of the self. While there are various theoretical perspectives regarding the concept of the self, there are two major psychoanalytic positions concerning its existence and meaning that deserve our developmental and clinical attention. One position, represented by a theorist such as Philip Bromberg (1996/1998) holds the "view that the self is decentered, and the mind as a configuration of shifting, nonlinear states of consciousness in an ongoing dialectic with the necessary illusion of unitary selfhood" (p. 270). Bromberg (1996/1998) argued that "...there is no such thing as an integrated self—a 'real you,'" (p. 195), but rather "...the capacity to feel like oneself while being many" (p. 195). Similarly, Frank Putnam (1997), psychologist, contended "...in a normal individual, specific state-dependent senses of self are sufficiently integrated with one another that the individual maintains a sense of continuity of self across state and context" (p. 164).

Earlier, Joseph D. Lichtenberg (1975) wrote on "The Development of the Sense of Self," cautioning that, "...'self', in my usage, always refers to self-experience, the sense of self. Sense of self, however, is explicitly not limited to conscious awareness, but refers to conscious, preconscious, and unconscious sensing. This total sensing is responsible for the *quality* of the sense of self—

its cohesiveness, its continuity over time, and its retaining an essential sense of sameness in the midst of developmental changes" (p. 460).

Antonio Damasio (1999) differentiated between three types of self: the *proto-self*, "...an interconnected and temporarily coherent collection of neural patterns which represent the state of the organism" (p. 174), the *core self*, "...a transient entity, ceaselessly re-created for each and every object with which the brain interacts" (p. 17), and the *autobiographical self*, "...a nontransient collection of unique facts and ways of being which characterize a person" (p. 17). When he considered "...the notion of a bounded, single individual" (p. 134), he attributed stability as the defining and central characteristic that assures its continuity of reference, while being able to change across time.

Daniel Stern (1985), in his classic book *The Interpersonal World of the Infant,* presented his ideas on the four subjective senses of self, each of which is supported in its development by four "different domains of relatedness" (p. 28):

- the emergent self— the infant's experience of "coming-into-being of organization" (p. 45),
- the core self—the basis of self-agency, self-coherence, self-affectivity, and self-history (p. 71),
- the subjective self—the infant's experience that s/he "has a mind and that other people have minds as well" (p. 124), and
- the verbal self—the child can objectify the self, be self-reflective, and comprehend and produce language (p. 28, 162).

In Stern's writings, he did not seem to reach a conclusion about *what is the self,* examining instead how the *sense of self* develops.

According to this decentered view of the self, the self is thought of in terms of both identity and multiplicity. Stephen Mitchell's (1991) view of multiple selves accounts for how we know ourselves, and of necessity how we vary ourselves in various relationships, as well as within one relationship in varying circumstances. He wrote (1993), "We are all composites of overlapping, multiple organizations and perspectives, and our experience is smoothed over by an illusory sense of continuity" (p. 128), but warned, "It is mistaken to assume that a digestion and blending of different versions of self is preferable to the capacity to contain shifting and conflictual versions of self" p. 105).

The other fundamental position regarding 'what is the self' is represented by those theorists who consider the self to be 'real', the existence of an entity. Freud's original notion of 'Ich', the I, would ultimately be translated by Strachey as 'ego'. Martin Silverman (1986) delineated how Freud used 'Ich' in four different connotations:

1) to denote the objective I, the "psychological entity one knows oneself to be;"
2) in the subjective sense, the I as interacting with others, "one's active, experiencing, operant self;"
3) the structural I as the "executive agency within one's psyche that assesses internal requirements and external constraints and demands and develops patterns of action that meet them ... and mediate between them;" and
4) as referring to "a person's self-representation ... that sets oneself apart from others as a unique, individual human being" (p. 182).

In 1900, Freud intimated that the word "ego" referred to the entirety of the psychic self. Yet, as his ideas developed, he conceived of the ego (1923/1955) as a structure evolving with the psyche for the purpose of mediating between the chaotic energy of the id seeking immediate discharge of excitation and the requirements of the world interfacing with the individual.

W. Ronald D. Fairbairn (1954) used the term ego in a similar meaning to Freud's original connotation, that is, as connoting 'self': "The pristine personality of the child consists of a unitary dynamic ego" (p. 107). He was resolute in his contention that this innate integrity of self was a "singular" and "unitary" whole, *a priori* to the exigencies of life, that this self existed from the very beginning of life and was *not* dependent upon experience for its existence. Richard Rubens (1994) suggested that Fairbairn's "relational/ structural model provides room for the most extensive and rich of notions of inner world" (p. 2), as Fairbairn "viewed the self not simply as the result of experience, but rather as the precondition for it.... the self is the pre-existing starting point for all experience and provides continuity in all that develops later in relationship to others.... The self expresses its selfhood and is shaped in the course of its development" (p. 2). Rubens (2003) further interpreted Fairbairn's view: "Psychic energy is object-seeking, the resulting conception of the psyche is that of a self-generated, unitary center of definition and energy, with the potential for, and the drive toward, self-expression outward into the object world, and the potential for experiencing that world, its own self-expression, and the resulting interaction between the two" (p. 4-5).

D. W. Winnicott discussed his concepts of the true self and the false self throughout his career. In his paper, "The Clinical Varieties of Transference" (1955-6/ 1975), Winnicott explained that when the adaptation from the infant's environment is not good enough, there can be no establishment of the true self as a differentiated and thriving entity. Instead, "there develops a *pseudo-self* which is a collection of innumerable reactions to a succession of failures of adaptation" (p. 296). While the false self is an aspect of the true self, it "hides and protects it, and it reacts to the adaptation failures and develops a pattern corresponding to the pattern of environmental failure. In this way the true self is not involved in the reacting, and so preserves a continuity of being. However, this hidden true self suffers an impoverishment that derives from lack of experience" (p. 296-7, see also 1960a/1965).

Winnicott examined the infant's true self potential in "Theory of the Parent-Infant Relationship" (1960b/1965), writing, "Infants come into *being* differently according to whether the conditions are favourable or unfavourable. At the same time, conditions do not determine the infant's potential. This is inherited... [yet] the inherited potential of an infant cannot become an infant unless linked to maternal care" (p. 41).

Heinz Lichtenstein (1961) defined the *concept* of identity as "the capacity to remain the same in the midst of change" (p. 193), differentiating that concept from the *sense* of identity... a consciousness of such continuity of sameness" (p. 193). In terms of the impact of the maternal relationship upon the emerging human identity of the infant, Lichtenstein advanced the idea that, "Out of the infinite potentialities within the human infant, the specific stimulus combination emanating from the individual mother 'releases' one, and only one concrete way of being this organ, this instrument. This 'released' identity is irreversible, and thus it will compel the child to find ways and means to realize the specific identity which the mother has imprinted upon it" (p. 208).

Though it certainly seems that Lichtenstein held to a unique identity, he extensively explored the *sense* of self in his paper "The Dilemma of Human Identity" (1963), capturing that dilemma in his statement, "When we talk about ourselves, we attempt to deal with ourselves as if we were, as Hannah Arendt calls it, a 'what'. But being a 'who', we are not properly capable of looking upon ourselves as a 'what'. In doing it, the who quality of our inner experience is lost. This is the type of problem I have in mind when speaking of the dilemma of human identity" (p. 174).

Heinz Kohut (1977), in his psychology of the self, stated: "My investigation contains hundreds of pages dealing with the psychology of the self—yet it never assigns an inflexible meaning to the term self, it never explains how the essence of the self should be defined.... The self, whether conceived within the framework of the psychology of the self in the narrow sense of the term, as a specific structure in the mental apparatus, or, within the framework of the psychology of the self in the broad sense of the term, as the center of the individual's psychological universe, is, like all reality… not knowable in its essence" (p. 310-311).

Still, he did address "the essence of the self" (p. 310), and suggested that "the examination of the question of the existence of a rudimentary self in earliest infancy [is undertaken] from a perhaps surprising starting point, namely, by stressing that the human environment reacts to even the smallest baby as if it had already formed such a self.… The newborn infant cannot have any reflective awareness of himself, that he is not capable of experiencing himself, if ever so dimly, as a unit, cohesive in space and enduring in time, which is a center of initiative and a recipient of impressions. And yet, he is, from the beginning, fused via mutual empathy with an environment that does experience him as already possessing a self" (p. 99-100).

Robert Emde (1983) examined the apparent contradiction of "how can there be a self before the development of a mental capacity for representation?" (p. 165). He introduced his notion of "the affective self" (p. 179): "Because of man's complexity and the fact *that no two individuals are born the same*, the general biological principles of self-regulation, social fittedness, and affective monitoring work toward the coherent uniqueness of each developing person. Thus, it seems a paradoxical truth of self that our heritage guarantees both our species-wide commonness and our individual uniqueness" (p. 179, italics added). Further, "Our 'affective core' ensures that we are able to understand others who are human… because our affective core touches upon those aspects of experience which are most important to us as individuals, it also allows us to get in touch with the uniqueness of our own (and others') experience" (p. 180).

Christopher Bollas (1989) put forward the idea that, "If we are to provide a theory for the true self, I think it is important to stress how this core self is the unique presence of being that each of us is: the idiom of our personality.

We are singular complexities of human being—as different in the make-up of our characters as in our physiognomies; our person design finds its expression in the discrete living villages... that we create during our lifetime. A genetically biased set of dispositions, the true self exists before object relating... depend[ing] upon maternal care for its evolution" (p. 9, 10).

Frank Lachmann (1996) argued that the "advantages claimed [in the postmodern tradition] for multiple selves as fluid, complex, and subtly textured, vis-à-vis singular self, are based on a static, simplistic, narrow definition of self" (p. 596). He defined the "singular-self process model" (p. 596) as "initiating, organizing, and integrating experience along the five motivational dimensions" (p. 596): (1) needs for physiological regulation; (2) needs for attachment and affiliation; (3) needs for exploration and assertion; (4) the need for sensual pleasure and sexual excitement; and (5) the need to react aversively with aggression or withdrawal (see p. 596). "These five systems, based on inborn needs, develop interactively with the environment from birth on. They contribute to the organization and integration of the self and are subsumed under it.... The self in this view is fluid, broad, and complex. It is fluid in that it shifts in different contexts as various motivations are activated. It is broad in that a range of motivations is encompassed. Its complexity is evident in the characteristic and pervasive themes that are consolidated in organizing a person's experience. It may or may not remain cohesive" (p. 596). This conception "implies *a striving for integration*.... Integration is not a melting pot that dissolves distinctions, but a mosaic that holds disparate facets of the self together. Integration does not entail pressure to yield up complexity, as critics of the singular self claim, but a tolerance for diversity" (p. 596).

Finally, Louis Sander (2002), considered by many to be 'the father of infant research' began his observational research with parents and their babies in the 1950s. His work is as alive and pertinent today as it has been spanning the decades. Many of today's infant researchers, like Demos, Stern, Brazelton,

Greenspan, Beebe, and Emde have made their own contributions following Sander's models or being inspired by him. He certainly has been pivotal to our understanding that as individuals made up internally of infinitely smaller cellular and biological systems, we grow and develop within dyadic systems of interaction, as well as within ever larger and more complex systems around us, which directly and indirectly influence that growth and development. Yet, he also highlighted the necessity of embracing uniqueness:

> ...uniqueness is a kind of complicated difficulty that has always seemed a hindrance to our understanding. But in dealing with ongoing processes in any given living system, we become confronted with the necessity to deal with the unavoidable actuality of uniqueness.... Given the uniqueness of each of us as individuals, in no two infant-caregiver systems will "process" be alike either.... Why not begin with uniqueness as a central principle in the organization of a living system (p. 34-35)?

Pregnant for the first time, I discovered the in utero photographs of fetuses by Lennart Nilsson (1990, with text by Lars Hambrger), which delineated the powerful process of intrauterine development. In my becoming-a-mother-self, these photographs did not depict the 'illusion of selfhood', but the dynamic growth of specific and unique individuals and their 'in potentia', prior to birth. From each of my children's births, being present, attuned, and responsive as possible to the unfolding of their very unique selves, and as they and I grew, and, years later, as I formed into a developmental psychoanalyst, I moved away from any either/or stance and instead looked for the 'truth' within the complexity of how each of these two fundamental views of the self could co-exist and inform each other. In concert with theorists such as Winnicott, Emde, Bollas, Lachmann, and Sander, I honored my stance that the self is real and unique; it *exists*. My evolving notions of development became based upon this profound existence of an innate, born self *as entity*, a *who* as each of us, what I came to call the *essential self*, essential in that this self is both unique to that individual and indispensable to its experience of life. Yet, in the spirit of Lichtenberg, Bromberg, Mitchell, and Sander, I experienced this self as finding its continuity and coherence of being and *moving towards* its development *as a process* within a complexity of self states, *a who in the process of how*, the flow or fragmentation of which emerges from the pivotal interactions with a providing or denying environment—*in between* self and other(s).

In my view, this theoretical deliberation concerning what is the self has reasons for being other than its philosophical intrigue or jockeying for viewpoint. For our patients, this 'debate' is core for their strivings. As traumatized children, bereft and alone and unable to escape their earliest overwhelming experience within their undifferentiated psyche/soma, or their 'self' being parceled into dissociated self-states whose default purpose was to defend them from the devastating nature and unbearable effects of his or her lived experience, the later adult anguished questions of *Who am I?, Why am I the way that I am?, Can I ever be what I want to be?* require answers.

Part Three

Shattered Glass

Models II and III *The Seven Keystones of Wounded and Traumatized Development*

The subject of trauma is plentiful but *why* and *how* trauma remains unresolved has not been explored to the same extent. Through dedicated research, my own personal experience, my own analysis, and later that of my patients', I became determined to unlock the puzzle. I delved deeply into what made up the facets of unresolved trauma: its interwoven experience with loss, its varied, taxing and stunning consequences, such as, Posttraumatic Stress Disorder (PTSD) and Complex Posttraumatic Stress Disorder (CPTSD), its myths, like closure and the idea that 'trauma is just a natural part of life', fueled by the false promises to be found in the passage of time. Especially, I looked to my models of the keystones of development to discern the various impacts of unresolved trauma upon each of them, particularly as they played out in the consulting room.

I began various formulations, the first three and four in no precise sequence. I expanded the possible dynamics, then moved them in and out of different orders, eliminated what was repetitious, then combined this thought-filled honing until I determined the six core reasons why trauma does not resolve:

- First, I found that no responsible and caring adult was available during the originating trauma to comfort, soothe, regulate, or process with the traumatized individual their traumatic experience, or later, its consequences
- Second, in fact, the perpetrator of the trauma was often a significant caregiver or someone who was supposed to be a 'safe island'
- Third, those to whom the child/adult turned for help either ignored, belittled, or denied the traumatic experience, thus re-traumatizing the individual
- Fourth, no discerning and protective caregiving adult intervened in the trauma's repetition

- Fifth, the perpetrator was not held accountable, nor was required to make reparations and usually was more protected than the victim, and,
- Sixth, alone in managing trauma's consequences, the child/adult became caught in an impossible dilemma, "fright without solution" (Hesse and Main, 2000, p. 1117), facing ongoing triggers and lasting traumatic reactions.

Exploring and processing in depth the developmental compromises that trauma imposes upon a child, adolescent, or adult patient is not for the faint of heart. But, as therapist and patient together bravely grapple with these impacts, life-changing opportunities are found on the path to healing and transformed development.

CHAPTER TWELVE

Trauma—Crash and Consequence

The Historical View of the Nature of Trauma

Originally, the word trauma was used medically to describe a severe *physical* wound caused by injury coming from external events. Joseph Breuer and Sigmund Freud (1893/1955) appropriated this word to describe how an injurious external event causes a severe *psychic* wounding, which has lasting emotional consequences, even though the memories of such events may no longer be retained in conscious awareness. Subsequently, Freud (1895/1955, 1898/1955) was convinced by his clinical work that only childhood sexual traumas were of consequence in the development of neuroses. After being shunned at the presentation of his revolutionary ideas to the Vienna Conference, Freud (1905/1955) abandoned his theory of sexual trauma in favor of presenting these traumas as existing in the patients' fantasies alone. In 1920, he delineated how patients who suffer from traumatic neurosis often have dreams that are basically a reiteration of the original trauma, complete with its affective charge. Noticing also that play and transference themes could have the same quality of trauma repetition, he proposed that *all* compulsion to repeat originates from traumatic experience: "an extensive breach made in the protective shield against stimuli" (p. 31).

Michael Balint (1969) assumed a three-phase structure to trauma:

1) in the first phase, "the immature child is dependent on the adult and, although frustrations in their relationships may occur which may lead to irritation and even to rage at times, the relationship between the child and the adult is mainly trusting" (p. 432),
2) in the second phase, "the adult, contrary to the child's expectations, does something highly exciting, frightening or painful; this may happen once and quite suddenly or repeatedly... there exists for a time a most intense, often passionate, interaction between child and the adult (or deep disappointment for the child)" (p. 432),
3) in the third phase, "the child... approaches the partner... and tries again to get some understanding, recognition and comfort. What happens quite often... is a completely unexpected refusal. The adult behaves as if he does not know anything about the previous excitement or rejection; in fact, he acts as if nothing had happened" (432-433).

In Balint's view, "all three phases are equally important for a proper understanding of the dynamic structure of a trauma" (p. 433). In terms of the analytic situation, Balint cautioned the analyst against participating in the excitation of repeating phase 2 in the treatment, but as importantly, in the event of such originating traumatic experience repeating in the transference, the analyst must not respond to the patient with "non-participating passive objectivity" (p. 434), as this would result in a re-traumatizing repetition of phase 3.

Other earlier theorists looked at trauma as well. Phyllis Greenacre (1965) concluded that, "Any condition impairing the mother-infant relationship at this time [first year to eighteen months] interferes with the foundation of object relationship, increases and prolongs primary narcissism, and tends to damage the early ego, with special harm to the sense of reality and often to the beginning sense of identity" (p. 148-149). Esther Bick (1968) explored the omnipotent defences that a baby must find to hold herself together when a containing object is unavailable, which, then, in adulthood, plays out in the embedded belief that the individual must 'do it all' by herself. These defences originally are the result of the baby's desperate strivings when the baby is too much on her own in managing distress. Joan Symington (1985) described the "catastrophic fear ... of a state of unintegration and spilling out into space and of never being found and held again" (p. 481) in lieu of the baby feeling a psychic skin that holds her and her various young parts of self together. To cope with such states of unintegration the baby attempts to hold herself by alternately 1) focusing attention on a stimulus that captures her attention, or 2) being in constant bodily motion, or 3) tightening or clenching muscular movements. Together, these actions might give the baby a sense of psychic skin, of being held together in the face of frightful unintegration.

Leonard Shengold (1978) defined soul murder as, "a deliberate attempt to interfere with another's person separate identity, joy in life, and capacity to love ... the child's almost absolute dependence upon an adult, most frequently a parent, makes possible a regimen of cruelty and seduction (overstimulation) alternating with indifference and neglect (deprivation) that provides the environmental matrix for soul murder...." (p. 419). Shengold (1979) went on to shed light on the repercussions of such traumatic experience: "Soul murder involves trauma imposed from the world outside the mind that is so overwhelming that the mental apparatus is flooded with feeling. (The same state can result as a *reaction* to great deprivation.) The terrifying 'too muchness' requires massive and mind-distorting defensive operations in order for the child to continue to think and feel. The child's sense of identity ... is threatened" (p. 538). But "in the resourcefulness of children, such a child can accomplish 'doublethink'" (imposed by the need for rescue during psychological torture)" (p. 540), and, thus, the child can love the torturing other: "Since the child 'can't understand what's done to her', her mind is unable to deal with, to work over, what is not understood and what may not even be allowed to register. It is this inhibition of the ego's power to remember and to test reality that makes soul murder so effective as a continuing force. The absolute need for good mothering makes the child believe in the promise that her parents and 'dear, kind God' will be good and rescue her, and to believe that *she* must be bad...." (p. 541).

Maria Bergmann (1992) looked at trauma as:

> ... a hostile blow from the outside world, evoking an immediate conscious feeling of being overwhelmed, helpless, disorganized and narcissistically injured. Typically the trauma victim is unable to put what has happened into words. Generally, intrapsychic reaction to severe trauma is characterized by damage to ego functions. Capacities for cognition, fantasy formation, verbalization and sublimation are reduced... defensive ego regression may lead to splitting in an attempt to disown the trauma, or to fusion with traumatizing objects in order to absorb the trauma.... Further, a reliable differentiation between acute and potential dangers may now be impaired, interfering with reality testing (p. 447).

Both Esther Bick's and Maria Bergmann's sensitivity to what constitutes the *experience* of trauma can be found in a much earlier paper by Martin James (1960) that has similar relevance to my work with Julia. James stated that in the first three months of life, "Premature ego development would imply that the infant, during the phase of primary narcissism, took over functions from the mother in actuality, or started as though to do so. This would not be phase-adequate behaviour under three months of age" (p. 290). Such premature ego development occurs because "Consistent failure to guard the [infant's] instinct-barrier happens when, for reasons either of her situation or of her personality, the mother cathects other things than her baby, and, as we say, 'has something else on her mind'" (p. 290). We can see the premature ego development occurring in Julia first in her fight to be breastfed, in "learning not to cry," and then in learning to feed herself.

Culled from trauma literature, various forms of trauma have been defined:

- ACUTE TRAUMA = a sudden and severe event of terrifying lived experience
- REPEATED ACUTE TRAUMA = numbers of or repetition of sudden and severe events of terrifying lived experience
- CUMULATIVE TRAUMA = chronic lived experiences of assault, deprivation, and/or neglect ("cumulative trauma is the result of the breaches in the mother's role as a protective shield over the whole course of the child's development, from infancy to adolescence—that is to say, in all those areas of experience where the child continues to need the mother as an auxiliary ego to support his immature and unstable ego functions" (M. M. Khan, 1963, p. 290).
- VICARIOUS TRAUMA = witnessing terrifying lived experiences in which one is helpless to intervene

Bessel van der Kolk and Alexander C. McFarland (1996) specified that, "Unlike other forms of psychological disorders, the core issue in trauma is reality" (p. 6). Complicating this reality is the subjective meaning assigned to these lived experiences and the judgments the child carries about him or herself as the result of this meaning making. van der Kolk and McFarlane demonstrated that the default defense system put in place as the result of trauma depends on the child's constitutional temperament, the child's age and developmental stage, environmental context, and the severity of trauma. These defenses can include: inability to accurately decipher the stimuli (assault or neglect), surrender, freezing, inability to modulate one's own arousal because one's physiology becomes a source of negative arousal or fear, avoiding and numbing, dissociation, hyperarousal with fleeing, and only much later, fighting back. This list, however, does not do justice to the raw experience of trauma and its aftermath, the price paid in the loss of protection and innocence and in the subsequent years of emotional vigilance traumatized individuals must endure.

Susan Coates and Mary Sue Moore (1997) defined trauma as "an overwhelming threat to the survival or integrity of the self that is accompanied by annihilation anxiety. Such a threat can be registered even in the neonate. Infants abused within days of birth show powerful fear and avoidant responses to the specific abuser both at the time and in subsequent encounters (see also Gaensbauer, 1995). When such emergency defensive reactions persist, they can interfere with the subsequent development of a flexible range of age-appropriate defense mechanisms and, ultimately, with the further development of the self" (p. 287). Together, Coates and Moore outlined a number of features associated with trauma, all of which were present in Julia and eight of which were present in Will:

- The transmission of intense, unmetabolized affect as an aspect of the trauma
- The multiple uses of imitation as means of managing traumatic experience
- The development of distortions in the self-structure as the result of imitation
- An impairment in the differentiation of self and other
- An impairment in symbolic capacity and in the ability to play
- Repetitive enactments of the trauma
- The preservation of a physiological memory of the trauma quite independent of representational memory
- An increase in characterological sensitivity
- The adoption of a hypervigilant stance

- The development of role-reversed behaviors in the primary attachment relationship (p. 287).

In more contemporary language, but similarly, Daniel Siegel (1999) and Frank Putnam (1997) have spoken to the nature of trauma, which:

a). causes the disruption of gathering self state coherence,

b). creates specialized self states in which the trauma is encoded in an effort to prevent overwhelming the individual's self system, and,

c). forces the individual to live in dissociated and fractured self states, which are use dependent.

This glimpse into this vastness of trauma literature can be captured in even more evocative ways. Bessel van der Kolk (1987) wrote, "The essence of psychological trauma is the loss of faith that there is order and continuity in life. Trauma occurs when one loses the sense of having a safe place to retreat within or outside oneself to deal with frightening emotions or experiences. This results in a state of helplessness, a feeling that one's actions have no bearing on the outcome of one's life. Since human life seems to be incompatible with a sense of meaninglessness and lack of control, people will attempt to avoid this experience at just about any price, from abject dependency to psychosis" (p. 31). Finally, Philip Bromberg (1994) spoke viscerally of trauma as "competing algorithms at the same moment[:] ... when your mother bounds toward you with fangs bared ... when your father approaches you with penis bared ... where your peer group suddenly becomes a pack of hyenas, stripping you bare while you are still alive" (p. 243).

Putting together my six elements of the unresolved trauma puzzle, we can see that unresolved trauma cannot be integrated but exists independently in dissociated states and in implicit memories, inculcated primarily in the right hemisphere. As such, it cannot be used for learning or as a reliable guide for discerning future threat or danger. For the child suffering unresolved trauma, his/her unprocessed terror experiences produce long-lasting consequences.

We can also deduce that if there is an attuned, empathic, caring, acknowledging, and intervening adult, a child or adult can recover from trauma. As this validating other helps the traumatized individual process the physiological and emotional responses to and repercussions of such experience, especially in partnering in holding the perpetrator accountable, traumatic experience can be made usable for learning and serve as a guide for future experience.

Now that we understand the basic difference between the nature of processed and resolved trauma and unresolved trauma, let us look at the impact upon development of unresolved trauma.

Development Consequences of Unresolved Trauma

From Sigmund Freud to Daniel Siegel the consequences of unresolved trauma are seen as raw, profound, complex, multifaceted, and, without intervention, long-lasting:

> In traumatic neuroses the operative cause of the illness is not the trifling physical injury but the affect of fright in the psychical trauma.... We must presume rather that the psychical trauma—or more precisely the memory of the trauma—acts like a foreign body which long after its entry must continue to be regarded as an agent that is still at work (Breuer & Freud, 1893/1955, p. 6).

> The emotional suffering, the stress-induced damage to cognitive functioning, the internal chaos of intrusive implicit memories, and the potential interpersonal violence created as a result of trauma produce

> ripple effects of devastation across the boundaries of time and human lives (p. 60).... Lack of resolution of traumatic events or loss from the past directly affects emotional experience (Siegel, 1999, p. 111).

One of my central assertions is that when the infant/child experiences trauma that, first, is affectively overwhelming, and second, remains unresolved due to the six core reasons I offered at the beginning of Part Three, especially the caregivers' perpetration of, or obliviousness to and/or belittlement or denial of the trauma, the development of the child's *essential self* is substantially hampered and his/her *sense* of self as *wounded* becomes established through a fundamental identification with the unresolved trauma. In turn, the child must then adapt to the subsequent requirements of the environment at the immense cost of his/her essential self. These repercussions of unresolved trauma may appear in patches or in more obvious and overarching ways.

Let us turn our attention to Model II, the Development of the Wounded Self when gaps, failures, and woundings occur and Model III, the Development of the Traumatized Self, which offers a visual depiction of the profound impact of sustained unresolved trauma.

Development of the Wounded Self

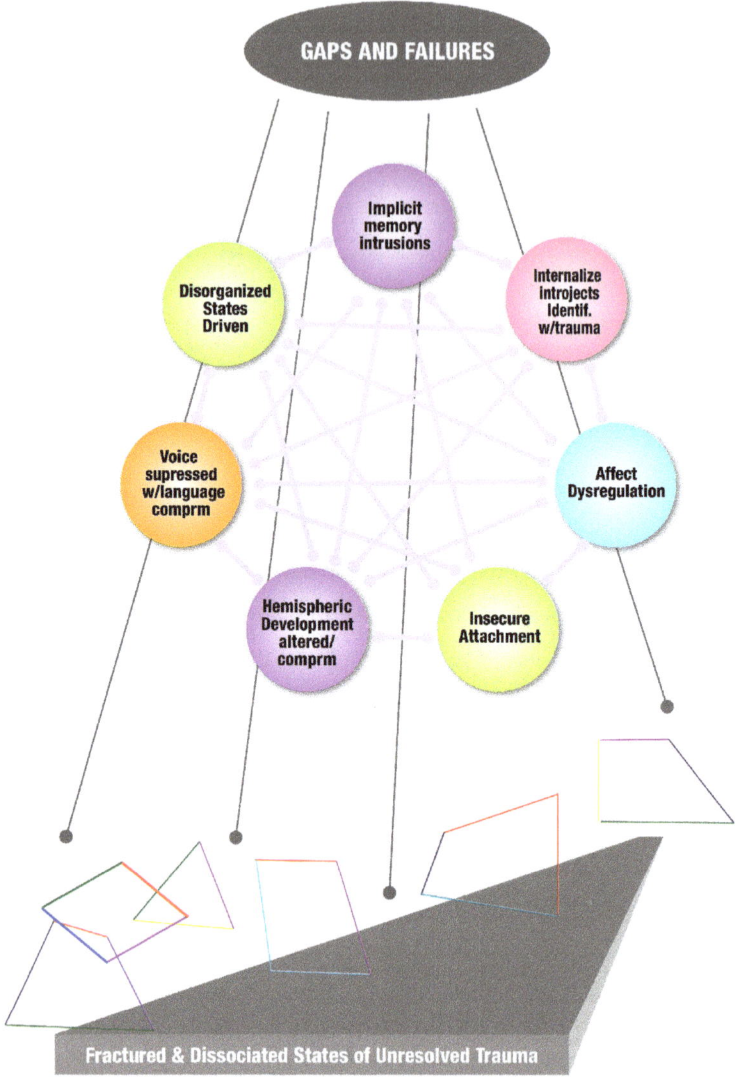

MODEL II - the Wounded Self ©Gwyneth Kerr Erwin, 2001

Development of the Traumatized Self

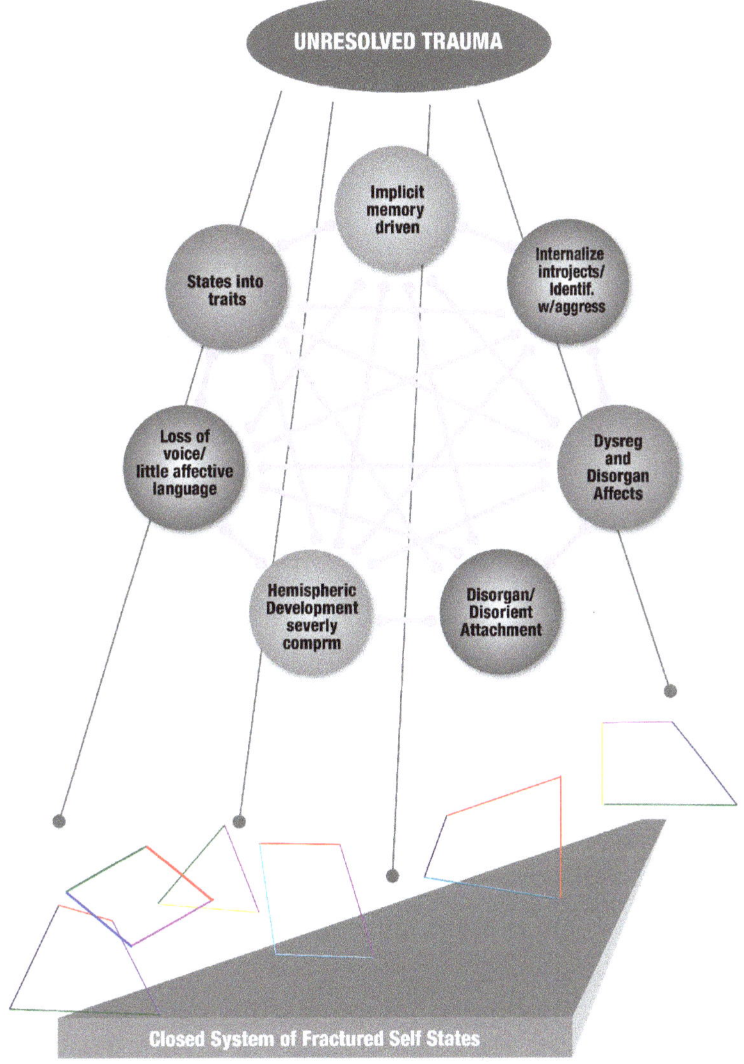

MODEL III - the Traumatized Self ©Gwyneth Kerr Erwin, 2001

The differences between Models II and III are not only qualitative, meaning worse in degree, but qualitative, worse in kind:

- the disorganized states of Model II have converted distressed states into personality traits in Model III;
- the implicit memory intrusions seen in Model II have given way to the traumatized individual being implicit memory driven in Model III;
- the internalized introjects we find in Modell II have placed the individual into a ferocious bind, either identification against the aggressor by becoming the victim, or identifying with the aggressor, acted out against others or imploding within, against the self, demonstrated by Model III;
- the affect dysregulation in Model II, difficult in and of itself, now becomes an internal storm of disorganized and utterly bewildering affects in the traumatized development found in Model III;
- the sub-categories of insecure attachment noted in Model II plays out primarily in disorganized and disordered attachment, such as reactive or traumatized attachment in Traumatized Development (Model III);
- the altered hemispheric development shown in Model II becomes severely compromised in the traumatized development as delineated in Model III; and,
- the suppressed personal voice and compromised expressive language viewed in Model II is lost with little expressive language available as shown in Model III.

CHAPTER THIRTEEN

The Impact of Unresolved Trauma Upon Development

Of utmost importance in terms of our understanding what we are dealing with clinically and interpersonally is that development, at its best or worst, does not occur evenly. One keystone may be mastered, another has a deficit, yet another exhibits a complete failure in meeting milestone requirements. Especially, when the wounded or traumatized individual has intervening developmental support from some pivotal source, s/he may be able to develop 'on top of' or 'around' other keystones. Think of a tree when its main branch sprouts auxiliary branches. Some may not grow, or are trimmed back, burned, or cut, yet the tree continues its reach for the sun. This, I interpret, is what Winnicott (1960b/1965), may have been seeing in his true self/false self portrayals. Survival of the self, at nearly any cost, is the primary driving force for humans, achieved through attachment proximity for love, safety, protection, and comfort, with thriving as the ideal. Now, we are going to take a deep dive into each of these keystones and the consequences they reveal that wounded and traumatized experience has upon development.

KEYSTONE #1 – Dissociated Self States into Traits

Any non-traumatized individual child or adult can become afraid, sad, angry, or experience loss while still maintaining a coherent sense of self as the self transitions between various affective and behavioral states. But with repeated and unresolved injury, neglect, and trauma, these resulting self states become engrained, and as they wire stronger and stronger neuronal pathways shift from being states into maladaptive character traits. For example, instead of a child being fearful or angry on occasion, the child becomes a fearful or angry child.

How does this happen? Bruce Perry, et al (1995) elucidated: "This process of creating some internal representation of the external world (i.e., information) depends upon the pattern, intensity, and frequency of neuronal activity produced by *sensing, processing,* and *storing* signals. The more frequently a certain pattern of neural activation occurs, the more indelible the internal representation. Experience thus creates a processing template through which all new input is filtered. The more a neural network is activated, the more there will be use-dependent internalization of new information needed to promote survival (see Cragg, 1975)," (p. 275).

The brain develops sequentially and in a hierarchy from least to most complex. To assist this development, there are what Bruce Perry, et al (1995) called critical periods of development and sensitive periods of development, during which times as we have seen with hemispheric development the brain and its central nervous system is being 'wired' and organized. The authors concluded, "Abnormal micro-environmental cues and atypical patterns of neural activity during critical and sensitive periods, then, can result in malorganization and compromised function in brain-mediated functions such as humor, empathy, attachment, and affect regulation" (p. 276), because "rather than a *deprivation* of sensory stimuli, the traumatized child experiences overactivation of important neural systems during sensitive periods of development" (p. 277). For example, "the child [who] is in a *persisting* fear state (which is now a 'trait')... will very easily be moved from being mildly anxious to feeling threatened to being terrorized. In the long run, what is observed in these children is a set of *maladaptive* emotional, behavioral, and cognitive problems, which are rooted in the original *adaptive* response to a traumatic event" (p. 278).

While we humans develop an array of psychological defenses and coping skills over the course of our lifetimes, we have three fundamental, biological defenses that occur in a developmental timeline. The first, occurring between birth and approximately two to three years of age is to freeze. Just as an animal who turns belly up and surrenders or plays dead in hopes the predator will go away, the young child similarly surrenders through 'tonic immobility' because s/he has not yet developed the sense of timing, the mobility, the strength, or the wits to flee or fight back. Once the child of 2-3 years of age develops a rudimentary sense of time (to get away) and space (somewhere to go), and working mobility (running), s/he exerts the second biological defense: fleeing and hiding. The third biological defense does not come on board until the adolescent child develops strength and can thus fight back. That does not mean that a younger child will not fight back, but the fighting is ineffective because s/he can be easily overcome physically by an adult or is punished in a variety of ways for voicing their objections.

Dissociation, Depersonalization, and Derealization

Depersonalization, the sense of unreality of one's very selfhood, and derealization, the sense of the external world as being unreal, are each an aspect of the dissociation process.

Dissociation occurs originally because the child's experience has become overwhelming to such an extent that as protection for his or her fledgling self, s/he has to "send away" a particular part of themselves for safekeeping. Dissociation of states serves as "the escape when there is no escape" (Putnam, 1997, p. 104), escape not only from traumatizing experience but from the affectively overwhelming state experience and as a "defense against fragmentation" (Bromberg, 1994, p. 244). Harvey Schwartz (1994) viewed dissociation as "... a self-hypnotic process that attempts to anesthetize and isolate pain. The mind is essentially trying to empty itself, to black out—in fact, to get rid of itself.... The mind is fleeing its own subjectivity to evacuate pain" (p. 191).

When the individual is 'successful' in dissociating aspects of his/her experience and the affective challenges within it, such "dissociative experience often remains unsymbolized by thought or language, lingering disconnectedly in somatosensory or iconic levels of memory... isolated, silenced, and hidden, dissociative experience continues to exert influence, but in a way that is cut off from full participation in the life of the individual intrapsychically and interpersonally" (p. 204). The often-resulting petrification of the child into what I call 'a system of fractured self-states' (Erwin, 2005), is the significant consequence "not of a shattering of a previously intact identity, but rather the developmental failure of consolidation and integration of discrete states of consciousness" (Putnam, 1997, p. 176).

In a less devastating scenario, with the intervention of available, responsible, and caring adults in the form of extended family members, teachers or foster parents, doctors, social workers, or various types of therapists coming into the child's life, what I have named 'the *wounded self*' (Erwin, 2005) can be formed, assisting the child as s/he functions despite a hidden internal system of dissociated self-states. This self is protectively dis-enjoined from its traumatized states and may even carry the *appearance* of an integrated self (see Winnicott's false self, 1960/1965). With added supports, this child may grow into a highly functional adult in certain non-affective and non-relational areas of life, but one who often feels fraudulent or at risk. However, the consequences of unresolved trauma become a living hazard for this individual.

Gary Whitmer (2001) conceptualized dissociation as an interpersonal defense rather than an intrapsychic one: "at its core [as] an impairment in the subject's ability to represent his or her own experience... what the subject recognizes as 'me' is determined by another's perceptions.... The harm that leads to dissociation lies in the mother's insistence that her interpretation of the child is the only interpretation..." (p. 812, 821). With repeated injury or neglect, traumatized states can become so engrained that they no longer function only as experience but convert into maladaptive character traits as we have seen from Bruce Perry's et al (1995) work, and may result in "... major abnormalities or deficits in neurodevelopment—some of which may not be reversible" (p. 276).

The younger the child the more likely dissociative responses occur. As we have seen in young children, their first and usual reaction is to freeze, which "allows the child the acuity to scan the environment for further threat and also hopefully serves as camouflage" (p. 280). Yet, in the face of subsequent nonverbal, verbal, or behavioral threat "the child feel[s] more anxious, threatened, and out of control. The more anxious the child feels, the quicker the child will move from anxious to threatened, and from threatened to terrorized. If sufficiently terrorized, the 'freezing' may escalate into complete dissociation" (p. 280). Dissociation affords the child an escape from overwhelming stimuli in the external world (as in daydreaming, fugue or depersonalization) and a retreat into or even feeling 'out of' the internal world (as in loss of consciousness). Perry, et al found, "The nature of the trauma seems to be important to the pattern of adaptation; the more immobile, helpless, and powerless the individual feels, the more likely they are to utilize dissociative responses" (p. 282).

Will dissociated, through derealization, many elements of the requirements of day-to-day living. Through depersonalization, he escaped the responsibility of his robust and courageous self, falling into the power of his superego attacks of his weak and cowardly sense of self. Pivotal to the understanding of Julia is a more complicated dissociative conceptualization, known as the Orphic Function. This concept was first captured by

Sandor Ferenczi (1932) as the automization of the personality. Nancy A. Smith (2001) built substantially upon Ferenczi's concept, coming to the understanding that, "Orphic functioning is neither pathological nor is it healing. Orpha should not be mistaken for a 'resilient' human spirit. Orpha does not attempt noble regeneration of life, it only preserves life. Orpha is an evolutionary necessity to insure our species' survival when attachment is impossible" (p. 5-6). Orpha thus represents: "In moments of extreme danger it is possible for the intelligence to detach itself from the ego and even perhaps from all affects... [and become] a vital life organizing instinct, felt by the patient as 'an unconscious guardian angel" (p. 5). Smith (personal communication) delineated ten aspects of Orphic functioning, which are briefly summarized as follows:

1) Orpha is one of the personality's critical responses to trauma, an innate maternal protective process, insistently causing the traumatized person to go on inhaling life.
2) Orphic functioning allows the traumatized person to navigate in the world despite trance and dissociation.
3) Orpha may be part of humanity's genetic grammar, to ensure survival of the species in times when attachment is impossible.
4) Orphic functioning is available at any point in human development when trauma occurs.
5) Orpha operates silently and efficiently outside the grasp of the punitive self and other. It is not called forth from an intersubjective matrix, but whenever one's internal psychic world is in crisis and external support is unavailable.
6) Orpha serves as a private intelligence, free of affects.
7) Orphic functioning is not to be confused with Brandchaft's concept of pathological accommodation (1995) but is to aid the individual

in a severe attempt to protect from further trauma and ensure s/he has no need of true attachment.

8) The earlier the trauma and the more severe, the more heavily Orphic processes rely on encapsulation of that trauma as a means of survival.
9) Orpha's concern is always *preservation* of the fragmented self, not *regeneration* of the self.
10) Orpha is dependent on receiving some assistance from the environment in order for growth to resume: to adapt to new conditions, allow for increased degrees of attachment.

For Julia, her Orphic internal "guardian angel" provided her the only glimpse of inner maternal care and protection in the absence of actual such care, and she depended on this presence as a guide to learning to be high functioning in her challenged experience.

KEYSTONE #2 – Implicit Memory Intrusions

Rita Carter (1998) gave us a perspective on the power and impact of memory: "The brain has 100 trillion connections joining billions of neurons and each junction has the potential to be part of a memory.... The human memory is... selective. Items of interest are retained better than those that are not... the brain also works by linkages. This is the basis of all mnemonic systems" (p. 175).

As we discussed earlier, **implicit** (also known as procedural and nondeclarative) memory refers to the conscious and/or unconscious encoding and retrieval of lived experience, especially skills and habits, emotional responses, and both reflexive and conditioned responses, particular to trauma. Experiences that are emotionally charged and arousing, and which are also repeated, increase neuronal firing and encoded neuronal pathways. Daniel Siegel (1999) explained: If the amygdala is activated, then the engram encoded at that particular time is thought to be marked as significant; this has been called a 'value-laden' memory.... This emotionally charged value-laden memory is thus made more likely to be reactivated among the myriad of infinite engrams laid down throughout life" (p. 48).

In **explicit** or declarative memory, the consciously encoded memory systems are altered over time due to subsequent influence, context, emotional valance, and the passage of time. But referring to implicit memory, van der Kolk and McFarlane (1996) showed numerous studies (see Bohannon, 1990, Christianson, 1992, Pillemer, 1984, Yuille & Cutshall, 1986, for instance) demonstrated that, "People's subjective reports of personally highly significant events generally find that their memories are unusually accurate, and that they tend to remain stable over time" (p. 281). Significantly, van der Kolk found no published accounts in the scientific literature [as of 1995] of intrusive traumatic recollections of traumatic events in patients suffering from PTSD that had become distorted over time, either in an experimental or in a clinical setting" (p. 282), possibly because "the imprints of traumatic experiences seem to be qualitatively different from memories of ordinary events... traumatic memories may be encoded differently from memories for ordinary events—perhaps because of alterations in the focusing of attention, or perhaps because extreme emotional arousal interferes with hippocampal memory functions" (p. 282).

Daniel Siegel (1999) came to similar conclusions as van der Kolk: "If events are overwhelming and filled with terror, a number of factors may inhibit the hippocampal processing of explicit memory, and therefore may block explicit encoding and subsequent retrieval. Such factors include divided attention, amygdala discharge, and release of noradrenaline and cortocosteroids in response to massive stress. Such conditions allow implicit memory to be encoded while explicit processing is impaired" (p. 47).

Trauma, early in childhood, which includes maltreatment and/or deprivation or neglect, "directly affects circuits that link the bodily response to brain function: the autonomic nervous system, the HPA axis, and the neuroimmune process... psychological trauma involving the blockage of explicit processing also impairs the victim's ability to cortically consolidate the experience... but the person may be prone to experiencing continually intrusive implicit images [or sensations] of past horrors... [and] autonoetic [self-knowing] consciousness of traumatic events is disturbed in individuals who have experienced trauma that remains 'unresolved'.... Some individuals may become flooded by excessive implicit recollections, in which they lose the self-monitoring features of episodic [explicit] recall and feel not as if they are intensely recalling a past event, but rather that they are in the event itself" (Siegel, p. 52-53).

Posttraumatic Stress Disorder (PTSD) and Complex Posttraumatic Stress Disorder (CPTSD)

While the nature of Posttraumatic Stress Disorder (PTSD) and Complex Posttraumatic Stress Disorder (CPTSD) and their relationships to States and Implicit Memory (and the other five keystones) will continue to be explored throughout this book, especially as they are exemplified in the clinical cases discussed, we need to understand their basic structures at this point. Posttraumatic Stress Disorder (PTSD) symptoms can be exhibited as:

- mental and/or physical signs of distress, including
    - intrusive thoughts and feelings related to the precipitating traumatic experience, which are provoked by traumatic "cues" or stimuli

- ¤ alterations in the usual ways a person cognitively processes (e.g, confusion, difficulties in focus and concentration)
- ¤ and feels physiologically (e.g.,, fear-based sensations in the body such as chills {parasympathetic}, sweating {sympathetic}, and disturbed sleep with accompanying nightmares

- avoidance of those cues and triggers
- increased "freezing," flight, or fight responses

Complex Posttraumatic Stress Disorder (CPTSD) has not yet been included in the DSM (see DSM 2013). But as Adrienne Schwartz (2020) pointed out, "According to the World Health Organization's International Classification of Diseases (ICD-11), a diagnosis of C-PTSD includes the symptoms of PTSD, but has three additional categories of symptoms: difficulties with emotion regulation, an impaired sense of self-worth, and interpersonal problems" (p. 4). Many researchers and clinicians (e.g., Dr. Bessel van der Kolk, Harvard University) are working diligently to have this diagnosis included in the next edition. CPTSD is a necessary diagnosis in professional opinions, including my own, because PTSD does *not* take into account the psychological dynamics and resulting significant symptoms that occur in CPTSD for traumatized individuals. Six clusters of symptoms are proposed for the CPTSD diagnosis: alterations in 1) affect regulation along with impulse regulation, 2) attention 3) self-perception, 4) interpersonal relations with others, 5) interpretation and meaning of experience, 6) and increased somatization. The most significant impact in CPTSD that differs from PTSD is what alters one's self-perception and why.

The essence of CPTSD lies in its ***interpersonal nature***, coming from repeated and prolonged exposure to an individual of significance, whether caregiver, person of authority, or partner, for instance. In such relationships, the victim has little or no chance of "escape," whether that be physically or emotionally. Foundational examples of CPTSD are various forms of abuse, deprivations, and neglect:

- physical (beatings, burnings, tortures),
- mental (gaslighting, accusing, undermining, ridicule),
- emotional (overt and covert),
- financial (stripping of independence, exerting control),
- and spiritual (hierarchial power).

Among the many consequences of such interpersonal trauma is what is called the deformation of the self, which results from the power, control, and influence that the figure of authority exerts overtly or covertly over the victim. Such traumatization often begins in childhood, even though it can occur at any phase of development. In CPTSD, the temporary loss of a coherent and stable sense of self usually leads to the following:

- subsequent loss of self-worth,
- depersonalization, derealization, dissociation,
- inability to take initiative,
- feelings of deep shame, fear, guilt,
- stigmatization, with a lack of safety and protection, resulting in a loss of trust in others,
- an internal loss of self-regulation exhibited in ongoing feelings of helplessness,
- loss of focal attention, a sense of purpose, and comprehensive functioning in the outer world,
- excessive accommodation, withdrawal, inhibited or exhibited anger,
- rumination of the reoccurring trauma at the expense of being able to concentrate on other required aspects of living,

- desperate reaches for help (which can tragically lead to re-traumatization as they are often met with denial, ignorance, or belittlement, accompanied by misguided renewed demands for acquiescence by others to the very person who is causing the CPTSD in the first place).

Will certainly suffered from both PTSD (early birth trauma and the automobile accident and ongoing hearing loss) as well as CPTSD (his sense of self as being weak and enfeebled). Will's father's retreat from a robust way of living and failure to intervene with his mother's rages and conflicts, along with Will's mother's alternating cocooning of Will due to her own agoraphobia and appropriating Will as her companion, all exacerbated his failure to live as an independent, high-functioning individual, both throughout his life and in his marriage. Julia carried active and debilitating PTSD and CPTSD from multiple forces, among them, her father's original excitation and terrorizing of her, her mother's inability to mother combined with the requirement of Julia to be something of a wife to her father.

KEYSTONE # 3 – Internalized Introjects and Identifications with Trauma

Identifications are used in the service of the growth of the self, by becoming internalized, synthesized, and integrated into the structure of the ego, thus enhancing both the self itself and the child's sense of self. On the other hand, introjects are internalized features of objects relations, which continue functioning in relation to the self as they did in the external world, through attaching to the superego.

When from the earliest moments of being the child's essential self was not only disturbed but traumatized rather than having available objects to grow their essential selfhood via first incorporation and later, primary identifications, the beginning processes of internalization become compromised with trauma-filled introjects (see Ferenczi, 1909, Jacobson, 1964). While introjects are also incorporated, they do not attach to the ego but to the superego and are made of the fabric of negative experiences that while taken in are not usable for self-growth. In short order, these introjects, like psychic barnacles, feel like the self, even though they are fundamentally the destructive projections of the others in our lives. W. W. Meissner (1971) explained: "Introjections [as] internalizations effectively alter the inner psychic structure in significant ways... introjects thus become structural components of the psychic system [the superego] but enjoy a certain autonomy that distinguishes them from ego components..." (p. 292-300).

First, these powerful introjects become incorporated through implicit memory encoding and are then stored as "somatic markers" (see Siegel, 1999, p. 143-44) in bodily egos (see Freud, 1923/1955, Novick, 1990). When such developmental failure occurs so early in life, the infant does not even have the opportunity to 'be inside' its essential self. Instead, the trauma is incorporated unconsciously into the infant's undifferentiated psyche-soma (see Winnicott, 1949/1975) through the firing and subsequent wiring of neuronal pathways, converting the essential self into what I call the *adaptive wounded self*, subsequently **felt** as his or her very self.

This early incorporation process of trauma, wherein the infant has internalized introjects rather than affirming objects, sets the stage for the infant moving into the primary identification phase already compromised. Instead of having objects with whom the child can identify for the purposes of growth of the essential self, "The child adopts the parent's 'procedural rules... this identification, then, is with a dyadic relationship *system* rather than with a single role..." (Seligman, 1999, p. 141). As Meissner (1971) depicted, "The introject exercises a particular influence on the subject's inner state and behavior, and the relations between subject and introject are as varied as the relations between two persons. The introject is the inner presence of an external object. Such a presence can only be recognized when it becomes conscious, but it may be active and effective when unconscious or subconscious as well" (p. 294).

When a child is left alone with unresolved trauma, her inner world becomes populated with introjected objects that continue to do their damaging work, just as they did externally. Bereft of healthy object relations who can serve her as identifications for the growth of herself, the child must preserve any residual integrity of being by identifying with her own traumatizing experience as testimony to the reality of her personal experience, hence, what I have named "the sheltered wound" (see Erwin, 2023, to come, also see Erwin, 2005).

We can see in Will's experiences, how deeply he struggled with what Peter Shabad (1987) described for such a child as: "The intangible, experiential quality of the traumatic theme is so difficult to grasp, the child often is not aware of what is happening to him, much less able to communicate it.... Here, the child does not only 'lose' the idealized parent, but he detaches from his own wishes that only lead to perpetual frustration.... Divided against his cherished hopes, illusions, and ideals, the child experiences the most devastating loss of all: the loss of his sense of integrity (p. 351).... More often than he either knows or would like, however, the child comes to rely internally on the same parents from whom he flees.... The introjection of an actual frustrating relationship with a parent seems to provide a more secure foundation for the development of the child's identity than longing for the actualization of an ideal relationship that never seems to materialize" (p. 353).

The consequences of such psychic loss are immense and complicated. In Julia's life, Shabad's (1987) portrayals can be applied in particularly poignant ways: "When the child's experience is that no one is there, he turns inward and immediately adapts to the perceived absence of the other by learning stoically how to go it alone and rely on his own resources, a self-reliance that all too often seems to be one of the residual casualties of growing up (p. 353)... the repeated aspects of the parent's history that have become entrenched in the parent's character and are continually enacted on the child; the helplessness engendered by the traumatic theme derives from the child's continued incapacity to change the parent into a wished-for figure" (p. 350).

This introjected frustrating parent of the child's early yearnings ultimately surrenders the child to an ongoing state of dissociation, what Shabad (1987) depicted as "a critical observer rather than a wholehearted participant in her own life, resulting in the sense of being on the outside looking in at herself, at her significant relationships, and perhaps most importantly, developing a sense of emotional alienation from the hopefulness of her childhood. The traumatic rupture of the protective illusion of innocence has a dissociative kick to it, as now the child-adolescent shifts his center of gravity from inside to outside, and from being present in the current moment to a braced preoccupation with entering the future... the transition from childhood to adulthood also is discontinuous, resembling a dissociative leap into one's adult identity rather than a graduated walking into it" (p. 353).

Working with patients who have formed an identification with such trauma in the absence of caring, validating, and protective others is the focus of another of my books *The Sheltered Wound* (to come 2023, also see Erwin, 2005). Individuals who carry a *sheltered wound* do so as an early and quite remarkable creative striving to gather a testimony of their personal truth to preserve the integrity of their compromised essential self in the face of ignorance, denial and belittlement of or true help with the trauma. This *sheltered wound* was *the* way to survive. Through the conversion of the trauma into an identification with the trauma itself the identity of the self becomes an adaptive *wounded* self to cope with the on-going and lived consequences of its lack of resolution.

KEYSTONE # 4 – Affect Dysregulation and Disorganization

In emotional dysregulation, the individual's arousal system shifts away from being able to maximize its emotional and physiological states within an open, processing range for relating and for pro-action (see The Arousal Chart, Lillas, 1994, Erwin, 2000), into experiencing increased excitatory arousal (the *hyper*arousal end of the continuum), characterized by increasing randomness, or into increased inhibitory dampening down (the *hypo*arousal end of the continuum), characterized by increasing rigidity. This dysregulation is *not* adaptive ultimately and reinforces its own maladaptive system. Whereas *recovery* from hyperarousal (rupture) or hypoarousal (disconnection) between the dyad decreases the disorganizing effects of a particular episode of mis-attunement and its emotional arousal, the repeated unavailability of recovery processes from the caregiver makes the infant/child a prisoner of its own emotional dysregulated arousal system.

Affect dysregulation is not a new concept; although the wording may not have been the same, the ideas were there. Max Stern (1951) followed a line of thought about anxiety, trauma, and shock, starting with Freud (1936) who discussed anxiety as a condition of excitation, a stimulus which is transformed into a traumatic factor, and in the face of danger "cannot be mastered by discharge" (see Stern, 1951, p. 179). Sandor Ferenczi (1932) found: "Shock is a destruction of the ability to offer resistance and to think and act in one's own defense" (p. 159) Daniel Stern (1951) himself explored, "the relation between anxiety and the condition of physiological shock… [and] a severe physical disturbance of the organism caused by overintense psychic activity" (p. 180) and concluded that, "Since shock was once experienced as reality, and as even signal anxiety can deteriorate into shock, the anxiety process includes a realistic element progressively gaining strength…. In anxiety we always experience [at least] a weak reproduction of the shock, felt as paralysis, and of the defense reaction, felt as tension, as urge to discharge" (p. 193).

I found the work of Harvey Milkman and Stanley Sunderwirth (1987) invaluable in my understanding and subsequently my ability to help Julia face and work with what happened to her in the face of terrifying experiences. Milkman and Sunderwirth highlighted the ferocious need for traumatized individuals to achieve some form of affect regulation, even if it becomes, paradoxically, severe dysregulation, and, ultimately, addiction: "One way of coping with disquieting factors is to immerse oneself in an activity that is incompatible with serious self-evaluation" (p. 15). For individuals like Julia, who experience *arousal* (on the sympathetic nervous system side), as a means of coping with trauma, such individuals "feel active and potent in the face of an environment that they view as overwhelmingly dehumanizing.... Their vast expenditures of mental and physical energy are designed to deny underlying fears of helplessness" (p. 19). The authors concluded that, "The repeated pairing of opposite emotional experiences, and their underlying physiological counterparts, may be the sustaining force behind all forms of human compulsion" (p. 104).

I was additionally assisted in my own formulations concerning Julia by Eleanor Armstrong-Perlman (1989) who discussed patients pursuing "alluring but rejecting objects—exciting but frustrating objects" (p. 223). "Given [the] absolute need for his parents, the child must somehow cope with and defend himself.... His total need does not allow a recognition of his mother as a bad object—a strategy that would solve the ambivalence, but at an intolerable psychic cost... [the child] employs the defensive process of internalization to remove it from outer reality, where it eludes his control, to the sphere of inner reality, where it offers prospects of being more amenable to control in the role of internal object (Fairbairn, 1952, p. 172)" (p. 226). However, this does not solve the problem for the child. "The child has altered only his perception; thus, when his mother is bad, he is left with the problem of rationalizing and explaining to himself *why* she is bad.... Obviously, his mother is bad because *he* is bad" (p. 227). To maintain hope in relationships, and to try to bear what is not bearable, the patient views these alluring but rejecting others as an ego ideal, externalized, "who must be submitted to at all costs" (p. 224).

My experience with Julia confirmed for me what Armstrong-Perlman found: these patients "cannot let go, no matter how maligned their experience. The need is compulsive, and the fantasy of loss is experienced as potentially catastrophic: The fear is that loss will lead either to the disintegration of the self, or to a reclusive emptiness to which any state of connectedness, no matter how infused with suffering, is preferable. Any anguish occasioned by these relationships is preferable to the feared anguish of the acceptance of the hopelessness of the relationships... to give up that hope may lead to a collapse of the self" (p. 224).

In the face of such severe trauma and its posttraumatic aftermath, Bessel van der Kolk and Alexander McFarlane (1996) explored six issues influencing how individuals dysregulate and process information. They are:

1) They experience persistent intrusions of memories related to the trauma, which interfere with attending to other incoming information.
2) They sometimes compulsively expose themselves to situations reminiscent of the trauma.
3) They actively attempt to avoid specific triggers of trauma-related emotions and experience a generalized numbing of responsiveness.
4) They lose the ability to modulate their physiological responses to stress in general, which leads to a decreased capacity to utilize bodily signals as guides for action.
5) They suffer from generalized problems with attention, distractibility, and stimulus discrimination.

6) They have alterations in their psychological defense mechanisms and in personal identity. This changes what new information is selected as relevant (p. 9).

Self-disorder in Heinz Kohut and Ernest Wolf's (1978) terms meant that the adult self may "…exist in states of varying degrees of coherence, from cohesion to fragmentation; in states of varying degrees of vitality, from vigour to enfeeblement; in states of varying degrees of functional harmony, from order to chaos. Significant failure to achieve cohesion, vigour, or harmony, or a significant loss of these qualities after they had been tentatively established may be said to constitute a state of self disorder" (p. 414).

Once again, I turned to my training from 1997 with Stanley Greenspan (1995, 1997a) who delineated five regulatory disorder types, which then helped me understand the tremendous consequences upon a child of environmental dysregulation or lack of any regulation. While there is also the necessity of considering original constitutional factors in the child, these regulatory disorders are either brought into being or enhanced by such environmental problems. These five types of regulatory disorder are:

1) Hypersensitive/Fearful = A bright, articulate, creative, insightful, empathic, and compassionate child who is overreactive to sensory stimuli. Hypervigilant, and mercurial, she is also shy and anxious/fearful, finicky, and often clingy in response to new experiences and people.
2) Underreactive/Self-Absorbed = The 'good' or 'easy' appearing baby who is withdrawn and internal. Passive, quiet, this child is more comfortable in his own fantasies than in reality. He needs to be wooed into interaction.
3) Hypersensitive/Defiant = This child has the same sensitivity as the Hypersensitive/Fearful child but uses defiance or stubbornness as

a defense against his sensitivity. Negative, controlling, into power plays, even simple activities become a trial. Very finicky in terms of touch.

4) Inattentive = Often mis-diagnosed as having ADD, this child is 'spacey', a wanderer, constantly on the go, having trouble with motor planning and sequencing, and finding words to describe things and feelings, along with difficulty with different types of attention because of challenges with processing, or reactions, or various sensory modalities.
5) The Active Craving/Aggressive Child = This child is *underreactive* to sensation, and so cannot use it as a signal for satiation or satisfaction. No sooner does this child get what s/he wants, then she is unable to take in what s/he has gotten and is off craving and pursuing the next thing. This type has considerable energy and tends to jump into experiences and think (if at all) later. This type covers the range from merely needing a great deal of stimulation and activity for their energy level to being strong-willed to being severely antisocial.

Will fell into the Inattentive type of dysregulation, with some features of Underreactive/Self-Absorbed. If he had not been born nearly dead from the umbilical cord being tightly wrapped around his neck three times, we cannot be sure that this form of dysregulation would have been realized. He might have been a Hypersensitive/fearful type instead, especially considering the near-fatal car accident he suffered at age eight. Julia was definitely Hypersensitive, vacillating between being fearful and stubborn/defiant.

Allan Schore (2003a) gave me a poignant look at how abuse and neglect played out in Julia's affect dysregulation:

> ...the abusive caregiver not only shows less play with her infant, she also induces traumatic states of enduring negative affect. Because her attachment is weak, she provides little protection against other potential abusers of the infant, such as the father. This caregiver is inaccessible and reacts to her infant's expressions of emotions and stress inappropriately and/or rejectingly, and shows minimal or unpredictable participation in the various types of arousal regulating processes. Instead of modulating she induces extreme levels of stimulation and arousal, either too high in abuse or too low in neglect, and because she provides no interactive repair the infant's intense negative emotional states last for long periods of time. Such states are accompanied by severe alterations in the biochemistry of the immature brain, especially in areas associated with the development of the child's coping capacities (p. 181).

Schore cited two important researchers in terms of how they saw affect dysregulation. The first, Robert Emde (1988), "defined pathology as a lack of adaptive capacity, an incapacity to shift strategies in the face of environmental demands" (p. 187), while in a similar vein, van der Kolk and Fisler (1994) "have argued, the loss of the ability to regulate the intensity of feelings is the most far-reaching effect of early trauma and neglect" (p. 187). This is the lived experience of affect dysregulation.

There are also certain categories of affect that insist upon a closer, but limited, look, especially as they relate to the two clinical cases presented. Of the affects explored in this section, several are the most critical to development, because they relate in elemental ways to the self—*who one is*—rather than *what one feels or does*. These are shame, loneliness, anger, anxiety/fear/terror, horror, and dread. However discrete these affective experiences are from one another, there is a profound tie between them, since to be utterly shamed leaves one abjectly alone (see Tompkins, 1963, Broucek 1982), in a state of terror, while a state of terror represents a state of abject alone-ness (see Schore, 1997) that produces profound and unmitigated shame.

Shame

"Impairments of affect regulation" Barnet Malin (1999) suggested, "lead to disorders of the self" (p. 375). He made an important distinction regarding shame and the disorders of the self, concluding that emotion is the better word to describe the subjective experience of shame; whereas, Tompkins' (1963) shame-humiliation was the better word for affective biological reaction. Malin conceived of emotion as: "... complex states that develop from the primary, innate affects.... Emotions may characterize both primary self-states and secondary defensive, or self-restorative states. Unlike affects, emotions such as shame cannot be present from the start of life and must emerge as objective self-awareness and self-object differentiation develop (Broucek, 1991; Lewis, 1993)" (p. 374). According to this distinction, Malin viewed "shame [as] the central *emotion* (italics added) in a disordered *sense of self*" and "specific affective and emotional disturbances as playing the central pathological role in *disorders of the self*" (p. 375).

Marvin Lansky (1999) has pointed out, "Shame is about the self... refer[ring] not simply to one type of affect, but to a complex emotional system regulating the social bond... what one is before oneself and others; one's standing, importance, or lack of it; one's lovability, sense of acceptability, or imminent rejection, as seen before the eye of the other or the internal self-evaluative eye of the self" (p. 347). He concluded, "Shame... is intimately concerned with disorders of the self" (p. 351).

Therefore, we can see from such theory-making that shame is often linked in ratio to the concept of self-esteem: that is, shame impacts one's self-esteem, and the level of quality of self-esteem can mitigate or increase the impact of shame. These lines of thought raise two pivotal questions, which are, when does shame appear? and what is its purpose? Various theorists (Ablon, 1990, Yorke, 1990, and Schore, 1997, 2003a), see shame in part as a necessary, even healthy, affect appearing later in the second year of life, for the purpose of socialization and civilizing the growing child, whereas Jacobson (1964) viewed shame as a reaction formation, requiring that the child be old enough to be able to be self-conscious, that is, as an object of observation for others, and therefore for himself. When this type of shame experience assists the child to modulate his own behavior and internal states in ways that lead to increased and positive social interaction, it is not damaging (see Schore, 1994, 2003a). However, Schore (1994) pointed out that shame is also evoked when the child's state is not attuned to accurately by the parent. "Shame-inducing interactions coupled with sustained parental anger and/or lack of repair of the disconnection lead to humiliation... [which is] toxic to the developing child's brain" (Siegel, 1999, p. 280 in referring to Schore, 1994).

Shame was a debilitating affect for both Will and Julia, especially as it concerned their senses of self-efficacy while simultaneously carrying the inaccurate burden of culpability. Shame is often the resulting affect when the individual feels incompetent (see R. White, 1960), occurring "when we cannot do something that either we or an audience thinks we should be able to do" (p. 126). Francis Broucek (1982) not only concurred that "... inefficacy experiences may be among the earliest releasers of shame.... There is an element of cognitive shock involved in the release of shame—whether it be the shock of the fact of the stranger [or mother in a 'stranged' state] or the shock of failed efficacy expectations *vis-à-vis* the environment" (p. 370).

Another significant aspect of Broucek's (1991) work concerned his distinction between the self as *subject* and the self as *object*. "Before the acquisition of objective self-awareness, if [and because] we receive healthy parental responsiveness, we [are able to] exist as pure subjects" (p. 46), meaning that our selfhood is honored and upheld in caring and respectful ways, leading to a pivotal developing sense of agency and self-efficacy. In the latter part of our second year, as we develop self-awareness, we also develop the sense of ourselves as objects for others, a developmental achievement that allows the others in our lives to exist as subjects and for us to fruitfully participate in both shared and differentiated experience. However, when we are shamed, we can no longer exist as a subject and an object with a sense of self and other, but instead become *objectified,* leading to a sense of repudiated self and dangerous other and the failed sense of self-agency and efficacy. Living within the experience of shame produces an incapacitating sense of loneliness, and ultimately in combination with fear and terror, a pervasive sense of dread (see below).

Loneliness

While Frieda Fromm-Reichmann's paper on "Loneliness" (1990) is psychiatric in style and concerned, ultimately, with the horror of loneliness and isolation experienced by psychotic patients, much of her thought is applicable to Will and Julia, both of whom suffered from various experiences of neglect, rejection, isolation, intrusion, and the stultifying loneliness that resulted from these experiences. The loneliness that Fromm-Reichmann described is "nonconstructive, if not disintegrative" and, which "... renders people who suffer it emotionally paralyzed and helpless ... the longing for interpersonal intimacy stays with every human being from infancy throughout life; and there is no human being who is not threatened by its loss" (p. 309). Such loneliness "is beyond anxiety and tension; defense and remedy seem out of reach. Only as its all-engulfing intensity decreases can the person utilize anxiety-provoking defenses against it" (p. 316).

Anger

Anna Ornstein (1998), in accord with Heinz Kohut (1972), offered the view of anger that is most pertinent to my work. She detailed the "defensive structures that... [evolve] in relation to chronic narcissistic rage, which is the legacy of traumatic disappointments and active traumatizations early in life" (p. 56). She also pointed to a significant distinction between destructive aggression and self-assertion arrived at by Stechler (1982, 1987) and Stechler and Kaplan (1980). They concluded, based on Stechler's (and others') longitudinal study with infants, and Kaplan's, et al corollary studies of the Boston University project at the James J. Putnam's Children's Center, that "assertion is accompanied by interest, excitement, and joy, while destructive aggression is associated with dysphoric affects of fear, distress and hostility" (see Ornstein, 1998, p. 55).

For a patient like Julia who was caught in the repercussions of the defensive structures caused by narcissistic rage, sadistic or masochistic behavior becomes manifest, either cycling within each or between these two expressions. Ornstein suggested, "Sadistic behavior (unleashing the rage at the frustrating other with physical and/or verbal assault) expresses the rage directly... narcissistic rage is also the motive for the masochistic and paranoid behavior... (haughty withdrawal, writing people off, holding grudges, collecting injustices as well as self-recrimination, depression, self-cutting, and suicidal threats) also express rage but... do so indirectly. Masochistic behavior, in particular, is a powerful accusation directed at the offender for the mental anguish that patients experience as having been carelessly or deliberately inflicted on them" (p. 56).

From either the sadistic or masochistic position, "patients are compelled to revenge themselves in order to reestablish self-cohesion and/or a damaged self-esteem.... Narcissistic rage, then... arises from a matrix of a fragmented self or a self that is threatened with fragmentation" (p. 57). Ornstein viewed the successful "'transformation' of the rage into a signal affect" (p. 57) as the result of structural changes, that is, "the consolidation of the self reduces the threat of fragmentation and narcissistic rage may then be experienced in the form of fleeting annoyance" (p. 57).

Anxiety/Fear/Terror/Horror/Dread

While the affective experiences of anxiety, fear, terror, horror, and dread may seem to represent but degrees on a single continuum, Allan Schore (1997) found fear and terror a right hemispheric response to threat, while anxiety is a later-developing left-hemispheric response. Terror, by his definition, is a state of abject aloneness under threat, a state that can be evoked within a mere 1/30th of a second, but one that can take hours, days, or weeks from which to recover (1997, see also Schore, 2003a, p. 263).

Bruce Perry, et al, (1995) examined the impact of traumatic experience on the neurodevelopment of infants and children, specifically in terms of the fear response to threat. To begin, Perry stated that, "The single most significant distinguishing feature of all nervous tissue—of neurons—is that they are designed to change in response to external signals... it is this capacity which allows the brain to be responsive to the environment (external and internal) to allow survival of the organism" (p. 274).

Thus, a child who is under repeated possible threats and is traumatized by assault or deprivation or neglect suffers from an "overactivation of neurochemical cues. Rather than a *deprivation* of sensory stimuli, the traumatized child experiences overactivation of important neural systems during sensitive periods of development" (p. 277). The psychobiological response to such fear and trauma can appear first as *hyperarousal* of the sympathetic branch of the autonomic nervous system, resulting in increased heart rate, blood pressure, respiration, muscle tone, and hypervigilance, expressed initially as crying, then screaming, but then in the somewhat older child, *dissociation,* where the child withdraws from fear-producing stimuli in their external world and into an internal world as a mechanism by which they move to numbing, freezing, avoidance, and/or compliance. As we have seen, the ultimate result of the brain's organization of neural systems is that for the developing child fear states convert into characterological traits.

Ehud Koch (2000) has considered dread to be "an extreme form [rather than degree] of fear that is induced by terror and horror" (p. 289), which is "manifested in the shapes of a 'dreaded self' and a 'dreaded state of the self'" (p. 289). His coinage of the "dreaded self" (p. 294) referred to "that representation of the self which one would hate to be fears one could become... states which dramatically challenge one's sense of reality, whether of one's being or of aspects of the external world" (p. 294-5).

Diverse types and degrees of experiences, such as loss, assault, natural and man-made catastrophes provide the origins for *dreaded states of the self.* The common threads running through these experiences are: "suddenness and unexpectedness; the potential arousal of intense and overwhelming affect; the loss of one's agency, experienced as acute helplessness or being out of control; and the threat to one's sense of what is 'real', either in oneself or in the external world" (p. 301). The impact of these experiences further depends upon "...the intensity of the traumatic events, the developmental/cognitive level at which they occurred, differences in temperament and defensive styles, and how the critical environment has responded at the time of these events" (p. 302).

Koch conceptualized three critical propositions about dread: the first was that any given individual may have "any number of shapes of the dreaded self rather than one unitary shape" (p. 302); the second was that these shapes "continue to develop and accrue over time" (p. 302-303); and three, that "each of these dreaded states speak to a range of salient, interacting, dynamic, and developmental issues; they are not simple responses to some 'original' [fixation] danger" (p. 303).

Koch made particular note of two aspects of the function of dread: dread as an affective response ("a sum of [unmanageable] excitation" p. 312) and dread as an affective signal ("of impending or potential danger" p. 312), that what has been will be again. Finally, what lies at the core of dread is "the experience of *horror* and *terror*... [with its resulting state(s) that stimulate] a wary *anticipation of repeating and reexperiencing the awful,* without the aid of an adaptive personal agency" (p. 312). Both Will and Julia suffered to substantial degrees these impactful affects via implicit memory encoding and retrieval and struggled in defenses constructed in childhood to manage them. Not until two to three years into our therapeutic work did their affective dysregulation begin to shift.

KEYSTONE # 5 – Insecure Attachment

Let us use Sidney Blatt and Kenneth Levy's (2003) ideas to understand that conversely to healthy development, the negative internal working models that are the result of implicit memory encoding lead to the distortions in relating that are the consequence of dysregulated and insecure attachments. Often, these implicit memory banks (Erwin, 2003) are unable to evolve into mental, and therefore, symbolic representations but remain as potential minefields to be triggered in the here and now interpersonally. There may exist little or fragmented and injured sense of self, combined with the sense of the other as threatening and dangerous or absent or disavowing, with the affective valance of relationships tumultuous, unreliable, and frightening, or despairingly empty. The degree of differentiation from these internal models is either little or none; instead, they are engulfing and intrusive. The possibility of integration is slim if at all, for what would be integrated would be a merger with these internal models, making it impossible for the individual to individuate in any way that would feel safe and viable. Finally, whatever Internal Working

Models (IWMs) or rudimentary mental representations present within the harmed child become increasingly *in*accurate, less able to be articulated, and conceptually simple and rigid, less comprehensive and certainly ineffective for interpersonal relating, since they are built upon traumatic early experience that created perceptual bias and was exacerbated by repeated disappointment or re-traumatization.

Daniel Siegel (1999) described secure attachment as "an inborn system in the brain that evolves in ways that influence and organize motivational, emotional, and memory processes with respect to significant caregiving figures. The attachment system motivates an infant to seek proximity to parents and to establish communication with them... attachment establishes an interpersonal relationship that helps the immature brain use the mature functions of the parent's brain to organize its own processes. [These] emotional transactions... amplify the child's positive states and modulate negative states.... Repeated experiences become encoded in implicit memory as expectations and then as mental models or schemata of attachment" (p. 67).

In contrast to secure attachment, we can see from the attachment research (Bowlby, Ainsworth, Main, Hesse) that when parents are trapped in angry, passive, or fearful preoccupations from past insecure attachment relationships, they are only able to supply a vague and irrelevant self narrative. In response, the child develops an ambivalent insecure attachment, as Will did with his mother, becoming emotionally isolated from that parent. When the parent is dismissing of attachment relationships and is emotionally unavailable and insensitive to the child, as well as providing a contradicting and brief or belittling narrative, the child forms an avoidant insecure and/or reactive attachment, as did Julia with her mother, giving up on seeking proximity to the parent. When a parent has suffered extreme and unresolved trauma, and exhibits chaotic and/or disoriented behavior, assault or neglect upon the child, and is unable to participate in reasoning or discourse in their narrative, as Julia's father enacted, the child will form a disorganized/disoriented insecure and/or traumatized attachment, their fear unable to be modulated or soothed because the parent is the very source of that fear. "The sudden shifts in these children's states of mind yield incoherence in their cognitive, emotional, and behavioral functioning.... Disorienting relationships create internal disorganization that in turn impairs future interactions with others, which disorganize the development of the mind still further" (Siegel, 1999, p. 109).

Erik Hesse and Mary Main's (2000) research suggested that "... disorganized/ disoriented behavior is expectable *whenever an infant is markedly frightened by its primary haven(s) of safety, i.e., the attachment figure(s)*" (p. 1102). These researchers concluded that, "...attachment must be closely tied to fear.... Considered in conjunction with constitutional factors and/or later intervening trauma, the relation between disorganization and repeated experiences of fright without solution may account for some of the emerging findings linking early disorganized attachment status and psychopathology" (p. 1117).

In each of the forms of insecure attachment, there is a failure with connection and repair. In the avoidantly attached dyad, connections are consistently infrequent and unsoothing; there is no repair. In the ambivalently attached dyad, connections are unpredictable and at times overwhelming and emotionally intrusive... repair in these situations may be overstimulating.... In a dyad with disorganized/disoriented attachment, interactions can be a source of overwhelming terror and despair... the caregiver the source of distress... the child is not given the opportunity to experience repair" (p. 116-117).

Two other complicating attachment experiences that occur for children are Traumatized Attachment, which results from early trauma compromises in (e.g. disorganized/disoriented attachment) or destruction of any form of attachment to primary caregivers, and Reactive Attachment Disorder

(RAD), the condition in which children are unable to form an emotional bond with their primary caregivers because their fundamental needs for comfort, protection, and caring are not met. We see in both, that without basic trust being established, hand in hand with the lack of affection and safety and kind, physical provisions, children do not have any expectation of care. Such deprivation may occur from removal from primary caretakers after an early bond was being established, prolonged separations from any caring environment, uninvolved and neglectfully damaging parents, multiple foster placements, institutional living. In these traumatized children, symptoms include various forms of non-responsiveness: listlessness, withdrawal, failures in expressions or seeking connection, and generalized lack of interest. Sub-types of RAD that have been identified include the *Inhibited* type, which demonstrates as avoidance, withdrawal, and resistance to comfort, and the *Disinhibited* type wherein children indiscriminately seek attention regardless of safety, lack of comprehension of boundaries (see Cleveland Clinic, 2018 and Mayo Clinic, 2022).

KEYSTONE # 6 – Compromised Hemispheric Development

Several researchers provide us with an understanding of how profound the consequences of unresolved trauma are upon wounded and traumatized hemispheric development. Allan Schore (2003a) demonstrated that, the consequences of an abusive environment are upon "the critical period organization of limbic cortical and subcortical connections that mediate homeostatic self-regulatory and attachment systems… [which] lead to a regulatory failure, expressed in an impaired autonomic homeostasis, disturbances in limbic activity, and hypothalamic and reticular formation dysfunction… trigger[ing] significant alterations in major stress-reducing neurochemicals, corticotropin releasing factor… and the glucocorticoid cortisol, especially in the right hemisphere that is dominant for the secretion of these hormones" (p. 252-253).

"An infant brain that is chronically shifting into hypometabolic survival modes and decreased heart rate has little energy available for brain growth" (Schore, 2003a, p. 253). With respect to hemispheric development and affect dysregulation, when the young child experiences unresolved trauma a "developmental overpruning [exerts] a toxic effect of overwhelming stress on the young brain: the release of stress hormones leads to excessive death of neurons in the crucial pathways involving the neocortex and limbic system—the areas for emotional regulation" (Siegel, 1999, p. 85). Daniel Siegel explained that, "The functioning of the mind... alters the physiological environment of the brain... a child traumatized early in life would have an alteration in physiological response, such that small stressors lead to large hormonal responses... which can lead to further physiological features that maintain the hypervigilant response over time" (p. 20). Conditioned fear-based experiences communicate to the brain through what Joseph LeDoux (1996) called 'the quick and dirty' route, a quick-response system between the thalamus and the amygdala, which in turn affects the hypothalamus, which controls the body's fight or flight response.

Rita Carter (1998) wrote that, "LeDoux proposes that the amygdala lays down unconscious memories in much the same way that the hippocampus lays down conscious ones. Similarly, when an event is recalled the hippocampal system will come up with conscious recollections while the amygdala-based system will produce a sort of physical reminiscence, reconstituting the body state—pumping heart, sweaty palms, and so on—that arose with the original experience" (p. 95). Carter clarified the mechanism in more detail:

> If a memory is burnt into the amygdala with enough force, it may be almost uncontainable, and trigger such dramatic bodily reactions that a person may re-experience the precipitating trauma, complete

> with full sensory replay.... Sometimes, though, the amygdala-based unconscious memories flood in without the corresponding conscious recollections that could pin them to a specific event. The irrational fear felt then may be vague... a thin cloud of anxiety—or it may be sudden or intense—a panic attack. If the feeling is provoked by a conscious stimulus, it may show itself as a phobia (p. 95).

We can see the ongoing consequences for hemispheric functioning of such early traumatic experience. For humans, the pre-frontal cortex, or Executive Brain, does not mature until the mid-20s. For adolescents, even in normal development, this immaturity of frontal cortical operation shows up in three areas of challenge: 1) the ability to plan effectively how to get 'from here to there', 2) the capacity to maintain focused attention, and 3) the ability to intervene with impulses. In healthy development, the parents' executive brain functioning serves the indispensable purpose of providing those mind and processing functions for the adolescent and young adult, either/and through earlier internalizations of the safe and care-giving provisions of the parents, the secure attachment to the parents, the affect regulation that has been internalized over time, and the collaborative, authorial dialogue between parent and child established from early in life. When environmental gaps or failures occur or any of the seven keystones of development are compromised, the cost to the growing child is the inadequacy of the parents' executive functioning, leaving the teenager or young adult to rely on his or her own unformed or inadequate prefrontal processing.

For Will, his mother's alternate indulgent cocooning with her various furies and his father's weakening approach to life at the most critical time Will needed his strength, left Will unable to plan his developing adolescent with effectiveness, or maintain focused attention once he was on his own in college, or to intervene with his impulses, such as in his early marriage. Julia, left on her own by her lack of mothering, and in reaction to a father who sometimes enticed her and sometimes terrified her, was provided some mediation by school success but only until she left for the east coast for college and became depressed. While she could usually maintain focused attention, when the traumas with Oscar occurred, her ability to intervene with her impulses disappeared.

These flashbacks are what I call implicit memory relivings. Carter described that, "Sometimes the memories [flashbacks] are fragmented, sometimes they are precise replays of some traumatic event... they are triggered by memories laid down in the amygdala, and bring with them their full cargo of both sensory and emotional associations" (p. 129).

Daniel Siegel (1999) helped us understand why this is so. The effects of intense (dis) stress "appear to be mediated by the characteristic neuroendocrine responses involving the immediate transient effects (lasting seconds to minutes) of noradrenaline release and the more sustained effects (lasting minutes to hours) of glucocorticoids such as cortisol, also known as 'stress hormones.'... High levels of stress not only transiently block hippocampal functioning, but excessive and chronic exposure to stress hormones may lead to neuronal death in this region, possibly producing decreased hippocampal volume, as found in patients with chronic posttraumatic stress disorder" (p. 50).

Bessel van der Kolk (2002) demonstrated that "people with PTSD have low levels of cortisol. The effect of increased secretion of norepinephrine, combined with decreased cortisol, renders people with PTSD more reactive to arousing stimuli... when people are frightened or aroused, the frontal areas of the brain, which are responsible for the analysis of experience and associating it with other areas of knowledge, are deactivated (Arnsten, 1998). Deactivation of the dorsolateral prefrontal cortex (which is responsible for executive function) in patients with PTSD interferes with their being able to formulate a measured response to threat" (p. 384-385).

Allan Schore (2003a) explained in neuropsychobiological terms, the effects of such trauma on hemispheric development:

> ...the effect of ambient cumulative trauma is enduring... the effects of early relational trauma as well as the defenses against such trauma are embedded into the core structure of evolving personality.... The developing infant is maximally vulnerable to nonoptimal environmental events in the period of most rapid brain growth. During these critical periods of genetically encoded synapse overproduction followed by environmentally driven synapse elimination... influence the critical period organization of limbic cortical and subcortical connections that mediate homeostatic self-regulatoryand attachment systems... [which] lead to a regulatory failure, expressed in an impaired autonomic homeostasis, disturbances in limbic activity, and hypothalamic and reticular formation dysfunction... [and] also triggers significant alterations in the major stress-regulating neurochemicals, corticotropin releasing factor... and the glucocorticoid cortisol, especially in the right hemisphere that is dominant for the secretion of these hormones (p. 253).

Van der Kolk's (2014) work at Harvard further demonstrated how Positron Emission Tomography (PET) scans and functional magnetic resonance imaging (fMRI) reveal "...that images of past trauma activate the right hemisphere of the brain and deactivate the left" (p. 44). The implications of these studies show the dynamics of implicit memory: "When something reminds people of the past, their right hemisphere reacts as if the traumatic event were happening in the present" (p. 45).

KEYSTONE # 7 – Voice Suppressed or Lost and Language Compromised

One of the most poignant consequences of unresolved trauma is the sad, wasteful, even tragic outcome for many children where their personal voices are preempted from coming into being or silenced in their development by neglect or abuse. The distinguished child psychoanalyst, researcher, and teacher, Selma Fraiberg (1982) sought answers to certain pivotal questions: "But what happens to an infant in the first eighteen months of life when his human partners fail in their protective function and he is exposed to repeated and prolonged experiences of helplessness?.... What means does he have to cope with extreme helplessness or to ward off 'something out there' which is uncertainly associated with painful experience? ...And if pain is associated with the figure of the mother herself in daily and repeated circumstances, how can he ward off the person on whom he is absolutely dependent and who is associated with pain and disappointment?" (p. 614).

Choosing twelve children out of a larger group of fifty who were being treated, Fraiberg made her choices based on those who were most impaired in object relations. For these babies, the mothers were "psychologically absent for a very large part of the infant's day" (p. 616), because of neglect, or suspected or actual abuse. The babies' characteristic behavior was that they each "avoided the mother through every system of contact he had available to him in a complete reversal of the social patterns that normally are exhibited at each developmental stage" (p. 616). These avoidances included: the babies never or rarely looked at their mothers, never or rarely smiled at their mothers, did not reach for her, did not signal the mother for comfort, and *did not vocalize* to the mother. In fact, these babies had learned that when their cries and screams and frantic gesturing were ineffective in drawing mother to them in ameliorating ways, the crying ceased. Others froze into immobility. Still other babies attacked themselves (head banging, being reckless, falling, colliding, etc.), and were able to "tolerate high levels of pain without wincing" (p. 631), or who seemed not to feel pain at all. When any of these states became too intolerable, the babies affectively disintegrated.

We have seen that in healthy development, as early as two years of age (see Brown & Hernnstein, 1975, Chomsky, 1980, Vgotsky, 1986, Carter, 1998, Crain, 2000) when a child begins to use semantic expressive language, his or her personal voice is being fully revealed, with authorial voice established by age three. But patients with unresolved trauma have had their personal voices preempted or silenced by neglect or abuse. Within the first two years of life, as traumatic experiences are encoded implicitly within the right hemisphere, there may be few or no words attached (van der Kolk, 1996). Unable to express or prevented from expressing the reality of their essential selves, "silence … [becomes] an attempt to protect a precious core of authentic experience from destruction" (Kurtz, 1984, p. 232, see also K. K. Novick, 1990). Even when semantic language becomes available to whatever degree, the implicit environmental threat may be such that the child is inhibited from placing the veneer of words onto his/her experience (Whitmer, 2001).

Kerry Kelly Novick (1990) captured the experience of what I call the loss of personal voice, in which language development continues but the expression of what I call the essential self does not:

> The exponential simultaneous development of cognitive, symbolic, and motor capacities has to be integrated in the self-representation for healthy development to proceed. The crucial mediator for this process is language. Naming of sensations and affects includes the body in the ego and self, making experience at all levels accessible to symbolic representation and the operations of the secondary process. If this does not happen, the toddler may develop a pathological relationship with the body, in which the body ego is not subsumed in the ego or the self. Verbal development continues, but without the resonance

> of feeling-states to ground it in the reality base of the individual's experience of his own body (p. 339).

When this loss of personal voice occurs, even during the acquisition of language, there is a double cause-and-effect result: the essential self of the child becomes a wounded self, with the essential self becoming hidden and personal voice becoming silenced. Such silencing and the continued absence of the interpersonal, elaborative communication so needed to nourish the growth of the essential self further deprives that essential self and reinforces the child's wounded adaptation, at the expense of authentic living. S. A. Kurtz (1984) in discussing his reactions to his patients' silences and what those silences might mean, wrote: "If the cohesive self of a certain stage of development... does not meet with the maternal response it requires to confirm its subjective reality, it may split off and continue—hidden and embryonic. Since the vitality associated with this split-off self is unavailable, its emergence and integration would animate the now depleted and distorted personality.... Silence, in this case, is an attempt to protect a precious core of authentic existence from destruction" (p. 232, see also Nacht, 1963).

A child's ability to be engaged in thought processes is the result of internalizing her experiences with her parents. As the child narrates life events with parents, s/he is able to engage in the narrative process within themselves. When parents deny, disavow, belittle or ridicule their child's traumatic experience, the child's unique, individual personal voice must go underground, in order to prevent further traumatization. If the trauma occurs in the first two years of life, the experience is encoded implicitly within the right hemisphere, with few or no words attached to it. Even when semantic language becomes available to whatever degree, the implicit environmental threat may be such that the child is inhibited from placing the veneer of words onto his/her experience.

Gary Whitmer (2001) pointed out that when the parents' version of the child is the *only* version permitted, the capacity for propositional thought is prevented from developing, and along with it the voice and language for such thinking. This is so, Rita Carter (1998) formulated, because, "Without some symbol, like a name [word], for an object [one] has nothing with which to hook the memories of it from storage. They may be brought to mind by sensory reminders ... but volunteer access to them, on demand, would be much harder" (p. 138). When the parent does not provide the potential space in which to assist the child in developing her own symbols for her sense of self and for experience, the child's voice and matching language cannot develop.

"Communication," Rita Carter (1998) pointed out, "is a matter of survival (p. 137). She discussed, "Just as each separate brain cell reaches out to make contact with others, so each brain is designed to communicate with its like. Our ability to enter the minds of others, by intuition and by speech ... allows us to create and live in the highly organized hives we call civilization, and as a species we can join in endeavors so grandiose that they alter our environment on a global scale. Language allows us to juggle ideas in a uniquely creative way, and our intuitive knowledge of others' mental machinations makes our relationships complex, subtle and deep. Language development changed the landscape of the brain radically because it annexed huge cerebral areas once used for movement and sensation. In doing so it created the asymmetry that distinguishes the human brain from that of any other animal" (p. 136).

Peter Shabad (1997), in discussing traumatic themes, has much to offer us in understanding both what I identify as implicit memory relivings and the understanding of the suppression of voice and compromised language:

> [S/he] both knows and does not know what is not there, and therefore, he both knows and does not know that he has actually

> experienced a trauma. To the extent that he is unsure of what 'really' happened, he must bring out proof of his experience to prove, paradoxically, that what occurred was not only his experience, but was a real event.... In order to secure a witness to his experience of trauma, and thereby transform it into an objective event, a person must continually re-create or 'make' the trauma over and over again. For the traumatized person, it may then not be easy to discern between trauma as his intended, omnipotently created experience and trauma as an objective event... the traumatic theme causes the child to transform his strangled communications into the belated effects of posttraumatic symptomatology. A person's unique constellation of psychological symptoms reflects the lonely, nonverbal journey of the repetition compulsion to bring out proof of his sufferings. From this perspective, symptoms are self-created communicative actions intended to build repeated memorials back to one's experience of trauma, so as to objectify the experience into an event..." (p. 355).

In terms of the languaging of trauma, Bessel van der Kolk (2014) reported, "Our scans showed that Broca's area [speech center] went offline whenever a flashback was triggered.... That doesn't mean that people can't talk about a tragedy.... [but] It is enormously difficult to organize one's traumatic experience into a coherent account—a narrative with a beginning, a middle, and an end" (p. 43). Van der Kolk concluded, "When memory traces of the original sounds, images, and sensations are reactivated, the frontal lobe shuts down, including as we've seen, the region necessary to put feelings into words.... At this point the emotional brain, which is not under conscious control and cannot communicate in words, takes over. The emotional brain (the limbic area and the brain stem) expresses its altered activation through changes in emotional arousal, body physiology, and muscular action" (p. 178).

Now that we have dived into the effects of gaps and failures and unresolved trauma upon otherwise healthy development, we focus on the challenge of diagnosis versus assessment and the provocative dynamics in the treatment experience of Will and Julia.

CHAPTER FOURTEEN

Diagnosis versus Assessment

Clinicians of every stripe turn to the process of diagnosis usually as a guide to the pathology exhibited by a patient, one that can offer parameters for understanding and treatment. As an activity, diagnosis seeks to establish cause and effect across a spectrum of conditions. For those in the mental health field, psychiatrists and clinicians not only classify mental disorders using the *Diagnostic and Statistical Manual of Mental Disorders*-5 (2013) and/or the *International Classification of Diseases* (2005) with specific criteria, but the diagnoses serve to "facilitate an objective assessment of symptom presentations in a variety of clinical settings—inpatient, outpatient, partial hospitalization, consultation-liaison, clinical, private practice, and primary care" (American Psychiatric Association, 2021). Diagnosis is also a necessary requirement for insurance coverage within the medical/psychological structure of the United States.

The term diagnosis originally derived from the Greek, meaning to discern, to distinguish, to know (see New Oxford American Dictionary). Thus, there are many calls by clinicians for revision, or more drastically an overhaul, a return to the psychodynamic model for the DMS, and other significant additions to improve its usage. One such new diagnosis has been proposed for the next edition of the DSM by Bessel van der Kolk (2017). His Developmental Trauma Disorder (DTD) addresses children who have suffered complex trauma, because "...PTSD diagnosis does not capture the developmental impact of childhood trauma" (p. 9), which are:

- Complex disruptions of affect regulation
- Disturbed attachment patterns
- Rapid behavioral regressions and shifts in emotional states
- Loss of autonomous strivings
- Possible aggressive behavior against self and others
- Failure to achieve developmental competencies
- Loss of bodily regulation
- Altered schemas of the world
- Anticipatory behavior and traumatic expectations
- Multiple somatic problems
- Lack of awareness of danger and resulting self-endangering behaviors
- Self-hatred and self-blame
- Chronic feelings of helplessness" (p. 9).

Van der Kolk's (2019) Developmental Trauma Disorder is "predicated on the notion that multiple exposures to interpersonal trauma, such as abandonment, betrayal, physical or sexual assaults or witnessing domestic violence have consistent and predictable consequences that affect many areas of functioning" (p. 10)... such children "lose the expectation that they will be protected" (p. 11). As promising as this new diagnostic category is, we, as clinicians, are left with those fundamental anguished questions from our patients and are challenged not only in working with such traumatized children and adolescents but mainly with the adults in our consulting rooms who carry this lasting unresolved trauma with them. In the spirit of a more humane and empathically accurate diagnosis we need to be able to turn to deeper and much more meaningful and non-pathological uses of this needed and valuable, but often perplexing, contradictory, even misleading activity.

A taskforce composed of numerous members of the American Psychoanalytic Association, The International Psychoanalytical Association, Division 39 of the American Psychological Association, the American

Academy of Psychoanalysis and Dynamic Psychiatry, and the National Membership Committee on Psychoanalysis in Clinical Social Work, such as Vittorio Lingiardi, Nancy McWilliams, Stanley Greenspan, Sidney J. Blatt, Robert Borstein, Robert Wallerstein, et al developed the first edition of the *Psychodynamic Diagnostic Manual* (PDM), (2006) as a diagnostic handbook to serve as a complement to the DSM and the ICD. The Second Edition of the PDM (2017) was described by its publisher, Guilford Press, as a 90% revised "authoritative diagnostic manual grounded in psychodynamic clinical models and theories. Explicitly oriented toward case formulation and treatment planning, PDM-2 offers practitioners an empirically based, clinically useful alternative or supplement to DSM and ICD categorical diagnoses. Leading international authorities systematically address personality functioning and psychological problems of infancy, childhood, adolescence, adulthood, and old age, including clear conceptualizations and illustrative case examples" (Guilford Press Website, 2017).

The rationale for the PDM-2 system was based on the idea that "A clinically useful classification of mental disorders must begin with a concept of healthy psychology... to understand symptoms we must know something about the person who hosts them and that mental health and psychopathology involve many subtle features of human functioning..." (p. 3-4). Further, "PDM-2 diagnoses are 'prototypical'; that is, they are not based on the idea that a diagnostic category can be accurately described as a compilation of symptoms... unlike the DSM and the ICD systems, the PDM-2 system highlights patients' *internal experience* of those conditions... it uses a multidimensional approach... to describe the intricacies of the patient's overall functioning and ways of engaging in the therapeutic process" (p. 6).

Nancy McWilliams (2011, 2020), one of the editors of the PDM-2 began her significant exploration into *Psychoanalytic Diagnosis: Understanding Personality Structure in the Clinical Process*, by writing: "For many people, including some therapists, 'diagnosis' is a dirty word.... The complex person gets flippantly oversimplified... the anguished person gets linguistically distanced... the troubled person gets punished with a pathologizing label... one objection to diagnosing is the view that diagnostic terms are inevitably pejorative... " (p. 7). However, she did also offer her five "interrelated advantages of the diagnostic enterprise" (p. 8):

- its usefulness for treatment planning
- its implications for prognosis
- its contribution to protecting consumers of mental health services
- its value in enabling the therapist to convey empathy
- its role in reducing the probability that certain easily frightened people will flee from treatment (p. 8).

McWiliams emphasized, "the DSM lacks an implicit definition of mental health or emotional wellness. Psychoanalytic clinical experience, in contrast, assumes that beyond helping patients to change problematic behaviors and mental states, therapists try to help them to accept themselves with their limitations and to improve their overall resiliency, sense of agency, tolerance of a wide range of thought and affects, self-continuity, realistic self-esteem, capacity for intimacy, moral sensibilities, and awareness of others as having separate subjectivities" (p. 9). McWilliams further pointed out, "Once I have a good feel for the person, the work is going well, I stop thinking diagnostically and simply immerse myself in the unique relationship that unfolds between me and the client... one can throw away the book and savor individual uniqueness" (2020, p. 7).

For me, I begin by savoring the uniqueness; after all, I am being invited into one of the most emotionally intimate relationships a person can have, providing the safety and trust necessary for this distinctive individual to partner with me in what we both hope will be a life-changing transformation. My developmental lens is ever-present, not as a fixed template from which

I work or as a mantel I place upon the patient, but because as a lifelong writer as well as clinician, stories are at the heart of the matter. When I read a book, I dive in, and swim. Characters' stories, made up of the rich fabric of the complexity of their experiences, always relationally based, reveal the narratives they carry, unconsciously or in vivid awareness, driving forward their day-to-day strivings, frustrations, and triumphs. I want to be compelled by their stories, viscerally affected by them, and care immensely about what is coming next. So, too, as a psychoanalyst with those who seek treatment, I want to be compelled, affected, and care.

In our initial session, I do an informal intake, but more I listen actively for three elements: their reasons for seeking help, the rippling of current time distress, within glimpses of early unfolding of pieces of history. My patients may bring their own notions of what is 'wrong' with them, they may feel an urgent need to be diagnosed: they are "a" or have a "something." The hope, implied or explicit, is to have some relief in their problems being wrapped up in a package that does not have to be ripped opened but speaks for itself, something that contains their years of suffering, something controllable, so they might not have to immerse themselves in their own painful tales, not quite realizing, but fearing, the complexity ahead.

There are other reasons, as well, to diagnose: conceptualizing the endeavor to come, working collaboratively with a psychiatrist, satisfying insurance requirements, testifying as an expert witness, for instance. Concurrently, like a mother, scooping up her newborn, I embrace this new being in my consulting room. We are on dry land, but we dive in and begin to swim.

My first analyst shared with me that she always asked in the first session for the patient's earliest memory, saying that the entire analysis was held in that memory. Indeed, that was true for me. My first conscious, explicit (unusual at that age, but probably due to the trauma involved), combined with implicit memory is vivid, even at such an early age. I was no more than fifteen months old, able to stand up in my crib in a converted service porch turned nursery that was tandem to my brother's bedroom. I could feel the Chicago sweltering summertime heat glaring through the two walls of windows. I was able to jiggle my crib on its metal wheels across the wood plank floor close enough to peer through the panes of the French door. I began calling "Mama," "Mama." I remember seeing that the solid door of my brother's room was closed and somehow knew, even then, that I was "far away." I began crying, "Mama!", "Mama!" I felt slippery to myself, though I didn't know that word then, but I was wet all over, sweat, pee, tears. After calling and crying, in one critical moment, I knew in the most profound sense that she was not there. Every cell in my body knew she was not there, and that she was not coming. Hardly able still to stand, I started calling as loudly as a toddler can "Ehya!" [Ella] "Ehya!" [Ella]. How long it took, I have no idea, maybe forever, but then there she was, my mother's cleaning lady, pushing against the humidity's stuck door and scooping me up, encircling me, patting me, crooning to me, saving me. She continued to do just that through the next few years as I struggled with asthma, pushing aside my mother's arms to reach for Ella who could make my breathing manageable until the doctor came.

My last analyst held that the analytic relationship *was* the analysis. In what became a truly transformative analysis, she diagnosed me with [ongoing] separation anxiety, even though I was in a deep and loving marriage in which we had several young children and successful careers. In one particular session, as she and I were exploring once again the whole notion of separateness and aloneness, I was finally able to find the perfect matching words for my 'diagnosis': "Separation and being alone isn't the problem! I have always been separate and alone. I learned how to do that. The problem isn't being separate *from*—it's being separate *with*." And in that moment, my final healing began.

Diagnosis is a complicated matter, with hundreds of thousands of words written and spoken on the subject. While I utilize it in the ways that are required or helpful, as a psychoanalyst I looked for a way to map visually where my patient began and how this unique individual with his or her unique story transforms in development over the profound course of our analytic endeavor. Based on my original models of the Seven Keystones of Development, I created The Seven Keystones of Development Assessment Map, which I use to shape a picture of my patients' developmental and relational experiences. This map is intended to be used as a collaborative instrument with the DSM or the PDM. I have found it a very useful unfolding 'portrait' for myself, for my patients, and for my students and supervisees, especially in the comparison it can illuminate between healthy and wounded and traumatized development. Further, it also provides a roadmap of where the work will need to focus as we begin to grapple with the nature of our patients' unresolved trauma and its consequences and the necessary healing and transformed development ahead (see Appendices for the Assessment Map for coping purposes).

Will's Assessment Map highlights the various dynamic forces and struggles of his psychological life. We spent years piecing together his narrative, so this assessment was built overtime as well. But it captures important reference points, so that at any point along our journey, I could locate him and me with him. Similarly, Julia's Assessment Map provided me a particularly beneficial grounding, especially when the road we were traveling became increasingly rocky.

The Seven Keystones of Development Assessment Map

by Gwyneth Kerr Erwin, Ph.D., Psy.D.

CLINICIAN'S NAME: *Gwyneth Kerr Erwin, PhD., PsyD.*	CLINICIAN'S SIGNATURE: *Gwyneth Kerr Erwin*
PATIENT'S NAME (OR INITIALS): *Will*	DATE (AND/OR RANGE): *Sample*

HEALTHY DEVELOPMENT

STATES	MEMORY SYSTEMS	INTERNALIZATION IDENTIFICATIONS	AFFECTS	ATTACHMENT	HEMISPHERIC DEVELOPMENT	VOICE & LANGUAGE
	☐ Implicit	☐ Mother	☐ Flow	☑ Secure	☐ Right	☐ Personal Voice
☐ Bridging		☐ Father		☐ Mother		
	☐ Explicit				☐ Left	☐ Expressive Language
☐ Transitions		☐ Sibling	Temperament Type:	☑ Father		
			☐ HF ☐ HD ☐ AC			☐ Circles of Communication Ave #
		☐ Grandparent	☑ Hypo	☐ Other	☐ Cross-Hemispheric	
	☐ Cross-Hemispheric					
		☐ Other	☐ Inattentive			

WOUNDED DEVELOPMENT

STATES	MEMORY SYSTEMS	INTERNALIZATION IDENTIFICATIONS	AFFECTS	ATTACHMENT	HEMISPHERIC DEVELOPMENT	VOICE & LANGUAGE
☑ Transitions	☑ Implicit Memory Intrusions	☑ Introjects	☑ Dysregulation	☑ Insecure	☐ Adaptive	☑ Personal Voice
Difficulties with			☐ Hyperarousal			☐ Altered
			☑ Hypoarousal	☑ Ambivalent	☑ Right	☑ Compromised
☑ Dissociated			☐ Mild	*Mother*		☑ Suppressed
		☑ Mother	☐ Moderate	☐ Avoidant	☐ Left	
	☑ Types of Memory Banks	*Hostile*	☑ Severe			
	Birth trauma	*Cocooning*	☑ PTSD	☐ Disorganized	☐ Split	☐ Expressive Language
☐ Depersonalized	*Car Accident*	☑ Father	☑ CPTSD			☐ Absent
	Bullying	*Bold then*	Types of:	Mother's:		☑ Halting
		compromised	☑ Shame	☐ Am ☐ Av ☐ Dis	☑ Primarily One-Sided (emotional)	☐ Stilted
☐ Derealized			☑ Fear			☑ Lack of Coherence
		☑ Sibling	☐ Anger			☐ Minimizing
		Overwhelming		Father's:	☐ Primarily One-Sided (cognitive)	
	☑ PTSD		☑ Depressive	☐ Am ☐ Av ☐ Dis		☐ Verbose
	Birth, car acc., bullying		☑ Immobilization			☐ Behavioral
	☑ CPTSD	☐ Other	☑ Fleeing & Hiding		☐ Cross-Hemispheric	☐ Symbolic
	Mother, bullying		☐ Fighting Back			☑ C of C # *1–2*

TRAUMATIZED DEVELOPMENT

STATES	MEMORY SYSTEMS	INTERNALIZATION IDENTIFICATIONS	AFFECTS	ATTACHMENT	HEMISPHERIC DEVELOPMENT	VOICE & LANGUAGE
☑ States into Traits	☑ Implicit Memory Driven	☑ Identifications with trauma	☑ Disorganized Affects	☐ Disorganized/ Disoriented Attachment	☐ Severely Compromised	☑ Loss of Voice
			☑ PTSD		☐ Right	
Characteristics						
☑ Fear based	☑ PTSD		*Fear, weakness*	☐ Mother		☑ Little Expressive Language
☑ Shame based					☐ Left	
☐ Anger based	☑ CPTSD	☐ Aggression Against Others	☑ CPTSD	☐ Father		
☐ Other			*Lost self*		☐ Split	☑ C of C # *0*
			Lost dreams	☐ Reactive Attach	☐ Cross-Hemispheric	
		☑ Aggression Against the Self				
				☐ Traumatized Attach		

The Seven Keystones of Development Assessment Map

by Gwyneth Kerr Erwin, Ph.D., Psy.D.

CLINICIAN'S NAME: *Gwyneth Kerr Erwin, PhD., PsyD.*	CLINICIAN'S SIGNATURE: *Gwyneth Kerr Erwin*
PATIENT'S NAME (OR INITIALS): *Julia*	DATE (AND/OR RANGE): *Sample*

HEALTHY DEVELOPMENT

STATES	MEMORY SYSTEMS	INTERNALIZATION IDENTIFICATIONS	AFFECTS	ATTACHMENT	HEMISPHERIC DEVELOPMENT	VOICE & LANGUAGE
	☐ Implicit	☐ Mother	☐ Flow	☐ Secure	☐ Right	☐ Personal Voice
☐ Bridging		☐ Father		☐ Mother		
	☐ Explicit				☐ Left	☑ Expressive Language
☐ Transitions		☐ Sibling	Temperament Type: ☑ HF ☐ HD ☐ AC	☐ Father		☑ Circles of Communication Ave # *6–8*
		☐ Grandparent	☐ Hypo	☐ Other	☐ Cross-Hemispheric	
	☐ Cross-Hemispheric					
		☐ Other	☐ Inattentive			

WOUNDED DEVELOPMENT

STATES	MEMORY SYSTEMS	INTERNALIZATION IDENTIFICATIONS	AFFECTS	ATTACHMENT	HEMISPHERIC DEVELOPMENT	VOICE & LANGUAGE
☑ Transitions	☑ Implicit Memory Intrusions	☑ Introjects	☑ Dysregulation	☑ Insecure	☐ Adaptive	☑ Personal Voice
except with fear terror – instantaneous to excitation			☐ Hyperarousal			☑ Altered
			☑ Hypoarousal	☑ Ambivalent	☑ Right	☐ Compromised
☑ Dissociated	☑ Types of Memory Banks	☑ Mother	☐ Mild	*Enlivening/terrifying*		☑ Suppressed
		Not able to mother	☑ Moderate	☑ Avoidant	☑ Left	
	Father threatening		☐ Severe	*'Dead' Mother*		☐ Expressive Language
☐ Depersonalized	*Father's sexual*	☑ Father	☑ PTSD	☐ Disorganized	☐ Split	☐ Absent
	intrusions	*Exciting terrifying*	☑ CPTSD			☐ Halting
	Mother's emptiness		Types of:	Mother's: ☐ Am ☐ Av ☐ Dis	☐ Primarily One-Sided (emotional)	☐ Stilted
☐ Derealized			☑ Shame			☐ Lack of Coherence
		☐ Sibling	☑ Fear			☐ Minimizing
			☐ Anger	Father's: ☐ Am ☐ Av ☐ Dis	☐ Primarily One-Sided (cognitive)	☐ Verbose
	☑ PTSD		☐ Depressive			☐ Behavioral
	Struggle over meaning		☑ Immobilization			
	☑ CPTSD	☐ Other	☑ Fleeing & Hiding		☑ Cross-Hemispheric	☐ Symbolic
			☑ Fighting Back			☑ C of C # *2–4*

TRAUMATIZED DEVELOPMENT

STATES	MEMORY SYSTEMS	INTERNALIZATION IDENTIFICATIONS	AFFECTS	ATTACHMENT	HEMISPHERIC DEVELOPMENT	VOICE & LANGUAGE
☑ States into Traits	☑ Implicit Memory Driven	☑ Identifications with trauma	☑ Disorganized Affects	☐ Disorganized/ Disoriented Attachment	☐ Severely Compromised	☑ Loss of Voice
			☑ PTSD		☐ Right	
Characteristics	☑ PTSD		*Fear into excitation*	☐ Mother		☐ Little Expressive Language
☐ Fear based					☐ Left	
☑ Shame based	☑ CPTSD	☐ Aggression Against Others	☑ CPTSD	☐ Father		
☐ Anger based					☐ Split	
☐ Other			*When feeling shame,*			☑ C of C # *1–3*
			loss of sense	☑ Reactive Attach	☐ Cross-Hemispheric	
		☑ Aggression Against the Self	*of self*	*To mother*		
				☑ Traumatized Attach		
				To father		

CHAPTER FIFTEEN

Falling Down the Rabbit Hole

The Impact of Unresolved Trauma Upon the Therapeutic Endeavor

Dynamics in Treatment: Will

While Will was making progress in the middle of our second year that seemed substantial and mainly grounded, the collision of his cousin's death, his wife entering analysis, and Will's mother's death ushered in a return to deterioration. After finding his voice delivering the eulogy at his cousin's funeral, his languaging faltered again, with lots of 'ums' and 'uhs' replacing words he could no longer find. One session, he held the journal out towards me. "Part of what I was trying to do yesterday was write down my feelings." He showed me a written list in the journal:

> a little depressed
> session a struggle to understand
> laughing/crying at same time—feeling the split (the part that wants to go
> out, the part that wants to stay home)
> "I—uh—it's all there—um—not easy to access consciously. I mean, I mean, it's all there—unconsciously—hard to connect with it—remembering—um—I—connecting with feelings—more mysterious and—ah—unpredictable—what it takes to do—um—that. Unpredictable. I—I—don't know what I'm trying to say. I was

> thinking about—um, um, um, the other day, I suppose—feeling—telling myself to feel—let go of it and to be—to let myself be spontaneous—follow through and call a bunch of prospects. That gets put off with anxiety. I tell myself, um, I say to myself, it's not an anxiety I have to carry around. Let my mother take that with—free myself up from it. And going through that—feels, uh, ah, good and um—but short-lived. I fall into the usual, what's comfortable, and go along until I come back in here."
>
> "That comfortable, cozy place is very seductive; it really pulls you," I said.
>
> He frowned, then smiled. "Yeah, it's very hard to—um—give up. I'm quick to justify it and think of it—you know, um, in a positive way. I need—it looks, uh, useful."
>
> After several labored back and forth exchanges about what role his mother played in this "comfy seduction," I asked Will, "And so, who do I become for you? The person to challenge you, to threaten that comfy place, or the one to rescue you out of it?"
>
> "Yeah! I think of you and the therapy as what will help pull me out of the comfort zone."

In the following session, Will confessed he had been agonizing about one of his sons, facing adolescence, who confessed feeling timid and weak. His son could not talk with his parents about this, only moan in pain and humiliation as Samantha tried bolstering him while Will stood by, flooded by his own feelings of being weak and inept. Will was overwhelmed with haunting memories of becoming immobilized time and again. His struggle in session to find a way to talk to his son led Will to share with me new levels of his anguish over his long-ago concerns about his manliness. His guilt about his lack of courage in being bold and robust combined with his current inability to reach out to his son all brought Will to a similar state of shame as his son's.

I was profoundly touched by his effort to be with the conflict and complexity of his feelings: "It's incredibly difficult to go into those experiences and feel what's there, isn't it?"

His voice constricted, the words squeezing out, "That—seems—very—painful—to—do."

His eyes brimmed over with tears as he worked to talk about his youthful yearnings and wonderings, about how there had been no one to talk to about such things, about how naïve and weak he was as an older boy. As we processed these painful memories and his son's anguish, Will began to empathize with his son's behavior accompanied by glimmers of how he might talk to him.

The grogginess that threatened to engulf me periodically, yet which I could usually overcome by helping Will feel his actual affect, reemerged with a fevered intensity as Will struggled with his own passivity. The earlier feeling that something was missing from his story, something raw but dismissed, now pounded at me. I kept searching myself internally, somewhat critically, for what I might be missing. At the end of what turned out to be a crucial session, as Will turned the doorknob to leave, he casually asked, "Have I ever told you they thought I was dead when I was born?"

In Will's throwaway line of "Did I ever tell you they thought I was dead when I was born?" his affect was completely absent, much as he had talked initially about the car accident, but I woke up with his disclosure, never to become groggy with him again. The story unfolded that at birth, the umbilical cord was wrapped tightly around his neck; he was blue, evidencing no signs of life. The doctor set him aside to work with the mother. A couple of minutes passed when Will hiccupped, and the medical team realized he was alive and "got him going." I was stunned as he talked at how our sessions paralleled, even replicated, that initial birth experience: every session, regardless of how the previous session had gone, I felt as though we were beginning again, with me wooing him, cajoling him into life.

During the ensuing weeks, he began to tolerate feeling the repressed terrors and pain of these pivotal life-and-death experiences, surprised that after all these years they had true and deep meaning for him. He cycled for months between his near-death birth experience, the near-death car accident, his early and failed marriage to his high school girlfriend. When he could not speak, he would pick up his drawing journal and write, I didn't know what. Tears would come, and he would then whisper, "when I came close to dying." In those brief moments, he could feel how truly frightened he was about so many aspects of trying to live. But significantly, he began carrying what we were processing from one session to another, successful transitions finally taking hold.

The patchwork of his life came together, for me, and for him. I could feel deeply how precarious life seemed to Will: he had almost 'not begun'; how unpredictably dangerous the world could be, a 'force' could crash into the 'vehicle' he was traveling in and nearly kill him; how risky it was to be active, to follow his curiosity, he could suffer his uncle's fate; his judgment might be horribly faulty, or lacking, he might "freeze," make the wrong decision, or be "too impulsive."

While his parents were affectionate and kind to him, his father took any way out of conflict and gave up when he experienced his own vulnerability, not able to help Will understand his own conflicts or impulses and how to manage either. His mother lived substantially housebound, contentious and suspicious, able to provide Will with soothing and cozy care but not able to support his resilience and purpose as he grew up and tried to face the world. While I was a new kind of analytic parent, believing in his potential strength, Will felt me in the transference alternately as the kind of 'father/mother' who might push him out into a dangerous world, insist he take risks he could not succeed in, or by keeping him in treatment, try to keep him by my side, beckon him back as he headed for the world of doing. What use, ultimately, was he going to be able to make of me? Our daunting task was to help him shift his identification with me as that analyst/mother/father who could help him become assured, bold, and safe in the world inside and outside his own mind.

Despite the profound nature of what he was processing in our sessions, his outer work world nearly came to a complete standstill. With this, his marriage teetered on shaky ground again, Samantha nearing the end of any patience, but with the clarity she was gaining from her own analysis, able to communicate her frustrations without going into a fury. Unfortunately, Will was still able to zone her out. One morning session, when he tried to zone me out as well, I confronted him, "Will, you know how you can stand on a train track and feel the vibration of a train coming, long before you can see or hear the train?"

He nodded.

I continued, "I feel like you're living your life like that right now, and after a while, you even go numb to the vibration on the track. You don't even recognize what it means when you see the train in your peripheral vision. But Will, now the train is barreling down the tracks and you are frozen, watching it come closer and closer."

His eyes filled with tears, his mouth twisted, and he said, "That's exactly it."

In the next session, I was so overcome with a momentary return to the grogginess and, even, a sense of grief, *his* unfelt grief? or *for* him? I didn't know yet, that I said, "You are enveloped right now in a thick fog, not even vapor. You've anesthetized yourself, and you're about to do the same to me."

As we processed the meaning for him of his life experiences, and of both the train and the fog metaphors, he experienced a renewed clarity of how dangerous it felt to be alive. We began tracking his energy shifts, seeing that whenever he did something successful or proactive, he would have a down shift in energy immediately after, zoning off into his fog. We discussed the secondary gains that existed in the closed system in which he and Samantha functioned:

1) how he could retreat in the face of her "bullying,"
2) how Will relived again and again the prohibitions against living a robust life,
3) how trapped they were within their concomitant and mutual need for him to tend the home fires, how that tending served his need to be cozy along with Samantha's historical need not to be abandoned, despite her desire for him to take care of her in worldly successful ways, and
4) how Will's failures and his passive-aggressive jabs at her then opened the way for Samantha to deliver the scathing punishments he believed he deserved. Once more, the fog, his and mine, lifted. And as it did, his burgeoning self emerged. So did his increased conflict.

Dynamics in Treatment: Julia

For what would be years to come in sessions with Julia, my challenge was to find for myself the ways to be present with Julia's rapidly shifting emotional states, tracking them, coming to understand each of them, along with the various purposes they served her as I also tried to manage and mitigate her dysregulation. Years earlier, my then supervisor had discussed how to maintain an "equi-distance" with patients. I trusted and respected her, but something in the concept felt off for me, especially due to my developmental ideas of working with my patients. Fortunately, she was someone with whom I could be open, so as I struggled to tease out what was bothering me, I found the words for the intuitive feeling that was the right for me: "equi-presence." Just as with developing children, a parent needs to stay "up close," supporting attunement, while also being regulated enough to offer necessary provision. So, too, was I convinced that as an analyst, instead of staying at a safe remove, I needed to be affectively present, moving with a patient in his or her state transitions without becoming dysregulated by them myself. As Julia ricocheted from state to state within our sessions, and from session to session, I focused on being "equi-present" and regulated with Julia's alternating terror and craving for excitation as she was compelled by the drama triggered in the relationship with Oscar.

I could feel frightened for Julia, but no sooner would my fear increase for her physical and psychic safety than she would move to a manic state, even more convinced she was in love with Oscar. His skin was particularly *irresistible* to her because it was tanned, smooth, and, especially, because it was hairless. Whatever internal protests might begin to form when she was with him, they would evaporate with his touch. I thought: *the idealized mother's skin?* Then Oscar's lovemaking was rough, overpowering, but exciting, like the relationship with Julia's father. I was keenly aware that she was in a profound replication, but also knew that if I did anything more than try to understand and gently narrate what "might" be playing out, and with that gingerly, she would flee. Try as I might internally to link this experience directly to a transferential response to me, I came to the conclusion again and again that this was her unconscious way of bringing her internal object world of traumatic identification and experience into the consulting room. There was no way for this to play out with me, only the many ways for me to come to know what had happened to her. My challenge was in truly becoming the new analytic mother who would learn *when* and *how* to intervene, someone with whom she could someday identify.

Julia made it clear to me in darker moments of almost 'confessionals' that she did not feel she would be safe from danger if she left Oscar. In session, she often buried her face in her hands, bowing under the shame she felt imagining what I must think of her. She proclaimed that she "knew" I was not judging her, that I could hold on to the "real" Julia. Yet, by my own countertransference feelings, I knew that transferentially Julia was casting me variously as the horrified mother, the frightened mother, the disapproving mother, and almost always, the observant but basically impotent mother. Julia also dreamt nearly every night about Oscar. Fights with him, against him, fights against the violence, while being swept up into the excitement of their fiery sexual life. Her conflict was enormous, as she struggled against the life of excitation he provided and the nudging knowledge that he really offered only danger. She told of a dream she had of him leaving her, driving away in a truck. In the dream, he stopped the truck a distance from her. She could not live without him: "I have no life by myself." She ached to feel joy in being alive, not dependent on a particular person for that. She climbed in the truck with him, and they traveled until they finally came to some kind of border, and she realized that there was nothing on the other side. The place they would be was empty for her. Like her mother. In the dream, she went no further with Oscar, returning home by herself, alone and bereft.

Throughout this tumultuous relationship with Oscar, Julia managed to see him only at work and on those nights when her children stayed overnight at their father's. While he acquiesced to these boundaries, Oscar was pushing for more and more contact. That crossed an internal line for Julia, her children having the first priority for her, and helped her, along with what we had discovered together about how her desperation drove her compulsively and how her terror to excitation conversion happened, to see other aspects of this replicating relationship. Julia was *beginning* to be affectively aware that her bond with Oscar centered around their "shared wound," as each of them had been young victims of incest and violence, and that, yes, maybe they were reenacting something together.

Under the sway of her sometimes manic defence (see Winnicott, 1935/1975), Julia confessed to turning the tables on Oscar (the oscillating shifts between masochism and sadism), tormenting him by being demanding, seductive, withdrawing, retaliating, and rewarding. Julia insisted it was in an effort to control Oscar, though a futile one.

In the next session, Julia anguished, "I have always lived an exemplary life. I had to. I tried never to make a mistake. I tried to make my father and mother happy. I tried to appear normal, like all the children of families who seemed to really care about each other, who were tender, who knew about real happiness."

Throughout the summer into the fall, Julia vacillated between staying with or trying to leave Oscar, their relationship a roller coaster ride. Again, Eleanore Armstrong-Perlman's paper (1989) helped me understand what was at stake for Julia and captured her excruciating dilemma for me, a dilemma evoked by "The Allure of the Bad Object:"

> ...the individuals cannot let go, no matter how maligned their experience. The need is compulsive, and the fantasy of loss is experienced as potentially catastrophic.... The patients cannot acknowledge the hopelessness of their relationships, or admit that the satisfactions they provide are partial and illusory, for to give up that hope may lead to a collapse of the self (p. 224).

Julia wrote an agonized letter to me:

> My attachments should begin to weaken to these people as I feel the pain they bring me. But it doesn't happen. I love them as always. There are explanations, I know. My neural pathways got linked up in such a way that I attached to my mother's emptiness. And my neural pathways got hooked up in such a way that I attached to the terrifying and oceanic experience of my father's sexuality. I translated terror into excitement. And I experienced it all as love.... I'm tired of feeling like

> an orphan. I come from bad people but I want to return to them. I come from a desert. I dig and scratch at the dry desert floor, and I find a trickle of water. This is thrilling. This keeps me going. Today, that has become life's meaning, finding the water, the small tokens of love in those who are almost dead to me. That is what feels real. That is how I am hooked up. Nothing else excites me. I do not speak another language.

Drama and trauma haunted the relationship with Oscar. One night, he toyed with a steak knife, as had her father, arrogantly talking to her of the joy and power of holding life and death in his hands. The next weekend when her children were with their father, Oscar caught a hummingbird, killed it and ate it, all in moments, in front of her, as she stood, immobilized. Doubled over in pain in the session, she cried, "He will never let me go." Now, she was startling awake nearly every night, seeing a faceless person watching her. Her feeling of degradation was profound: "I will never be human again." Bodily sensations flooded her. The shadowy faceless figure standing over her was playing with himself. She was tingling, vibrating. Feeling panicky inside. She would lie still, play dead. She was cornered. She wanted to kill him, but instead she said she was "scurrying around [internally] like a terrified mouse, scrambling for my life." If she did anything, she would be exiled, exactly what had happened in her life. It would never be over. She was dehumanized, put into an inhuman place.

In the following session she shared an experience she had as a young girl of twelve years, being in the family boat in the channel where the tankers came across the Pacific from the Far East. Her father anchored the boat in the channel, while Julia was consigned to stay awake all night on alert, bell in hand, to ring the alarm if she heard a tanker. Her father got emotionally "high" on such escapades. For Julia, as she fought against sleep all night, it meant death: she would not make it, she would go down when a looming tanker crushed their small excursion boat. The recurring message: *I cannot have life, joy. I am responsible for everyone else's life.* And if she were to stand up to her parents, tell the truth, say what she knew, or draw attention to their insanity, she would be disowned.

In the despair we grappled with every session, the hopeful signs of life in Julia at this time were her fierce commitment to our work and her eager utilization of understanding once she grasped a concept or the meaning of her experience. Once she 'got it' she began working with it. I shared with her Ferenczi's notion of the Orpha function, one which is not for the purpose of the individual's growth but for pure survival, 'marching on', which I had read about in Nancy Smith's (2001) paper. Julia 'filled in the blanks' herself: "Well, that's who I am most of the time." She shared memory after memory when she issued gentle but commanding orders inside herself to "Play dead," or "Now it's time to smile," or "Time to get up, get going, do this and do that." She confirmed for me this hovering presence I often felt with her. At session's end, Julia said, "I do want to attach to you; I want to grow, but it is terrifying to give over any part of this 'job'." I could feel a shift in the room, in the very air, the "forceful wind" of her Orpha self, as though this aspect of Julia's self was considering turning over to me some of her responsibilities.

In this session, too, she finally could tell me more about the kind of degradation and punishment she experienced earlier in her life and as late as into her adolescence. In an all too typical interaction, she would be in her bedroom—begging. Her father would have a belt or a hanger. Her supposed 'mistake' or 'infraction' was infinitesimal, unknowable. She was to take off all her clothes, bend over naked, so he could beat her until she bruised. No one at home or school, her mother, her teachers, the school staff commented or did anything, even though the bruises clearly showed to any of them, at least those on her legs. The beatings felt very sexual to Julia. She felt vial; her father was literally salivating. Yet, her father was the only one who taught her, inspired her, engaged with her, believed she could do anything. Finally, in emotional paralysis, she could feel herself emotionally join him: "I'm in worse than hell—falling, floating, eternally, in black outer space. I'm in shock, alone in the universe, the only sentient being, trapped eternally, having to stay alive to experience it—timelessly, endlessly." Either because of a crumb of affection or his forcing himself upon her, sickening her, she could glimpse how quickly this hell had to be converted into something she craved. No longer could she feel her rage or terror; instead, she was consumed with fervor and craving need. Telling me this, she felt nauseous, nearly crushed under abject shame. Many times, I alternately felt heartbroken for her and in a fury with her father.

Julia's father—the specter. Her terror of him juxtaposed against her fear of being alone. Which was worse? The only life she had was with him. She was flooded with grief in sessions, incredible sadness. The orphan, literally and psychically. Then, I might feel somewhat puny against such formidable internal objects yet awed and touched by her willingness to try to "give up" to me some measure of her Orphic functioning. But I also felt brave, the only one holding her hope. As she wept, while squirming against nearly unbearable shame, she told me she had a small sense of a cord of light running through her—maybe in her stomach. I wondered: Is this a new umbilical cord? Up against all the guilt, the desire, and fear of destroying her mother and father from her hate of their corruption, she had a dim sense that maybe somewhere she had a light. That maybe, *they* were not the light of the world.

The first of the year, she spoke again about her dream of the little girl pushing a cart, leaving the walled city behind. That little girl needed a mother; she was a ragamuffin. In considering the dream, she felt there was a secret tragedy, for which there were no words. She was walking away from the walled city, without a home, and nowhere to go but ahead on a dirt path, pushing a cart that was much too big for her. She thought she had to flee to keep the inhabitants safe.

As we talked that day, she said she was not so sure. Maybe they made her leave to keep them from having to see. After she associated to the dream again, I mentioned that I had the image of the little girl being like the town crier who was not allowed to shout out what she knew. Simultaneously, we each went to the Phenobarbital story, the purpose of which was to snuff out her crying. The atmospheric sense of prohibition, the sense that the mother could not stand the stimulation of Julia's crying, permeated the room. Julia could not stay with much about her mother for very long; it was too bleak and empty. But what we each noticed was that with me she was now able to be the 'town crier', and I was listening.

In between our next sessions I received a voice mail from her—she was in the terror and paralysis. She was shaking all over, having just had confirmation that the only member of her family with whom she still had contact (a cousin) had proven to be a pedophile with young adolescent men. The family history repeated and repeated. She felt like a timid mouse, a wimp. She could not confront him; instead, she avoided him. She was leveled. Her mind scrambled for days reliving his visits to her home, as she scoured her memories for any possibility that she had ever left him alone with her son. By the next session, she was immersed again with memories and feelings of her father. Experience after experience, she was trapped with a monster, alone in the requirement to please him, entertain him, soothe him.

She had a recurring dream throughout her life. In the dream, she was a child, and her family was leaving the southwest, moving to California. Through the rearview mirror, she saw an enormous truck barreling down on them; it would kill them. She said, "Those days, the air, the bleakness still bear down on me. They haunt me." Another childhood recurring dream: a large snake is crawling up her left arm; he sinks his fangs into her small shoulder. She will die. "Is that the incest?" she asked me. She covered her face with her hands, then emitted a childlike moan.

Back to medieval times. She returned to the image of the earlier dream, but it was changing. It would be May Day, she said now. She would be five, and I, sixteen. We were on the path together; the cart was fading from view. There were ribbons in my hair. She was running off collecting leaves and flowers, then running back to me. We made eye contact, over and over. In spite of our gladness, we both knew what had happened back in the walled city. Something terrible. Something she saw, something she knew, but could not tell. She knows I am with her.

In that moment, she had a profound first glimpse: it [the terrible secret] was not about her! She did not need to be punished. She asked if I could move my chair closer to her. I did. She turned her head and as her eyes gazed into mine, I said, "Hmmm," nodding. She softly matched my 'hmmm'. She began swaying slightly left to right. I made an "ahhh;" she responded. She got a little more animated, and said, "oohhh." I matched her. Annaliese Riess (1988), (as did Beebe & Lachmann's 2002 work), served as guide for me: "The powerful role of the eye and of face-to-face behavior... affects greatly the formation and the nature of human relationships" (p. 399).

Moment's later, Julia's mind formed a picture, one she could give words to:

> My father is 'tanked', fucking my mind, torturing me. He seems ten feet tall with fangs, claws. I desperately need someone to help me. I'm back in my room, no way out. I need a 'very big thing' to help me. Oh! [she notices] there's this creature—like an abominable snowperson. Furry. The abominable snowperson bites my father, makes him backup, won't even let him stand in the doorway. It makes him leave. I am trembling all over. (long pause). The snowperson is you! You pick me up and hold me in your big furry arms. We time travel away, to safety.

The life-long tide that threatened to drown Julia begin to ebb.

She increased her sessions to five times a week. The next session, moments after lying down on the couch, she sat up, turned, and looked at me. "I want to sit up from now on. I think I can bear having you see me." At her request, I moved my chair so that I was sitting fairly close to her, with she and I facing one another. Taking a minute to adjust to 'being seen', she said, "I do not want to hide in the couch in shame anymore." This interchange was validating to my contention that while the couch could serve multiple positive and useful purposes, the gaze that developmentally impaired patients needed more often required face-to-face contact, the "gaze" of interest and hopefully delight in the analyst's eyes providing a profoundly new object experience.

Julia found an old letter from her father. We spent weeks, session by session, going through the letter with me reading it aloud just a few lines at a time, all she could tolerate in any one session. His letter began:

> We obviously have a problem, which is an ancient one, and which I thought was resolved... so we can both be winners. The solution is two-fold. It requires that we increase the positive elements of our relationship as well as decrease the negative ones. Let me start with some inarguable assumptions that can serve as "ground rules," the first being that we love and respect each other very much; this is the positive aspect. On the negative side are the old pains that occasionally rise to the surface and boil over uncontrollably; such elements need to be eliminated. A third assumption is that we are both ok; our dealings with the rest of the world proclaim this. A first step is to be sure that we think this way not only about each other but also about ourselves in our special relationship.

The letter went on for many pages, each sentence triggering either pain, anger, humiliation, or confusion. Together, we discussed all that her father wrote, with Julia free-associating to every sentence, digesting each of them, struggling to find her truth within all he said. As she sorted out her feelings and memories, she began to feel a bit stronger, but prematurely bolder.

One weekend night after work, while her children were having dinner with their father, Oscar began drinking at dinner, enough so that he could not drive. Julia drove him home, thinking that he was enough "out of it" that she would be able to leave easily. Instead, once she helped him into his apartment, he grabbed a bottle of whiskey, blocking her exit. He guzzled the liquor, emptying the bottle, smashed the bottle to the floor, while escalating in both his errant attempts at lovemaking and his threats. She struggled to get away but was no match for him with his taller height and bulkier weight. He forced her into the bedroom, with one hand around her throat, squeezing, the other holding the jagged edge of the broken bottle near her neck. She could barely breathe, and quit resisting, going limp. As they reached the bed, he passed out on top of her. For quite some time she lay still, not daring to stir. Finally, it seemed he was truly 'out,' and although his weight was nearly dead weight, she worked inch by inch to wriggle and squirm to get out from under him, and then fled.

CHAPTER SIXTEEN

The Complexities of Risk

Risk is no small matter, ethically, legally, or interpersonally. Risk is something that therapists face every day, even if it is not ordinarily felt. Risks for patients are enormous: the risk of taking another chance, the risk of trusting, the risk of hope, the risk of commitment, the risk of love, the risk of loss. This chapter does *not* give a paint-by-the-numbers solution (as there is *no* such thing!) to the risks involved for each partner in the therapeutic endeavor. Instead, I take a hard, close up and personal look at the emotional, cognitive, psychological, heart, soul, and even physical risks involved in doing the deep and strenuous work concerning the consequences that result from developmental gaps, failures, and unresolved trauma.

Will:

Will's profound fundamental risk was to choose to live. Everything else was subsumed and informed by that risk, from the miniscule to the momentous. During our treatment, at every phase, in every session, risk was in the air and choking Will, literally even from using his voice. Risk began at his birth, soon followed by competition with his sisters for position, the cloying but stultifying environment provided by his mother in the face of the frequent absences of his father who Will adored. While Will was robust enough to jump off his garage roof at five years of age, the jump came with the price tag of a broken arm. Still able to persevere, he could use his cast as a playful weapon. The car accident when Will was in second grade altered the trajectory of his life with Will curling up inside, as well as in the cocoon his parents created, and from which he never emerged despite some futile attempts in later adolescence. Life echoed the refrain: you are not safe.

There is grief in shifting our stories: we lose the familiarity of our emotional environment; we might even lose a sense of who we are—and are not sure who we will become. The therapeutic endeavor with Will presented him with an intense dilemma: would his urge to learn to live actually cause him psychical or physical death? As enticed as he was by the hope that he could become the vital, bold, proactive man he dreamed of being, that hope was quickly dashed by his fear that I "was leading him down the garden path." Despite invaluable insights, we spent the majority of working through time in treatment on the teeter-totter of why not? And because!

Will came in on a Monday and agonized over how the weekend had fallen apart, both in terms of his energy and focus and in his interactions with Samantha. He knew he needed to talk to her about his dwindling set aside monies. As he described his Saturday, he began the day helping out a friend with a home woodworking project. He stayed afterwards to visit, followed by a visit to another friend who lived nearby who he had not seen for a long time. One of the themes throughout the marriage to Samantha was that he had friends, and she did not, that he got to do things he liked to do, while all she did was work. This particular Saturday, when he came home to grab a bite to eat, she insisted he was home to stay, and began a critical rant about his abandonment of her. When he noticed groceries in the back of their van, he merely commented, "I see you left your purse in the front seat." Their swords were drawn, Samanatha's pointed and aggressive, Will's passive and testy. The rest of the day deteriorated even further. Samantha, angry and burdened, withdrew, Will's energy collapsed, and even their evening turned into a squabble over Will wanting them to enjoy themselves for awhile after dinner with some wine and conversation versus Samantha wanting to clean up right away. Sunday, Will turned compliant, working on projects around the house that Samantha wanted done, but he was not emotionally present or engaged.

I asked him where *he* felt he had gotten derailed, and he said it was with the comment about Samantha's purse and not retrieving it for her or immediately helping with the groceries. I offered the suggestion that I thought it had happened earlier, when he was dreading telling her about the dwindling finances by 'hiding out' with his friends late into the afternoon. He 'got it' and together we noticed at each turn how he and then Samantha kept each other in their old systems of failure, hurt, jabs, and punishment, ultimately, energy loss and emotional fog for Will, and withdrawal, then attack, for Samantha. Toward the end of the session, when he was talking about the conflict after dinner, I asked, "What did you want?"

"I wanted to go for a walk with her and extend our time of being together, get closer. But she wanted to clean up."

"What did you say, or do?

"I helped her clean up, zoned out in front of the TV, and then went to bed."

"What might you say if you were speaking your real feelings?"

"Oh, something about how I'd like to go for a walk, and it was a nice dinner."

"Try again, I know it's scary but say what you really mean."

He was quiet for a minute, and then said, eyes glistening, his mouth twisting, "You fixed the most wonderful dinner tonight, and I feel much closer to you. I'll clean up in a little while, but right now, I'd like to go for a walk with you and tell you about the things I was avoiding earlier." He flushed a bit, cocked his head, and asked, "How was that?"

"Perfect." Tears welled up in my eyes.

In the remaining sessions of the week, Will's energy restored and did not fade, and he reported functioning the way he wanted to in his work hours. Still, he made no mention of talking to Samantha, so I knew we were in for many more vacillations between taking risks with their specter of failure and their occasionally felt but seemingly illusive benefit of growth and self-realization.

Julia:

The day after Julia fled from Oscar's drunken provocations, he was calling, apologizing, telling her how much he loved her, that he knew she would never be able to leave, that they were meant for each other. In our session that day, she agonized again: "Why did I think I could handle that? When am I going to be strong enough to leave him? Why do I keep doing this?"

I had the intuitive sense that the time was ripe to take the risk with Julia of changing her story. *I* talked that day, sharing with her how her trauma, implicitly encoded and encapsulated, split between terror and craving states, had not ever been able to be used for learning. As such, it could not serve as information to help her know what *not* to do the next time. I explained that part of repeating was trying to understand the trauma, so that it could either be processed and made usable as a resource or expelled. Another force of the repetition was to try to have a different ending to an all too familiar story. But the erroneous belief at play is that to have a different ending, one has to hold on to the same story. I also told her of how I had been thinking of various ways we could begin to intervene in its repetition. Was she ready to see if we could find those ways?

From this conversation and our subsequent intervention planning, Julia took the bold step of telling Oscar she could not see him for a while. Julia had no in person contact with him for the next month, other than at the hospital. In his phone calls he begged, promised to get help, therapy, go to AA. In our sessions, she struggled to come to terms with her kaleidoscopic feelings, mostly not giving in to believing his promises or her fears of what he might try to do to her, or her children, if she actually left.

At the end of the month, we discussed her readiness to end any phone contact. In this session, I felt the moment had finally come that if I took a position, she would not leave treatment. "This is it,' I said. "Once you do this, there's no going back."

She nodded, gravely. "Okay."

Julia secured a new position in a hospital forty miles away, and decided not to give her boss any notice, something she felt chagrined about. She was incredibly frightened, believing that Oscar would never let her go.

After the next session, she did not pick up the phone at home any longer and instructed her children not to answer any phone call as well. She could not yet consider disconnecting the line and getting a new one, as keeping the phone and her voice mail would be her main way of tracking Oscar and what she was sure were his threats. She would return only those calls she chose to return, and none of his. She called his voice mail after our session and told him the relationship was over, for good.

Oscar did not believe her. Over the weekend, on her voice mail, he pled, joked, pressured, and then threatened. When she did not arrive for work on Monday, and there was no word of why not, he turned dark with malevolent scorn. In a flurry of phone messages, all of which she listened to, he told her she would not ever get away, that, in fact, he would ruin her life, or kill her, that she would never know where or when—it could be today or tomorrow. Hysterical, she called me, the only urgent page she had ever sent me. During my return call to her, we decided she would pack some things quickly, confide in her ex-husband, gather the children from school and stay at her ex-husband's house until she could plan what to do.

I was frightened myself at the possibility of a real threat to Julia's life. For the next *three days*, Julia lived inside of abject terror. She did not come to sessions, hiding instead in Greg's house, having her sessions with me over the phone. She confided that she was unable to eat, finally even to keep down water. She felt she was falling into an endless abyss, where the torment would never end.

Her ex-husband was upset, even angry, but came through. He parked her car in a different location and ferried the children back and forth to school and friends. He installed a security system, complete with panic button. The messages from Oscar were unrelenting. She listened to each of them, in panic, but was equally terrified not to track him. Still, she was able to resist returning any of his calls.

Finally, I said to her that I wanted her to come in for a session, even in her pajamas, but if she absolutely could not, I would come to her. When Julia arrived in person for her session, she was gray, lips chalky, and her face expressionless. Deep circles accented her pale and staring eyes. Her mouth was parched, her lips cracking. I got her a glass of water, and a spoon, coaxing her to accept small sips throughout the session. I fed her as I would a dying baby bird with a medicine dropper. Not lost on me was that I was feeding the Phenobarbital baby, emerging from her coma. She was able to keep down the water. My chair close to hers, I clasped the hand she reached out to me, as I told her that this was not going to be the end of her life. I hoped silently that I was right and feared I might not be.

The next day, Julia said she was considering surrendering everything, her job, her reputation, and the last vestiges of her community, in order to file rape charges against Oscar. Within minutes, she agonized over all she would lose of what she had left, and said, "I can't do it." She railed against Oscar, against her father, her mother, against her own nervous system, hardly able to bear the shame and regret she felt at her own weakness, her need for aliveness at any price. Internally, I agonized over her myself.

She then confessed that she had seen him following her in his car, even to my office. In the session, I exhibited a conviction and strength I did not entirely feel. I began locking the door between the waiting room and the several consulting rooms in our suite during sessions, especially at night. Although I was beginning to suspect that Oscar, as dangerous as he appeared to be, would have as much or more to lose than Julia, and might be full of greater threats than he would ever carry out, I was afraid now not only for Julia, but for myself. Dissociation was not one of my defenses. Rather, what I had struggled with much of my life was being flooded and not having ways to get away from too-much-ness of feeling. During this time, I came to learn again, in even deeper ways, the power of regulation. Instead of searching for safety in the fresh allure of 'equi-distance', I worked intensely to find safety in my 'equi-presence' with my own and Julia's affective states, sensing when I needed to be fully present affectively and when I needed to have internal protection of knowledge and then the action at my disposal.

The phone messages from Oscar continued unabated, some mixed with his reassurance that he would, of course, never hurt her, others with raw and increased threats. Many times, as she had in the past, she saved them, replaying them for me in the consulting room. She was desperate for me to believe her, to know the reality of the "cause" of her terror. Each session, we processed her fears, as well as the wounded grief that had brought her to such a point.

After two weeks, Oscar's phone calls subsided in quantity, the threats being replaced by his assurances that he loved her and would never hurt her. In fact, he would *wait* for her return. If she did not, soon, though, he would "bother her for a very long time."

The waiting consisted of fewer calls for a two-month period. Then, after this so-called break, Oscar began a new spate of terrifying calls lasting nearly a week. The trauma began all over. Julia nearly collapsed. Oscar's threats, that she "would never get away," nor would she "really want to," forced her to consider again filing charges, but once more she felt she could not prove her case and that he was in a much more powerful position of being able to harm her. Terror and panic enveloped her: "This will never stop; he will never let me go," she could barely whisper. She came to sessions, feeling to me like a 'rag doll'. Every session, she was lethargic or emotionally paralyzed.

Trying to shore her up, I shared a word picture of how I might hold and protect this little rag doll. Amazed, she told me of her early childhood comforting object, a rag doll. When she was nearly three, her mother cut it into pieces, to "break me of the attachment to it." She believed the same thing was about to happen to her or me: we would be cut into pieces, or I might get "sick of her" and cut off the relationship. It did not matter what we worked with. She and the terror were unmovable. By Wednesday, I was feeling impotent, helpless, that the threat was too real. That even if he wasn't going to kill her, he was going to torment her, endlessly. My own hopelessness was rising.

The next morning, I received a message from her that she could not come in. She was exhausted. Giving up. I wondered what I was going to do—how I was going to 'move' her. I called her back, leaving her a message saying I understood exactly how impossible it seemed to find a way out, but as difficult as it might seem, she had to come to session. In that moment, I decided we would no longer talk about Oscar, even though we regularly worked with the introject of her father which Oscar represented. She called back very soon, leaving me her message: "All right, I'll come in. But it won't do any good." I wondered that myself, for the first time.

She arrived looking as hopeless as she felt, and as soon as she sat down, she began detailing her terror of Oscar again. I interrupted her: "We are not going to talk about Oscar. We are going to talk *only* about your internal object world, which is now terrorizing you far more than he ever could." Throughout the session, Julia was inevitably drawn back to talking about Oscar, and, each time, I forcefully intervened, bringing her back to the powerful forces at play inside of her. Well into the session when she once more pulled back to talking about Oscar, I became exasperated:

G: Julia, he's a punk, all bark, no bite [I hoped].

Julia jumped: "You called him a punk!

G: [recovering]: Well, he is. And as it turns out, that's all the power your internal objects have. When you were a child, these threats were very real. The only power they can have now is the power you give them inside.

J: You called him a punk! (she kept repeating). (Color returned to her cheeks.)

The bogeyman began to shrink.

Toward the end of the session, Julia and I talked about the various ways she might intervene when the terrorizing internal threats came into play. And she decided it was time to stop listening to Oscar's messages. As she left the session, she smiled for the first time in weeks, "I'm glad you knew what to do."

While this sliver of the struggle for Julia was won, the battle, let alone the war, was not yet ended, although that session proved pivotal. Over the ensuing weeks, we worked with various dynamic implicit memory processes of hers, especially focusing on the conversion of her terror into arousal.

In addition to this intense work, I also prepared Julia for what I was certain would be on-going cyclical threatening calls from Oscar. I again compared Oscar's cycles to Julia's father's manic and depressive cycles, with Julia finally finding the parallel process between the two men 'eye-opening'. By the time the next two-month increment was reached, and Oscar's calls increased to up to ten or more a day, Julia could say, "It's the two-month mark." His calls still made her feel fearful, and she hated them, but she was able to go about her life without collapse. And bravely, she began to make room for examining her own sadistic impulses—identifying with the aggressor *against herself*, as well as the sadism of wanting to get even, terrorize, torment Oscar, her mother and her father, the source of her "jabs."

Part Four

Treatment—Mending the Looking Glass

Model IV The Seven Keystones of Transformed Development

Many formative years ago, facing another blank page, I struggled one night to breathe life into my own writing voice. In my frustration, I heard the echoes of my original wounding: "There isn't enough of you to 'fill' a dissertation. Who do you think will care about what you have to say?" Fatigue, then anguish, gripped me, and I thought, *There's no end to that litany of words; though they aren't even very original, just repeating and repeating, they carry tremendous confusion and conflict: "You're too much __________,"* (fill in the blank), and/or, *"You're not really much of anything at all."*

But I could also feel the press of time, and my heart's desire. I slipped a CD into the player, and moments later, Yo Yo Ma stroked his musical voice into the air. I let the music wrap itself around me and then envelop me. I picked up my pen and began with the flow writing I vowed (and often failed) to do every day: "If I were an instrument, I would be a cello. Deep, lush, full, yet delicate and capable of a light touch. An instrument to be taken seriously, one that can pull at your heart-strings, never frivolous, like a flute or a piccolo, or even a violin, a show-offy instrument, or a harp, lyrical but finicky. A cello can stand alone, and be held. It can sway and be crooned, but it has weight and range. And isn't the challenge of the cellist to play her instrument, both for the cello's 'voice', its innate shape and sound, reverberating against string and wood, *and* for the cellist's 'voice', yes, interpreting, sounding the written notes, but also through her sensibilities, insight, and touch, rendering music that is like no one else's? I want to be free to gather my bow/pen and glide it across the page, finding with my mind the exact rhythms, word-notes, and pace of my song."

In the consulting room, I often think of my therapist self as just that instrument, allowing myself to be played by the uncertain hands of my striving patients, in search of their own rhythms, word-notes, and pace of their songs. This sensitivity, this receptivity, this resonance is the creative force vibrating at the center of the exacting analytic endeavor. We come to this work, trained through rigorous study and practice, primed to listen in 'the talking cure' to our patients' music, whether snare drum and cymbals, trumpet or saxophone, the faint tinkle of the triangle or the rippling of the piano, reverberating in return with our dissonance and harmony. Together, we variously compose and orchestrate a lullaby, a madrigal, an aubade, a serenade, a chant, a drone, a dirge, an opera, a cantata, a ballad, and finally and hopefully, a new morning song.

The question whispering beneath these multitudes of notes is: How do we capture in something so artful, so 'invisible' as music wafting through the air, the gritty nature of the treatment and healing of trauma and transformation through the developmental lens?

CHAPTER SEVENTEEN

The Therapist's Responsibilities

In the simplest of terms, the patient's responsibilities consist of showing up reliably (and hopefully on time) to do the work and paying for the therapist's time and expertise (but not her heart—that is given) per their jointly agreed upon fee arrangement. The therapist's responsibilities, on the other hand, are complex and immense. In not fulfilling them, they can be the deal breakers.

Often, our consulting room is 'the last house on the block', meaning that our patients may have tried several therapeutic modalities, spiritual practices, 'going it alone', different relationships, changing careers, moving locations, any or all of these usually ending as failed efforts to find the help they sought. In my opinion and experience (despite those who carry a perhaps vehemently held opposite position), the therapeutic relationship is a *real* relationship. By this, I am not implying that it is social, or dual, or inappropriate in any way. A real relationship is also not made of up mainly of theory-making and implementing technique, intrinsically vital in the work itself, but which needs to be reserved for consideration outside of the consulting room.

What I intend by a real relationship is one that is authentic, especially based on the therapist's willingness to be as fully emotionally present as possible, filled with genuine caring and, and as importantly, to own those times of fissures and their effects and offer repair when her/his own presence temporarily wobbles. The therapeutic relationship is unique, unlike any other, in which a patient is held in the sacred space of being known, eventually, utterly, but at his or her pace and timing, as defenses melt (not jackhammered away) within the skillful ministrations of someone who wants to be emotionally and psychologically involved. The therapist's most important responsibility is to protect that sacred space of meeting the patient wherever s/he is in full support of the shared therapeutic endeavor.

- **TRUST**

At the heart of every treatment is trust, the previous lack of it in the patient's life and the building of it in current time. On that basis, the therapeutic journey rises and falls on the trustworthiness of the authentic therapeutic and 'real' relationship. At the beginning of treatment most patients, eager, even desperate, for help may seem to be trusting and relieved. The referral they received was from a reliable friend, family member, or other treating professional or s/he was drawn to the therapist's website or blog. But even in the first session, 'tests' (see Weiss & Sampson, 1986) are being conducted, often unconsciously, by the patient's highly sensitive and radar-like attunement to the subtlest nuances of the therapist's presence, his/her voice, language and tone, manner, pace, expressions, gestures, and the holding environment in which they meet. Our patients are individuals who have experienced trauma, to one or another extent, long ago or ongoing, and have been re-traumatized by the vicissitudes of life. As such, why should they trust us? Their disappointments have been substantial. And their yearnings are profound.

Neville Symington (1996) put it so well as he discussed his work with a psychotic patient, his ideas applying to any patients who have suffered unresolved traumatic lives: "...what is of concern to the patient ... is not what the analyst says but, rather, the inner emotional attitudes of his heart" (p. 367).... There is an unconscious knowledge and communication operating all the time in an analysis. This *is* the analysis" (p. 370). The patient *must* "...force me with all the strength in her being to be the analyst she needed" (p. 375).

The patient's many tests will tell the tale. This is not a neat and tidy process, especially in the earlier stages of treatment when these tests are being made by the patient, unconsciously and consciously, for assessing the therapist's trustworthiness, or when an entrenched implicit memory bank must be relived until it is thoroughly and successfully decoded. These tests tend to grow in consequence as time goes on and the treatment deepens, with the stakes ever higher. As I have shared, Will said at pivotal moments that were stretching him in gathering his courage and becoming less timid that I *might* be "leading him down the garden path." Julia could not tolerate any hint of the negative transference reaction and needed me to attune, adjust, adapt, and respond in an empathetic way to those hints as soon as I could.

Trust, therefore, is at the heart of every one of the Seven Keystones of Development.

- **THE SEVEN KEYSTONES OF THE THERAPISTS'S RESPONSIBILITIES**

Each Keystone requires weighty responsibilities of the therapist, just as the original import of nurturing the development of a new baby rested on the trembling shoulders of the parent.

Keystone #1—States

Understanding the complexities involved in the patient's state systems and working to build bridges between them where none have existed before is one of the many requirements the therapist needs to shoulder. A patient may have a flow of some states and not of others, s/he may have the repeated experience of 'landing' in a cluster of particularly challenging states, having no immediate way to transition to a desired state, yet another may have a panoply of dissociated or fractured states. The therapist's early tracking to decipher and track those state shifts, followed by an active partnering with the patient to understand his or her own state architecture will be invaluable to both.

My favorite writing of Sigmund Freud's (1895/1955) consists of his conceptualization of a three-aspect traumatized psychical structure, which provided me with an invaluable map to the nuclei of trauma of my patients' systems of dissociated or fractured self-states. In the first, the linear, chronological order of such traumatic themes can be traced in reverse, "The freshest and newest experience in the file appears first, as an outer cover, and last of all comes the experience with which the series in fact began" (p. 288).

In the second, also linear, any concentric stratification around the nucleus helped me understand that each "particular stratum [is] characterized by an equal degree of resistance, and that degree increases in proportion as the strata are nearer to the nucleus" (p. 289). I could see that with patients we were working through the tender relinquishment of their secondary and then primary defense organizations. Rather than become discouraged by my patient's increased 'resistance', I viewed that as a hopeful sign, encouraging my patients in their strivings that we were nearing the very core experience of dissociated state systems we needed to access for their productive resolution and linking.

In the third aspect, realizing that "the linkage made by a logical thread reaches as far as the nucleus and tends to take an irregular and twisting path, [which] has a dynamic character ... this logical chain ... contains nodal points at which two or more threads meet and thereafter proceed as one ... it can happen that there is more than one nucleus ... which has an etiology of its own but is nevertheless connected with the first" (p. 290) helped me know that all roads, even tangential, or seemingly irrelevant ones, lead to 'Rome'.

This last, non-linear and dynamic arrangement, along with the "morphological two stratifications mentioned previously" (p. 290), made Freud's earliest work immensely relevant and practical in my work with fractured state systems: "We drop threads and pick them up again; we follow them as far as nodal points; we are constantly making up arrears; and every time we pursue a file of memories we are led to some side-path, which nevertheless eventually joins up again. By this method we at last reach a point at which we can stop working in strata and can penetrate by a main path straight to the nucleus of the pathogenic [traumatic] organization.... With this the struggle is won, though not yet ended. We must go back and take up other threads... but now the patient helps us energetically" (p. 295). How exciting and rewarding this analytic enterprise becomes for both clinician and patient!

Keystone #2—Memory Systems

A significant aspect of my original contribution to the psychoanalytic theoretical and clinical field consists of discovering how to decode what I came to call "implicit memory banks" (Erwin, 2000, 2005), the exciting partnering work with the patient that leads to effective interventions, what I have termed, 'bending the river'. Inherent to crucial trust building is my finding that the usual judgment that when a patient is 'acting in', defensive, resistant, or enacting, what is usually occurring instead is an implicit memory reliving. While these are inevitable and inevitably painful (not only as they play out in the therapeutic relationship but as forms of tests), they can become immensely valuable to the therapeutic couple because through their 'decoding' and resolution they can lead to profound understanding of the patient's implicit memory experience and the hopeful intervention in its future repetition. The word of caution I want to extend to clinicians is that treatment is difficult enough than to 'invite' or foster such relivings as 'grist for the mill', particularly by viewing the patient's experience as *only* the patient's experience. My position speaks to the need for the therapist to provide a protective barrier (see James, 1965) for the patient against re-traumatization by recognizing and authenticating whatever role the analyst might play, even inadvertently, in an enactment or reliving and by leading and being actively involved in its resolution (see Balint, 1969).

The power residing within the combination of state systems and implicit memory cannot be emphasized enough. Although they each have their own independent integrity of dynamics, they are intrinsically inter-woven. Implicit memory activity is use and state dependent, and our state systems are built within implicit memory, to be activated for future use. The relivings of traumatic implicit memories are ruinous in the patient's life so the relief s/he experiences when understanding how their own memory system works and that they can be intervened with and made usable and not just played out is substantial. Becoming knowledgeable of memory systems, their capacities and operations, and leading the way to decoding them with the patient (see Chapter Eighteen) is a significant responsibility of the therapist.

Keystone #3—Internalization & Identifications

The therapist must also earn the trust of the patient in order to become a source of healing identifications for the patient. The individual who is entrusted to our care has had a lifetime of internalizing all too often mainly the introjects of the disappointing or detrimental others who continue to wreak their destructive influence upon the patient internally. There certainly may have been intervening others who provided nourishment and validation for our patients and those caring and respectful others who did contribute to the growth of the self, due to their object ties. But still, the reason our patients are in our office is that those facilitating and loving others could not mitigate the harm that introjects exert. For many patients, one of the complexities of risk is whether to trust the therapist's ministrations, whether the affirmative encouragement and guidance is 'real'. In time, as the patient internalizes the attuned and caring ways the therapist treats the patient through the reliable provisions of affective attunement and new object relating, and partnering the navigation through the shoals of ever deepening waters, s/he will discover an entirely new realm of self-care and self-worth.

Keystone #4—Affect Regulation

As we have come to understand, one of the primary deficits most patients demonstrate is the inability to self-regulate. We can see this in their state systems and the lack of bridging and transitions between them, as well as in the thrust of implicit memory relivings. I can confidently argue that the therapists' initial responsibility is to spend a great deal of time and effort in regulating the patients' dynamic affective experiences and shifts in treatment, both in the consulting room and through necessary out of office contact. Certainly, that endeavor includes the therapist's dedicated tracking of the patient's affective life in session through affective attunement, and by so doing provide the regulation that the patient lacks, giving the patient the new object experience of a regulating other who can be internalized and identified with. The therapist's ability to regulate their patient's dysregulated affects overtime forecasts the ways and manner that the patient will eventually be able to make use of that new regulation for her/himself.

I am aware of those clinicians who might argue that this is 'beyond the analytic/therapeutic frame', but I encourage those clinicians to recognize that if they are not willing to provide such provisions and leave it all in the lap of the patient, ultimately the treatment will be arduous and not succeed in the developmental ways that are so vital to the patient's healing. Within a lengthy treatment that is focused on resolving trauma, healing affect dysregulation is a requirement and sometimes is the main work for a year or two, followed by its intermittent use as the treatment necessitates. I recognize and respect those clinicians who do not want to do such deep and absorbing work for a variety of legitimate reasons, but for those who undertake these intense and compelling cases, affective regulation is the necessary bedrock for all the other work. Our patients with unresolved trauma or developmental difficulties or failures did not have and may never have had an attuned other who was dedicated to understanding their emotional life and providing the caring ministrations of regulating them as babies and growing children, so that they could internalize those as their own regulating system. Providing that new object relationship is life saving and supports the healing that our patients so dearly require.

Keystone #5—Attachment

Evident from the very beginning of treatment are the manifestations of the consequences of the patient's repeated dysregulated affects and insecure attachments. Secure internal working models of attachment are unavailable to the individual, the result of implicit memory encoding, leading to future distortions in relating. As we have seen, these implicit memory banks are unable to evolve into mental, and therefore, symbolic, representations, but remain instead as potential minefields to be triggered in the here and now interpersonally.

There may exist only minimum or fragmented and injured senses of self, the sense of the other as absent or disavowing or threatening and dangerous, with the affective valance of relationships felt as tumultuous, unreliable, and frightening, or despairingly empty. The degree of differentiation from these internal models is either little or none; rather, they are intrusive and often engulfing. The possibility of integration is slim, if at all, for what should be a merger with secure attachment internal models, which as we have seen, makes it impossible for the individual to individuate in any way that would have been safe and viable. Finally, whatever rudimentary IWMs or mental representations might be present become increasingly *in*accurate, less able to be articulated, and conceptually simple and rigid, less comprehensive and certainly *ineffective* for interpersonal relating over time, since they are built upon early experience through already encoded perceptual bias, and then provocatively reinforced through repeated disappointment or re-traumatization.

In each of the forms of insecure attachment, there was a significant failure with both connection and necessary repair after rupture. Amini et al (1996) have suggested that the reason psychotherapy is effective in fostering long-lasting change is because "an attachment relationship [is] capable of regulating neurophysiology and altering underlying neural structure" (p. 232, see also Fonagy, 1999, Cicchetti & Toth, 1995). Margaret Parish and Morris Eagle's study (2002) found that, "the relationship that forms in long-term psychotherapy clearly has many qualities of an attachment relationship" (p. 280).

In developmental work, it is imperative for the therapist to provide:

- the attunement,
- affect regulation,
- effective work with the patient's state systems,
- decoding implicit memory 'relivings',
- along with the therapist's availability, consistency, reliability, and authentic presence over several years of treatment so that a secure attachment can be achieved.

Keystone #6—Hemispheric Development

The truly wondrous result of this significant developmental work over time is that our patient's traumatic neuronal pathways can actually be rewired to a noticeable extent with new, supportive, and facilitating ones laid down. Instead of the right hemisphere, loaded with mostly non-verbal and multi-sensory based cocooned traumatic lacunas, being used primarily for relivings, the decoding of and interventions with those static stressors now allows for cross-hemsipheric communication. Implicit Memory material can now be used for learning as it is combined with all that the patient has acquired in explicit memory throughout their lives. This is one of the most promising results of fully informed depth psychodynamic treatment: we are not starting from pure damage or from scratch. The phase of integration of the right and left hemisphere with rewiring and resolution of implicit memory banks opens the way for exponential improvement and healing with all of the patient's attributes, skills, and knowledge coming together in transformative development.

Keystone #7—Voice and Language

In long-term therapy, the patient does a great deal of talking and the therapist does a great deal of listening, carefully and actively, sorting and realizing in ever deeper ways the nature of the patient's concerns, conflicts, and yearnings. When the therapist speaks, the patient may be highly attuned, even vigilant, about all the nuances embedded in the therapist's words (and other expressions), searching for hidden meanings, evaluating what is true and what might not be.

In that patient's early life, long before semantic language, there was voice: often *not* the parents' crooning words providing soothing and comfort to the baby's upsets expressed in cries and body language, often *not* the words of delight and reception to the baby's coos and smiles. In these developmental gaps and failures, the parent's words were too often harsh, critical, and demanding or demeaning and loveless.

One of the main avenues to healing is to be found in the thoughtfully aware and responsible use of the therapist's personal voice and rich, elaborative, sensory-based language. This voice is not only for processing, clarification, and interpretation but is to be used for genuine communication between herself and her patient. Under the umbrella of authentic interpersonal exchanges, non-verbal and verbal, a vital environment is established for the patient's personal voice to emerge and begin to articulate his or her narrative. As the patient's voice is embraced by herself and received by the therapist, expressive language then becomes increasingly available to the patient, so his or her newfound "authorial voice" (see Wolf, 1990) can help shape a new future.

In addition to the responsibilities found in each of the Seven Keystones of Transformed Development, there are crucial and foundation-building processes that are indispensable to therapist and patient alike.

- **PROCESSING, CLARIFICATION, AND INTERPRETATION**

Processing is at the heart of the therapeutic dynamic, a complex and shared activity made up of minute-and-broad-brush-strokes of conversation, which are not just a parallel of non-verbal and verbal exchanges, but what I call "elaborative languaging." This is what Stanley Greenspan (1999) called "circles of communication" (p. 332-333). In his version, the initiator opens one circle with the second member responding while the initiator responds next to close that circle. I build on his description in that within each exchange there is an elaboration of what the previous person has communicated: meanings are teased out, built upon, with each therapeutic partner enriching the dialogue and its intrinsic meaning. These interpersonal dialogues are rich in sensory-based language and congruent emotional valence to support understanding, presence, and true knowing between the participants.

Just as a child seeks a parent's resonance with his or her young experience and receives the caring response s/he needs, so too do our patients seek the processing dialogue s/he needs, in the same manner. More significantly, in trauma, a child or adult does not receive the processing care s/he needs, which is one of the six pivotal reasons trauma remains unresolved. Processing is the vital dynamic by which we comprehend our experience, past and present, and in this opportunity, we are freed of its unresolved consequences and find a path toward reparative action.

Clarification is an action that either partner can take with the therapist's responsibility consisting of making those clarifications safe. The patient may need to let the therapist know where the therapist might be off track, mis-attuned, or unclear about what the patient is trying to communicate, yet speaking in this way may hold formidable risk for the patient. S/he may feel that the therapist will be personally offended or that the patient is overstepping a boundary. The therapist may need to bring clarity to muddled waters, to expand and enhance the patient's thoughts and feelings, and at times, to guide and teach, but this endeavor can also be filled with perilous possibilities: the clarification may be premature or 'blinding'. Timing is everything, as we well know, with that timing being an exquisite component of clarification, even when the patient is in desperate need of clarity. Will's mind "swirled" when he became muddled, and while he deeply wanted to understand, such understandings were fraught with his insecurities, timidity, and conflicts. When clarification is well-timed and delivered with respect and kindness, for example, delving into the nature of states and implicit memory and their operations, such clarity can lead to building bridges and fleshing out successful interventions.

Years ago, I had a life-altering experience with my analyst over the course of a year and a half, which came to inform my responses to future patients' need for verification. My analyst was not a particularly self-disclosing therapist, especially in the early stages of our work together. But she was exceedingly present emotionally. In about year two, she became noticeably (to my radar for nuance) at a remove. I asked, "Are you alright?" to which she brightened and replied, "I'm fine." I was still too cautious to push beyond this brief and unsatisfying exchange. Six months later, the experience repeated itself, so I ventured a little further: "You seem distracted, which is unusual. Am I the problem [heaven forbid!]?" This time her voice became a touch stern as she insisted, "Gwyn, I'm fine! And no, you are not a problem." Somewhat reassuring but definitely not elaborative or soothing. Another six months passed, and by then our relationship had significantly deepened with my trust in her growing as well. While I peppered what I was about to say with several disclaimers, "I'm not trying to be intrusive," and "I don't mean to cross any boundary, but... this is the third time in a year and a half I've felt this particular kind of shift in our connection." Then, I gulped and spoke my emotional truth, "Each time I have had this sense that you were experiencing some kind of loss and you really needed to be somewhere else." My heart was pounding out of my chest as I felt I had just risked our entire relationship.

Her eyes moistened with the beginning of tears and her mouth quivered a bit. She had a velvety kind of voice, and it now dropped a few tones: "Gwyn, you're right, amazingly. I guess it is time for me to tell you that in each of those times, someone important to me was dying. Today, it's my best friend." A long silent pause 'spoke' of the weight of what she was sharing and her trust in me to share it. Finally, "I want to be here with you. I am able to be here with you. When we are finished with our time, I'll be going to her." Neither her nor my breath could hold. She finished with: "You are changing me. All for the better. And I thank you."

Other than with my husband, I had never had such a profound exchange of validation with someone in my personal life. These moments, brief as they may be, can be life changing. I did not need the details of her losses. The validation and affirmation and trust between us were what I needed. Fully present, each of us grew, immeasurably. Our patients need that kind of soulful exchange at just the 'right' moments, partially so the patient does not end up feeling crazy in their own valid but unacknowledged perceptions, and partially because clarification is an essential catalyst of growth for each of the therapeutic partners.

- **INTERPRETATION**

Ah! Interpretation! The second royal road, supposedly, and classically held as the analyst's domain. The stereotype became: the analyst sits in hovering attention, listening in rapt thoughtfulness to what the patient unfolds. At just the most salient moment, "the point of urgency" (M. Klein, 1932, p. 51, see Bion, 1959), the analyst delivers his interpretation, which then ushers in a healing experience for the patient. In this scenario, which does have its value, the positions of the therapist and patient are hierarchical, because the therapist is the one who knows. Yes, there are those instances where I have felt that if I sat on a rock for a thousand years, pondering, I never would have come to the 'xyz' realization I desperately needed, so that in those moments my analyst's interpretations were invaluable. So, too, can be those occasions when a parent delivers an 'on-high' message of praise, admonition, or warning. Developmentally, however, the best interpretations are those the child or adolescent comes to through an elaborative language exchange with the parent. In my experience and opinion (though not exclusively), the same is true for therapist and patient.

Ivri Kumin (1989) captured the emotional consequences for the patient of incorrect interpretations as: "a painful or frightening disillusionment which repeats, on a small scale, similar misunderstandings or empathic failures suffered in past relationships. The patient's reaction not only mimics his past affective response but also recapitulates whatever defensive solutions he found to the past environmental lapses.... To the patient, the incorrect interpretation feels like the return of the repressed, projected into the analytic situation. The well-integrated patient feels as though the analyst has dropped the ball; the poorly integrated patient feels as though he himself had been dropped" (p. 142, see also Davies & Frawley, 1994).

For both Will and Julia, while there were any number of critical times where they needed me to lead the way, and I did, they each needed to know they could lead the way as they struggled to put together the pieces of their own psychological puzzles. Insight came as the result of perhaps months of exploration, processing, and clarification, not simply as easy 'Aha' moments but as the multifaceted comprehension of and appreciation for how their minds worked and the reasons for the roles fulfilled by others and themselves day to day.

George Atwood, Robert Stolorow, and Jeffrey Trop (1989) saw the "negative therapeutic reaction" as resulting from those instances "wherein the patient's emotional needs are consistently misunderstood and thereby relentlessly rejected by the therapist" (p. 557):

> Such misunderstandings typically take the form of erroneously interpreting the revival of unmet developmental longing as if it were an expression of malignant, pathological resistance. When the patient revives such a longing within the therapeutic relationship, and the therapist repeatedly interprets this developmental necessity as if it were merely a pathological resistance, the patient will experience such misinterpretations as gross failures of attunement. Consequently, traumatic psychological injuries are repeatedly inflicted, with impact similar to the pathogenic events of the patient's early life (p. 557-558).

Kumin (1989) spelled out the variety of incorrect interpretations, incorrect because such interpretations may be cognitively correct but empathically false. These include:

- comments which are true but premature (and therefore emotionally overwhelming),
- comments which are true but limited to manifest content (and therefore banal),
- comments which are true but ignore developmental considerations (and thus ignore the destructive meaning of the interpretation itself within the transference),
- comments which are true but are not made tactfully enough to preserve the patient's self esteem (Poland, 1975, Glenn, 1978),
- comments which are true but compulsively clever, and so pre-empt the patients' capacity to be creative in the analytic work (Winnicott, 1971), and
- no comment at all when a potential interpretation is at the 'point of urgency', and so deprives the patient of an opportunity to establish a link to the analyst (Bion, 1959), (p. 143).

Chief remedies among incorrect interpretations is their repair of resulting ruptures, pivotal in terms of fostering transformation.

- **RUPTURE AND REPAIR**

Rupture is confusing and frustrating, painful, and sometimes ruinous, with the patient often shouldering the blame, just as a young child does to preserve the parent as "good enough' and 'usable'. Rupture's other side of the coin, repair, represents the profound opportunity for healing and growth, particularly where there was none before. Those occasions of repair are, more often than not, the turning of a corner in treatment, because they come from the therapist's thoughtful and non-defensive awareness of having missed the patient in attunement, mis-interpreted that patient, rushed the patient, or not shown up with his or her emotional presence at a critical juncture. In my view, the therapist carries the greater responsibility for repair in part due to training and expertise but more due to caring for the patient while 'doing no harm."

In Steven Frankel's (2000) *Hidden Faults: Recognizing and Resolving Therapeutic Disjunctions*, Frankel bravely revealed the vulnerabilities inherent in the analytic endeavor. He offered a riveting and substantial dive into the nuanced dynamics of the analytic relationship as he examined not only the nature of therapeutic disjunctions but their visceral experience in his practice. To begin, Frankel demonstrated that "disjunction ... is a failure in interpersonal engagement" (p. xii). More specifically, "Disjunctions occur when therapist and patient differ in their perceptions or level of emotional engagement or collude to minimize their differences in ways that obstruct therapeutic progress" (p. 31).

Sharing with the reader his own momentary 'failures' in perception, attunement, understanding, and analytic inaction, Frankel used six cases to examine in depth the causes of disjunction. He explained, "Represented in disjunctions are transferences, countertransferences, and projective identifications.... Disjunctions are built of conscious and unconscious elements. Work with disjunctions, however, is organized around the product of these inner states, the actual discrepancy between the therapist and patient's experiences of one another" (p. 33). On a more experience-near level, he wrote: "...a disjunction is likely to be a hall of mirrors. Once you enter you really cannot tell what is inside of you and what is outside. Usual frames of reference are readily lost. As therapist and patient slip away from each other they are equally likely to lose their internal bearings, to give up their sense of themselves" (p. 40).

He then demonstrated how disjunction was recognized, sometimes first by his patient, other times by himself. Repairing a disjunction became the transformative experience he called conjunction (Frankel, 2005), leading to creative development. This road to analytic repair could feel anything but transformative, worthwhile and indispensable though it actually was:

> Recognizing that a disjunction exists can feel cataclysmic. It is often profoundly disorienting. The therapist no longer understands the patient. The patient no longer feels the therapist comprehends his or her experience.... The process of working through a disjunction is entirely collaborative. Therapist and patient need each other to determine what exists: who each of them is, how they are similar and, most especially, how they are different. To accomplish this end, therapist and patient need an honest dialogue. Both minds, the patient's and the therapist's, must be exposed and probed.... This collaboration has another benefit. It progressively creates a bond between the therapist and patient. Here self-disclosure adds to the authenticity of the relationship upon which the therapy is built.... The act of recognizing and working with disjunctions, and especially extreme disjunctions, is usually generative. It leads to new levels of understanding.... Sustaining this effort requires enormous commitment to the therapy and to one another by both therapist and patient. The consequence of this profound interpersonal experience is that therapist or patient, and more likely both, begin to change (p. 88-89).

In a similar vein, George Atwood, Robert Stolorow, and Jeffrey Trop (1989) suggested, "impasses in psychoanalytic therapy... provide a unique pathway—a 'royal road'—to the attainment of psychoanalytic understanding" (p. 554). Whether this royal road is available or not, "facilitat[ing] or obstruct[ing] the progress of the therapy depends in large part on the extent of the therapist's capacity to become reflectively aware of the organizing principles of his own subjective world" (p. 555).

Beatrice Beebe and Frank Lachmann (2002) focused their work with patients utilizing three principles of salience: 1) ongoing regulation, in which both partners actively contribute to the regulation of the exchange, moment-to-moment, including interactions in which the patient narrates and discloses while the analyst attends, reflects, describes, and questions, 2) disruption and repair, which organizes violations of expectancies and ensuing efforts to resolve these breaches, and 3) heightened affective moments, those interactions that are organized when the person experiences a powerful state transformation, either positive or negative.... Heightened affective moments can provide opportunities of new experiences (see p. 4-6).

Rupture, as threatening as it can be, and repair, as redemptive as it can be, usually rises and falls on the subjective experience (unconscious or conscious) of both therapist and patient. This is once again the realm of 'tests' and implicit memory relivings for each partner of the therapeutic couple and as such ripe for the derailment of treatment. In my view, the therapist holds the greatest responsibility for repair; in my experience, I have never known a patient who "could not go there," but I have consulted with any number of therapists who themselves "could not go there." The culprit?

• COUNTERTRANSFERENCE

Historically, countertransference has been viewed as the analyst's 'unfinished business', that is, the analyst's unanalyzed response to the patient's transference, in this case resulting from the conflicts, unconscious or conscious, that remain unanalyzed within the analyst. Sigmund Freud (1910/1955) offered two positions in regard to the notion of the analyst's countertransference: the first, "We have become aware of the 'counter-transference', which arises in him as a result of the patient's influence on his unconscious feelings, and we are almost inclined to insist that he shall recognize this counter-transference in himself and overcome it" (1910/1955, p. 144); and the second, "In my opinion, therefore, we ought not to give up the neutrality towards the patient, which we have acquired through keeping the counter-transference in check" (1915/1955, p. 164). In the 1950s, various theorists (see Heimann, 1950, Racker, 1957, Kernberg's, 1965 totalist perspectives) argued that countertransference was concerned with the analyst's total response to the patient, even that such responses could be considered valuable avenues for understanding the patient through "all the feelings which the analyst experiences towards his patient" (Heimann, 1950, p. 81).

In the way that I work, Wilfred Bion (1963) had much to offer me in considering the meaning and use of countertransference. Bion spoke of passion, that "component derived from L [love], H [hate], and K [knowledge]. I mean the term to represent an emotion experienced with intensity and warmth though without any suggestion of violence" (p. 12-13). Such "passion is evidence that two minds are linked" (p. 13). By means of this emotional passion, presence and resonance with the patient and his or her emotional experience is made available to the analyst, both verbally and nonverbally.

Over time, as I continued to consider countertransference and nonverbal communication, I found great value in Joyce McDougall's (1978) thinking, "With regard to traumatic events stemming from even earlier periods before the acquisition of *verbal* communication the detection of their existence becomes considerably more complicated—to the point that we may only become aware of the traumatic dimension through the unconscious pressure it exerts upon the analysand's way of being and speaking, and thus eventually, may only be accessible if captured through our *countertransference reactions* (p. 174). "The question becomes," she asked, "is how to understand and make use of such countertransference affect" (p. 178). Her answer: "These analysands frequently use language as an *act* rather than a symbolic means of communication of ideas or affect... revealing the effect of a catastrophic failure in communication which has occurred at a time when he was unable to contain or work through, psychically, what he was experiencing (p. 178).

For Evelyne Albrecht Schwaber (1992) her efforts to move away from a hierarchical position with her patients, noticing her "tendency to look at the psychic stirrings within the patient, [as] basically set apart from and outside my participation" and her "reluctance to recognize my unwitting participation in another's ongoing inner experience" (p. 352) helped her discover that, "Sometimes, our patients make their feelings more directly known, in ways that may become so intense and immediate that we are at risk of stepping back, to regain for ourselves what we may feel to be a more comfortable distance" (p. 355). In doing so, "We may thus spare ourselves the intensity of the patient's pain or wishes, of the closeness, and keep away from resonance with our own pain or wishes" (p. 355).

Schwaber made the poignant point that, "Countertransference interferes when, knowingly or not, I won't let go of the supposed wisdom of own vantage point." In contrast, she learned "to find the patient's world. And in so doing, seek resonance with my own... whatever our impact, *it is from the point of the patient that its exploration and elucidation assume the central focus*" (p. 358).

I have respected colleagues who would never share any aspect of their countertransference with a patient, reserving it for their own private knowledge or personal analysis or supervision. Others might admit (under pressure) to a patient that s/he was having a countertransferential response, assuring the patient of her intention to seek consultation, but refusing to discuss any aspect of it with the patient, thus depriving the patient of processing and clarification (and perhaps her own dignity or position). In my clinical experience, I have found repeatedly that dealing with my countertransference as beneficial messages from a patient can not only provide significant relief to the patient but become a curative experience.

• SELF-DISCLOSURE, SELF-REVELATION

Hand in hand with countertransference, we need to consider the activities of self-disclosure and self-revelation. Traditionally, either was considered a potential breach in treatment, burdening the patient with aspects of the analyst's inner or outer world. Over the decades, while some clinicians still hold a strict boundary on such sharing, many theorists (see E. Schwaber, 1992, O. Renik, 1999, S. Frankel 2000, 2005), have found true therapeutic value for the patient in the thoughtful and responsible revealing of their actual or emotional experience. Owen Renik (1999) offered a significant guideline: "I think it is of the utmost importance that we acknowledge that the clinical psychoanalytic situation is ordinarily real. What the analytic treatment relationship can be, within ordinary reality, however, is extraordinarily candid. That requires courage on the part of both participants. In order to be candid, a patient needs candor from his or her analyst" (p. 536).

Arnold Richards (2018) detailed ideas concerning disclosure and revelation even further: "There are different *kinds* of self-disclosure. There is *inadvertent* self-disclosure, which, as we all know, is inevitable. How we dress, how we furnish our offices, the color of our skins, whether we are thin or fat, the tone and cadence of our voices—all are there for the patient to observe. *Deliberate* self-disclosure covers the more-or-less intentional sharing of such matters as our own thoughts and preferences, the details of our life experience, our family relationships, and, most important, our feelings about the patient. In the context of the analytic process, I think it is crucial to separate our feelings about the patient's habitual ways of responding, his or her choices, relationships, and so on from other aspects of our personal and clinical experience. This is the category that I call self-revelation, as opposed to self-disclosure. The latter refers to the exposure of facts about the analyst's life; the former refers to the revelation of the analyst's feelings.... There too the conservative view is concerned with whether the resulting disclosures are deliberate or inadvertent; self-revelation is not on the table. The less conservative view is that self-revelation is inevitable and may be therapeutic; this is Ehrenberg's (1995) "intimate edge," and Renik's (1999) concept of playing with our cards face up.... I tell my supervisees that this category of self-disclosing—better, self-revelatory—remarks should be avoided early on in the treatment, lest the patient bolt. It can, however, be helpful later on, once there is a solid working alliance and especially at times of impasse.

With Will, the awareness and 'revelation' of his feelings, in concert with my expressions of concern, warning, support, and encouragement brought him to the alive inner presence of himself and in his presence in his own life. With Julia, my transparent accessibility and responsiveness gave her the first experience of processing her lived experience, while the use of my fear for her and frustration with Oscar's threats began to shrink his power, giving her the sense that she could tackle the challenges of leaving him.

As essay of mine, "Weather," published in *Psychoanalytic Perspectives* in the spring of 2011 offered analogies to the way I apply my countertransference, self-disclosure, and self-revelation with my patients. In part, it read:

"I love weather—storms, tornadoes, twilight breezes, heat for egg frying, snow, wind, and rain—but I do not live in it.

Except.

I open my office door, walk to the waiting room, and welcome the weather coming in to be analyzed, hours of weather to come. My patients and I, pair by pair, will warm, then freeze, seek shelter from sheets of rain, look for bunny tracks, name each spring bird and umbrella plant in this forest preserve called psychoanalysis, leap into mounds of leaves soaked in years of tears or crisped by critical voices, transporting us to earlier times, cracking the ice that has formed around hearts long ago broken, still trying to mend, searching for the sun that might bring a lightning melt, reminding us that joy can be found if we strive.

My patients are my wind, blowing me to the ever colder North and the chop of Great Lakes, forcing swim strokes to the safety of a boulder where we can look out and see how long we have been treading deep and treacherous waters; to the unremembered East, except as we relive it in our current psychological locale; to the South, beckoning with its warmth to reaffirm its promise that help is here and healing nearby, but we have to weather the weather and learn to bend the wind to our wish and our will; to the West that foreshadows the mourning of the ends of days, followed by a new morning that, like spring, offers forsythia. We stand beneath the umbrella plants of language, just like the fairies do, straining to form the magical words that might speak our experience; we embrace the trees of knowledge to understand all we have survived and to find where we stand now; we follow the night stars or the arc of the sun to compass our ways to a different future.

And every hour after hour, day after day, year after year, I learn more about weather than I ever thought possible. While my responsive nervous system is my gift, reading every nuance of temperature and barometer, tracking currents, each lift of air, it [can feel] a curse and prefers climate. Not here, though, not in this office. On those early mornings when the alarm rings too soon, and I slip my feet out from under the bed covers, struggling to recognize the hardwood floors as being of this house, not the ones of my earliest bedroom, I [turn] to the day with its elements that will engage, challenge, threaten, console, and transform, and I learn again to love the weather. And to live in it" (p. 17).

Countertransference and self-disclosure and self-revelation are some of the richest avenues for therapeutic understanding of our patient's lived experience, historically, traumatically, and in the here and now. Often, the psychological pressure our patients exert, unconsciously as well as consciously, non-verbally and verbally, is equivalent to our baby's or child's cries—they are intended to stir us, to beckon us, to command us to action as we tend to their strivings. Our greatest responsibility in providing a reliable, trustworthy, and responsive holding environment for our patients' developmental transformations lies in the conscientious and creative use of our countertransference, self-disclosure, and self-revelation.

CHAPTER EIGHTEEN

The Healing Power of the Therapeutic Relationship

"It" is all about the relationship. This is true from the beginning of life. Every child needs parenting from a committed, aware and attuned, loving and protective mainstay caregiver. The lack of such a dependable and enduring relationship and the consequences of that deprivation of presence, intermittent or consistent, is the primary reason patients seek treatment. Our patients may be children or adolescents, crying out in a poignant array of unmet needs. They may be young adults trying to find their ways in an ever more uncertain world. They may be full on adults, concerned with careers, families of their own or the single life but regardless of their status impacted by triggers that overwhelm them. They may be elders trying to come to grips with life changing or ebbing away. In each and every instance, even in the face of the manifest content with which they present themselves, the haunting refrains echo from those earlier years and all that followed in kind. They needed a mother who loved them. They needed a father who loved them. They still need a someone like that.

Now in our consulting rooms, in essence, the care they need is the same. Not that we can become the literal mother or father, but we do have to provide those fundamental parenting functions of proximity, safety, comfort, and protection, often for the first time in their lives. And we need to come to love them. "IT" is this relationship within clinical treatment, the earnest work together a hard-won journey within both a therapeutic and real relationship so unique and so valuable as to change and heal the patient, and, in many ways, perhaps the therapist as well.

• OUT WITH THE OLD/IN WITH THE NEW?

This therapeutic relationship is central to healing, for among other facets the therapist provides are new object experiences for the patient, especially in the face of implicit memory relivings and the visceral transferences and countertransferences taking place within them. Milton Viederman (1991) focused on the "real relationship with the analyst . . . writing, "A psychoanalysis is an intense personal relationship for both patient and analyst" (p. 455), and as such, "The analyst's status as a special person involved in the patient's growth through understanding gives him centrality in the patient's life as a participant, as an agent of change in the achievement of desired goals" (p. 454). Bessel van der Kolk (1996) also addressed the analytic relationship in regards to the treatment of trauma: "Much of the treatment of victims of trauma is intuitive; it depends on both a sensitive understanding of the unique issues that make every individual different from all others, and clinical knowledge about the accurate timing of appropriate interventions. What occurs between a patient and therapist is a function not only of a particular diagnosis of the patient, but also of the unique and personal relationship between patient and therapist" (p. 539). Yet, as Lewis Aron (1991) cautioned, "It is only through the analyst's very similarity to the old objects that the patient can imbue the analytic relationship with meaningfulness and the necessary interpersonal affect which gives the transference its power" (p. 104-105).

While both patient and therapist can 'enact' in the transference and countertransference aspects of the patient's traumatizing relationships, I do not hold to the notion that everything 'is grist for the mill.' As I have said, the patient has lived a lifetime in that mill, and part of our purpose is to come to know how that patient was originally traumatized without our becoming the re-traumatizing figure to find out. While occurring within this alive relationship are necessarily inevitable interpersonal relivings ultimately usable for decoding and transformation, there is also the necessity of new object relating, which provides crucial healing opportunities and relational internalization into the patients' object world. As we saw in the previous chapter, it is imperative that the therapist take responsibility for ruptures based on inadvertently and temporarily hurting or failing the patient, understanding the role they may have contributed to any implicit memory relivings, and taking an active part in repairing those ruptures. Consistent and authentic new object relating is vital to the patient's being able to gain trust, comprehend and relinquish perceptual bias, decode the 'bogs of quicksand' in which they sink, and with the analyst plan for effective means of intervention, leading to the opportunities for actual and transformative change.

John Fiscalini (1988) captured this dual function of the analytic relationship:

> "First, the analyst relates to the patient's neurotic intrapersonal and interpersonal patterns [of the wounded self] in ways that consistently contradict transferential expectation (or provocation) [perceptual bias]... this aspect of the new interpersonal interaction is characterized by the patient's repeating old patterns [implicit memory relivings], but with the analyst consistently relating to them in a new way.... At some crucial point.... the patient attempts new non-transferential ways *[the real relationship]* of being more in line with his or her true needs, perhaps modeled after that of the analyst [identification] or perhaps emanating spontaneously from the patient's autonomous self or center [the essential self]. Again, the analyst responds in ways that, for the patient, are new and different; that is, unlike that of other significant figures (past and present)" (p. 138-139, paraphrases in brackets added).

Louis Sander (2002) posed a pivotal question, one which I hope to answer within the pages of this book: "How can we, as unique self-organizing individuals, remain 'distinct from' an 'other' at the same time that we must be 'together-with' that 'other' in order for our 'system'—which is sustaining life for us—to maintain its essential coherence and wholeness?" (p. 19). He applied the concept of coherency to the therapeutic endeavor: "Achieving a coherent sense of 'self-as-agent'—differentiated, valid, and competent within one's context of life support—brings us to a key goal of both the developmental and the therapeutic processes" (p. 19). Let us examine how the therapeutic relationship provides the essential coherence and wholeness that leads to healing and transformed development.

The Healing Relationship Within the Seven Keystones of Development

- **States**

The spectrum of state architectures we encounter in our practices is as wide, deep, and varied as each of our patients' individual temperaments and personalities. This spectrum may be peppered with discontinuities between states, their bridges never being built or having been broken. These states may range from such lack of bridging to the fracturing of entire state systems, depending on the kind and degree of unresolved trauma. Our knowledge and skillful work with the nature and activity of states is crucial in helping our patients gain mastery of understanding their own inner structures and how they operate. When patients become familiar with the fundamentals of state systems and transitions, their relief is palpable, and they become both advocates for and eager participants in working with them. This partnership deepens and enriches the therapeutic relationship as healing unfolds.

In healthy development, the individual maintains the sense of essential self even as s/he moves between state experiences. In fact, I define the psychological health of an individual as the coherency of the essential self as it flows among diverse affective, physiological, mental, and behavioral states of being across time and within state space (Erwin, 2001). Frank Putnam (1997) explicated in detail what I find are the components of this definition:

1) the ability to sustain [the essential self] in a desired state [of being] in the face of distractions and destabilizing stimuli
2) the ability to recover from disruption of a state [of being] by reactivating the desired state
3) the ability to match the appropriate state [of being] with the contextual demands of the situation [and in social and intimate interactions with others, without losing one's coherency of the essential self] (p. 161, brackets added).

Conversely, when trauma occurs that remains unresolved, the individual finds a solution where there seems no solution by unconsciously dissociating states that are affectively overwhelming and physiologically over-arousing. One of the challenges in analysis is accessing these fractured states in ways that are not re-traumatizing and that build bridges between them. The therapeutic relationship provides the necessary holding environment in which initially the therapist finds the particular ways for each patient to establish affect regulation. Using states effectively and ultimately creating new state bridging is completely 'use-dependent' on such regulation.

How does the therapist help the patient begin to regulate, first with the therapist's help, then overtime by internalizing those provisions into self-regulation? The process I developed many years ago began in my work as a writing and creativity mentor, but which eventually I honed in my work with patients:

- The first task is to support the patient in session in being able to tolerate their affective experience, especially their powerful vitality affects. I slow everything down and talk quietly and softly about "being with" whatever s/he is feeling. I assure her/him that I am with them and that together we will be able to bear and cope with whatever they are experiencing. There is no need to judge or act on anything. This exchange ushers in a *purposeful* state shift and the ENTRANCE state shift leading to many others.
- In this "being with," I help regulate their breathing, even if all they can do at this point is follow my breathing. Within minutes, their breathing usually begins to regulate. Steady, eased-filled, relaxed breathing—no counting, no labor—just easy, quiet breathing.
- Next, we NOTICE. In that noticing, we are initiating the ability to think with feeling and feel while thinking. We notice what their bodies are feeling in various sensory modalities, the sounds they pick up, what pictures they are seeing in their mind's eye, inside the present moment. My beloved grandmother, Anna Nowak, was the first person who taught me about noticing when I was just a little girl. We would go for delicious walks in the neighboring forest preserves where she shared her immense knowledge of birds, plants, trees, and the invisible fairie world inhabiting these precious preserves while she taught me *how* to notice, not just *what* to notice, and what to use that noticing for: to step softly so as not to scare away a feeding hummingbird, or to step firmly to be aware of the crunch of the gold, yellow, and burning red of autumn's leaves. She gave me a magically imaginative and realistically safe world that I have been able to use every day in countless ways ever since. She offered me regulation, which I learned early on to help others with even when I was a child. I have been teaching "noticing" for decades for many numbers of writers, creatives, and eventually traumatized patients. (Janina Fisher, has an excellent section in her

workbook, *Transforming the Living Legacy of Trauma*, on the noticing brain, 2021, pp. 51-55.) In this noticing, let time flow and stretch. No matter what comes up, the noticing offers our patients a momentary observing ego, which becomes more and more stable and available as this work continues.

- FLOW and FOCUS. As we assist our patients in being present and noticing in the flow of feeling (a right hemisphere activity), we then direct their focus (left hemisphere) when we sense we have landed on something significant. In focusing, the therapist needs to be aware of the quantity of feeling a patient can tolerate and stay with while also thinking. This is where the therapist's affective attunement of 'stop and go' is invaluable. If the experience becomes "too much" (see Arousal Chart), this is the point to use the soothing, dampening down features of the parasympathetic nervous system to bring the patient back into an open, processing sphere; if the patient is shutting down or withdrawing, this is the moment to use features of the sympathetic nervous system to help bring the patient up to an open processing sphere (use the Affective Questionnaire results, see following section on Affect Regulation).
- Then, we consider what, if anything, to DO with what we have noticed. This provides an opportunity to exercise the patient's propositional thinking and early authorial voice in the tentative beginning step by step process of choosing. Choice making is an entire endeavor it and of itself, one we will see demonstrated in the remainder of this book. Such choice making is pivotal in becoming masterful at state shifts and free of unresolved trauma. One step (with its own state experience) followed by evaluation, iteration, choice, another step, followed by another evaluation and perhaps series of iterations, and so forth. Life changing.

- And finally, an EXIT state shift, either to one state practicing sequence in session, or at the end of session to emerge back into the patient's outer world. This detailed process may be engaged with and practiced hundreds of times over sessions, and with such practice, the process becomes more efficient and usable in the patient's world outside of treatment.

On the road to this achievement, though, are the triggering of implicit memory relivings, which can offer therapeutic opportunities for decoding state fractures and finding ways of recovering from such state-dependent relivings. Decoding and intervening with implicit memory relivings is central to and instrumental in building bridges or links between dissociated or fractured states. Since states are use-dependent and implicit memory building encodes state experience, providing access to and linking disparate states is a necessary enterprise for moving toward the health of the self. The therapeutic goal is to be able to 'visit' traumatized states for the purpose of understanding their meanings and functions without having to 'live' in them or being 'sideswiped' by them.

- **Memory Systems**

To know that one is traumatized is not enough, or even to have that understood by a healing other, or to work diligently but vaguely in a 'working through' process. The patient desperately wants and needs to know *what it means, what happens to them in the moment,* and *what to do about it.* Through my own experience, research, and within my clinical work, I was fortunate to discover a great deal about what these implicit memory 'banks' mean, how they get triggered in any given moment in very individual, idiosyncratic ways, and evolve new and innovative conceptualizations and processes of working with them effectively. Indeed, we can do something about them, actually intervening in their playing out, intervening with their reliving, and ultimately, altering them, thus so they can be used for learning and change instead of repeating. In the process, we access and repair fractured state systems, finding injured, lost, and hidden aspects of the self, all there in the dynamics of the wounded self in service of protecting the essential self.

There are ever unfolding valuable avenues for approaching the treatment of trauma: PTSD, and CPTSD, such as EMDR (in which I am trained and which I did use at certain points with Julia), ACT, EFT, CBT, DBT, Somatic Psychology, art therapy, music therapy as well as pharmacological or hypnotherapy treatments and the trailblazing techniques established by Judith Herman (1992), J. A. Chu (1998), Gabor Maté (2003/2011), Bessel van der Kolk (2014), Peter Levine (2015), Adrienne Schwartz (2020), and Richard C. Schwartz (2021), among others. In this company, two of my original contributions to psychoanalytic psychotherapy treatment concern innovative ways of working with unresolved trauma delineated in my Seven Keystones of Transformative Development (see Chapter Twenty) and the new pathways I discovered in the 'decoding' of and intervening with what I came to call implicit memory 'banks' (Erwin, 2003). As an overview, to be followed in illustrative depth in Chapter Nineteen, the implicit memory conceptualization and process is one I offer to my patients metaphorically as 'bending the river'.

Years ago, as I learned about explicit memory and the power of implicit memory to understand what was playing out with various traumatized patients, I found, not uncommonly, that the first two opportunities of working with implicit memory 'banks' was first, the benefit to them and to me of viscerally feeling what that experience was like for them. As such experience was invariably repeated, I understood it in ever more complex ways and was able either to bring to them, or help them find, the emotional language to narrate that experience. For the first time in their lives, they were able to share with another what had happened to them and to have that other be a bearing witness for the previously unbearable (see Poland, 2000). This, in and of itself, promoted healing.

The second opportunity was in the processing of their traumatic experiences that we engaged in together (not just once but repeatedly), usually as therapeutic 'Monday morning quarterbacking,' but valuable enough since this after the fact processing had been so absent in their originating experience, which contributed to the trauma remaining unresolved. In such profound resonance (see Siegel, 1999), I was able to help them recover from the reliving through soothing and regulating, bringing my affective *presence* to our relationship, which provided some healing to the psychical *absence* they had lived with for decades. But, as I fostered recovery from their implicit memory relivings, I realized these were often the only opportunities most therapists and patients found to understand and recuperate from the reliving of implicit memory banks "till the next time."

The third opportunity built upon the first two: together, patients and I planned how to intervene with their relivings at the very point that they became aware of an anticipated triggering. Comprehending the triggers was not a perfect science, since there was a broad variety of possible triggers that could catch them unawares. We worked to establish intervening strategies that could be effective, physiologically and emotionally, in helping the patient regulate, as well as behavioral strategies for intervening in the acting out that often accompanied the driven nature of the implicit memory.

There was trial and error and failure in these interventions, because what seemed workable in the safety of my office and within the calm of our moments together did not necessarily transition into triggered experience. In these failing instances, I needed to function as an empathic and regulating other, withstanding their dismay, and modeling and teaching for their identificatory purposes how to become soothed and make another attempt. Despite the successes we did have, and the obvious rewards of understanding, recovery, and future planning, a tremendous amount of anguish existed for each of them when they were unable to prevent their implicit memory response from activating the next time it was triggered. I needed to find additional ways of decoding these 'banks' and create substantial opportunities for intervention.

One day as I was struggling with how to help a patient, I thought of how useful it was for me personally in various circumstances to break large tasks or challenges into much smaller steps. I realized in that moment that while there were times when pre-planning with a patient how to intervene before such a 'bank' was triggered had been somewhat successful, it basically was 'too large' a task. I also was acutely aware of how demoralizing it was for patients when they became swept up again in a reliving despite their best efforts. So, I turned to the actual procedural steps of the implicit memory bank.

I discovered a fourth opportunity within these procedural steps (Erwin, 2005). With my then patient's eager collaboration, we played psychic detective, taking an implicit memory bank and breaking it down into its smallest steps. Once we were fairly sure we had unearthed all the steps and then sequenced them in order, we looked for where transitions occurred between the steps, paying particular attention to the affective shifts occurring within those shifts. I came to appreciate why it was so nearly impossible for someone to intervene once they were in the throes of any one of the steps/states, since those state experiences were ripe with overwhelming affect. But in the moments of shift (like a breath), between the steps, where one affect or state shifted into another, there often existed a subtle but noticeable 'exhale' of one affective state before an 'inhale' of another.

I discovered that these were where rich opportunities existed. I realized that if one intervention failed earlier on in a reliving, another transition was just ahead, with its own opportunity for intervention. Subsequently, careful planning for each of these transitions led me and various patients to find that once even one small intervention worked, such success helped them regulate within the transition as well as finding that they could intervene in any acting out that often accompanied the subsequent driven nature of their reliving. The success of the following transition opportunities then became exponentially possible (see Procedural Steps Planning Pages in the Appendices).

In the presence of this exquisite and most tender of therapeutic processes, I felt the power and the majesty in this creative and healing discovery. In these decoding endeavors, I found the "something more than interpretation, those profound 'moments of meeting'...the 'moving along' process that alters the intersubjective environment, and thus the *implicit relational knowing*" (see D. Stern et al, 1998, p. 909). Implicit memory banks, traumatized and traumatizing though they may be, hold not only the problem but the *solution* where we thought there was none.

Decoding and intervening with implicit memory 'banks' is the new 'royal road' where previously there have been only problems without solutions. As I came to discover that such decoding was possible by making immediate use with the patient of such implicit memory relivings, the patients experienced for the first time in their lives both profound relief at how they made what I called "emotional sense" and a renewed belief in themselves (and an eagerness) that they could actually *intervene with* and *change* these internal minefields. Not that this was an easy endeavor. But such new autonoesis (self-knowing) gave my patients the courage to try and try again with me until they were successful.

- **Internalization and Identification**

Internalization (Meissner, 1976, 1979) is the *process* by which *who they started out to be* is built up. As we can see this transformational process utilizes external relationships, interactions, and forms of regulation for the purpose of building the *structure* of the internal world, thus setting the tone for the *experience* of the inner world (see Meissner, 1971). By implication, internalization refers to the movement of structural elements in the direction of the integration with that part of the psychic structure that is seen as most central to its inner identity—the ego.

W. W. Meissner (1992) in discussing the therapeutic alliance and the real relationship pointed out that "... from both sides of the analytic relation, objective qualities of the participants come into play continually to shape the quality and course of the interaction between them (p. 1069-1070).... There is a developmental aspect of the interchange between therapist and patient that involves mutual cuing and reciprocal relatedness that reaches back to the earliest strata of mother-infant interaction for its foundations" (p. 1071).

The identification with us as the new object and with healing is not a smooth and straightforward road. Instead, it can be disheartening, with many 'starting overs', necessitating finding innovative ways to pave the road ahead with a sense of possibility so the patient can experience that the psychical death they fear of who they think they are is actually an implicit memory relived along with the fear of the unfamiliar (see Erwin, 2023 to come). Being able to serve as an identificatory figure occurs because of various endowing capacities of the analyst coming into play with the patient's strivings, including the willingness to go to places within our own internal worlds that we find challenging. Malcolm Slavin and Daniel Kreigman (1998) talked of our patients "tapping into the fault lines in our identity, our conflicts—they take us someplace that is obviously hard to go. But we go there and often change in the process, because having a relationship with them requires it. They are worth it" (p. 281).

The following endeavors of the therapist are those I consider *necessary* as provisions in fostering the patient's identification with us:

- the therapist building and building again and again, the trust necessary for the patient to consider identifying with this new 'object', including through resolving any of her own limitations in or impediments to emotionally intimate relating

- the therapist's willingness to be consistently affectively present, an 'equi-presence' with all the oscillations and vicissitudes of the dynamics in the treatment, while regulating the patient's affect so the patient can internalize such regulation over time
- the therapist's respect and caring, and ultimately love, for the patient
- finding new ways of being within the dyad, for the patient and for the therapist
- the therapist's capacity to patiently foster a secure attachment through affective attunement and dependability over time
- the therapist's capacity to be the witness to the patient's experience and, with the patient, to bear what has always been the unbearable
- the therapist's appreciation of what is at stake for the patient
- to understand and navigate the balance between knowing when to allow the patient to lead the treatment and when the timing is right for the therapist to lead, intervene, confront, and set limits
- the therapist's capacity to repair ruptures, including through taking responsibility for her own part in any breach and,
- the therapist's collaboration with the patient in,
- acknowledging and working with transference and countertransference experiences in terms of the meaning such experience has for the patient and the therapist in any therapeutic reliving
- helping the patient tolerate the discoveries of how his/her fractured dynamic structure functions, especially as it plays out in the interpersonal matrix
- 'decoding' implicit memory banks
- creating links between implicit and explicit memory for the purpose of using the implicit for learning
- assisting the patient in the development of his/her own voice and helping him/her build the capability for elaborative 'emotional language', while crafting a coherent autobiographical narrative.

- **Affect Regulation**

The developing child's co-created regulating experience and the development of object constancy, object permanence, and object usage finds their parallels in the therapeutic endeavor as well. Just as with the infant/baby/growing child and parent, can the patient experience that she can truly be who she is and find in her therapist an affectively attuned, caring other who can offer such profoundly affecting regulation in a new object tie that the patient can come to trust enough to internalize and identify with life-giving identifications?

The therapist's regulating ministrations may offer the first opportunity for the patient to experience comfort and regulation *while* processing. For example, with Will, my willingness and patience in providing him open-ended sessions for a season, which allowed him to find his own pace and rhythm and to 'locate' himself within time and transitions, led to Will being able to keep track of himself in new ways outside of treatment. With Julia, experiences such as my alive, engrossed, but very nonverbal presence over many months while she drew her story (see Chapter Nineteen), provided the holding environment in which the rest of her story could be found. Yet, when my personal voice was active in reading her story back to from the beginning as she created it, session after session, the space was carved out in which she could resonate with her story and find herself within it. Outside of sessions, our regular voice mail processing of even minor details of her day-to-day living, as well as my affective attunement, gave Julia her very first sense of "going-on-being" (Winnicott, 1949, p. 145) with another in her life.

I think it is accurate to say that affect *dysregulation* has been part and parcel of each of our patient's experience. The developmental gaps, failures, or traumas any one of them withstood has left them with defensive reactions rather than true regulation. The pivotal reason that affect regulation must be achieved in the therapeutic endeavor is that without it not only is the therapeutic alliance prevented from successfully developing but delving into the traumatic sequelae in a patient's experience becomes fraught with the possibilities of re-traumatization.

As we examined in the section on States above, affect, implicit memory, and affect are inextricably related and use dependent upon each other. As suggested, the Arousal Chart (Lillas, 1994, Erwin, 2000) is an immensely useful medium through which therapist and patient can track affect and state charge and their shifts. Once the therapist and the patient have become very familiar with the affective movement of the patient in the face of stimuli, the Affective Questionnaire serves as an indispensable companion in finding those sensory modality opportunities for regulation that are geared to mitigating the patient's sensitivities and sensibilities In our collaborative work, when the patient is engaged with the therapist in learning regulation and finding intervention possibilities within implicit memory relivings, the answers found in this chart supply effective tools.

THE AFFECTIVE QUESTIONNAIRE

What Soothes You?
What Enlivens You?

by

Gwyneth Kerr Erwin, Ph.D., Psy.D.

SO = Mark those items (and any you would add) with an **SO** for those activities that help you become soothed when you've become distressed (anxious, worried, angry, afraid) or "hyperaroused" (THE RED ZONE).

EN = Mark those items (and any you would add) with an **EN** for those activities that help you become enlivened when you've become depressed (or tired, cynical, fearful, giving up) or "hypoaroused" (THE BLUE ZONE).

REMEMBER YOU ARE TRYING TO COME BACK TO AN **OPEN, PROCESSING SPACE** (THE GOLD ZONE!)

VISUAL (sensory modality #1)					
	watching a fire in the fireplace		fluorescent lighting		order
	watching fish swim		lamp light		clutter
	watching the sunrise/sunset		candlelight		something far away
	being near trees		sunlight		something close up
	bright light		twilight		something busy
	dim light		darkness		something still

Add yours					

AUDITORY (sensory modality #2)					
	the sound of water		soft voices		shouts
	the sound of music (name instrument/s)		loud voices		clutter
	the sound of humming		crying		poetry
	the sound of breathing		laughing		stories
	heartbeat		whispers		

Add yours					

ORAL (sensory modality #3)			
	Taking slow, easy breaths		"Chewing" on (gum, hair, strings, buttons, coins, pencil, pens)
	Sucking on hard candy		"Crunching" on (pickle, olives, pretzels, chips, ice, hard candy, nuts)
	Sucking on something cold (ice chips, popsicles, frozen edibles)		Eating something sweet
	Sucking or licking (lips, tongue, inside of cheeks)		Eating something salty
	Whistling or other noises with your mouth		Eating something tangy/sweet-sour
	Biting nails, cuticles		Eating something bitter
	Sipping something hot (cocoa, tea, coffee, warm milk)		Alternating flavors (sweet to salty, for example)
	Drinking something cold (milkshake, ice water, carbonated sodas, milk)		Eating alone
	Drinking something hot (cocoa, coffee, tea)		Eating with others

Add yours			

SMELL (sensory modality #4)			
	something sweet		something crisp, like fall air
	something woodsy		something fresh
	something floral		something sour
	something pungent		something tart
	fire in a fireplace		something like baked bread

Add yours			

TOUCH/KINESTHETIC (sensory modality #5)			
	twisting/stroking your hair		rubbing skin/clothing
	moving objects in your pocket		fidgeting (with a straw, paper clips, fingers/nails, etc)
	cool shower/bath		feeling a breeze
	warm shower/bath		sitting near someone
	having a massage		sitting alone
	petting a dog/cat/other animal		feeling something itchy
	drumming fingers		feeling something soft
	jiggling foot		feeling something smooth
	jerking muscles		

Add yours			

MOVEMENT/VESTIBULAR (sensory modality #6)			
	rocking		running
	shifting/squirming		riding a bike/horse
	pushing back chair on two legs		tapping toes
	exercise		dancing
	lifting weights		tapping an object
	scrubbing/cleaning		yard work
	rolling neck and head		stretching/shaking
	cracking knuckles		walking/hiking
	bouncing or jiggling		sports

Add yours			

- **Attachment**

The attachment process offers a dynamic opportunity for patient and therapist to understand and work through the patient's original attachment systems and to forge a new secure attachment with a caring, present, and reliable other. Michael Balint (1936), in considering the final goal of treatment, wrote: "For those who were obliged to suffer severely from the 'confusion of tongues', whose capacity for love was artificially wholly stunted by lack of understanding in their upbringing, quite a peculiar situation arises. Everything turns on one decision. Shall one regard all past suffering as over and done with, settle account with the past for good, and, in the last resort, try to make the best use of what possibilities there are in the life still lying ahead? This decision to begin to love anew is very far from easy" (p. 215).

For Will, on the road to a secure attachment with me was the regularly intruding ambivalent attachment with his mother. Could he trust my encouragement of his living an emboldened life, or was I "leading him down a garden path?" Or, as we sank into deeper levels of the analysis, was I beckoning him into an alluring cozy, cocooned place that would hold him hostage psychologically as had his mother, or would I help him find his essential self that "was in a box?" Ultimately, could he invest enough in our relationship and the treatment to really come to care in his life, "to love anew," (Balint, p. 215), or would the intensity of those feelings be more than he could tolerate and thus too frightening, so ambivalence would once again offer his solution where he could not consider any other solution.

Many years ago, after I presented my work with Julia at an analytic forum, a colleague who I greatly respected and enjoyed, gave me quite positive feedback on my work with Julia. At the end of his remarks, he rhetorically asked, "I wonder how it will go when the negative transference comes in the room?" (see Valenstein, 1973). Indeed. I found out the very next session. What I discovered through Julia's and my intermittent and brief sojourns into the negative transference was that while we made productive use of such instances, they were actually terrifying for her when they emerged with her needing me to understand and repair them as soon as possible.

I came to know early into our work together that Julia could not have made me into the transferential figure of either her mother or her father without that having an iatrogenic effect, re-traumatizing her. I also could not be the mainly 'interpretive' analyst, as such a stance would have inadvertently objectified her and produced spirit breaking shame (see Kumin 1989). Our real relationship of connection, communication, and caring aided me in coming to understand with Julia the traumatic life she had lived, especially as it was re-lived in her relationship with Oscar, with my responses to her "revival of unmet developmental longing" (Atwood, Stolorow, & Trop, 1989, p. 557), becoming key to Julia establishing a secure attachment to me, leading to her healing.

- **Hemispheric Development**

With unresolved trauma, inherent operations of the brain become concretized and rigidified in the right hemisphere as that trauma is encoded in fractured state systems. Then, the taking apart of perception does not automatically come back together to form whole percepts. Rather than "... the brain's integrative function to 'put it all together' being on board, carrying out idiosyncratic tasks of basic adaptation, [providing] an organizing force at the most complex levels of human experiencing..." (Sander, 2002, p. 27), the brain 'organizes' distorted and split apart perceptions from repeated intense traumatic experience into implicit memory neuronal pathways, usable only for being re-triggered in the current moment.

Fortunately, we know now that long-term and effective psychotherapy and psychoanalytic treatment 'rewires' those neuronal pathways. As Allan Schore (2003b) addressed that when we, the analytic dyad, are successful in "identifying nonconscious right brain perceptual biases, and use interactive repair... that disconfirm[s] the patient's perceptual biases, and allows for the emergence of a right brain system that effectively regulates the intensity, frequency, and duration of negative and positive affects ... reorganizing insecure internal working models into secure models ... that allow for a developmental progression of the ability to maintain a coherent, continuous, unified sense of self" (p. 279-281), healing can occur.

Such healing takes place on the hemispheric level because the "dyadic affective transactions within the working alliance cocreate an intersubjective context that allows for the structural expansion of the patient's orbitofrontal system and its cortical and subcortical connections. Orbitofrontal function is essential not only to affect regulation but also to the processing of cognitive-emotional interactions and affect-related meanings" (Schore, 2003b, p. 264). The hope in analytic treatment is the rewiring of previously maladaptive hemispheric development, "the creation of new neuronal linkages, then, allows the internal constraints of the dynamical system of the brain to change" (Siegel, 1999, p. 306).

The affective regulation and building of secure attachments in and of themselves began to re-wire the neuronal pathways of both of my patients' brain hemispheres. In developmentally based treatment, the firing of previous traumatized pathways are re-lived and reworked within the therapeutic and emotionally real relationship, perceptual biases based on dysregulation and insecure attachment are decoded, granting space for using affective cues as signal opportunities and for new templates, or mental representations, for use in the patients' worlds. Rather than existing primarily in a dampened down narrow range of parasympathetic response to stimulation (Will), or in a hyperaroused, excitatory sympathetic response to stimulation (Julia), the individual develops a much wider range of regulating responses, finding within open, processing states, true possibilities for relating. The resolving work with implicit memory 'banks', fractured state systems, and suppressed voice all adds to this re-wiring.

- **Voice and Language**

And then there is the matter of personal voice and affective 'elaborative languaging,' not just the patient's but the therapist's as well. Leo Kovar (1994) reminded us that, "those seeking out the talk therapist are regarded as suffering from disorders of the talk itself.... I am not referring to failures of communication, but rather to an impoverishment of talk. The communicators generally understand each other all too well, including their attempts singly or mutually to make their communications devious or obscure, where the effort toward obscurity and befogging the other is the communication itself" (p. 555). W. W. Meissner (2000) pointed us to the evidence that while "the patient's discourse [should be taken] at face value... [it is] but the tip of the iceberg of reference and implication.... The analyst listens not merely to the words and the meanings they express, but also to the tone, pace, affective coloring, nuances of expression, restful or disruptive movements, facial expression, tears, sobs, sighs, groans, chuckles, laughter, etc" (p. 320-322, see also Stern, 1984, Poland, 1986, Greenspan, 1999). So too, I contend, does the patient.

For our patients to find his or her own personal voice and affective 'elaborative language', the therapist, within the provision of emotional safety, must be willing to speak, not in professional jargon, or at a safe remove through "incorrect interpretations" (Kumin, 1989, p. 141), but in the brave and revealing atmosphere of her own personal voice and elaborative language. Such pivotal moments with Will consisted of: when I spoke with the emotional authenticity of my personal voice of the vibrations in his life as like a "train barreling down on him," or of when I kindly but firmly confronted him about his avoidance of the consequences he was mindlessly creating in his relationship with Samantha in his lack of work activity and the diminishment of his later saved monies, and when I used my deeply disturbed sense to communicate my concern in affectively charged metaphor, one which he could *hear* and *feel*. With Julia, the day I called Oscar "a punk" out of my exasperation, was a significant turning point in shrinking his threatening presence into something she could finally face, and then leave.

Kovar (1994) inspired me with, "[The analyst] must *en-vision* the words spoken. Bare by themselves, they must be clothed pictorially, not with stills, but with movies" (p. 556). The therapist of the word, at his best, gives his patient a gift that cannot be purchased.... True concern entails the attending to highly detailed complexities of what is listened to and equally careful judgments as to what ought to be said in response.... The talking therapist must have the desire and the aptitude to talk to his patient in such a way that this tangible gift-giving becomes almost palpable" (p. 569).

In the therapeutic setting, even with traumatized patients, the capacity for amodal perception (Stern, 1985), that ability to perform cross sensory modal matching can be tapped as the patient makes use of the therapist's communications within the emotional elaboration that takes place between patient and therapist. First through incorporation, then into the realm of new identifications, the ways in which the therapist communicates her caring and perceptive therapeutic actions, nonverbally and verbally, provide a new opportunity for the patient not only to name her experience but begin to recover her personal voice and matching affective language.

The techniques and tools recommended in this chapter and throughout the book are substantially effective and can lead the way to deep psychological change and healing. At the heart of it all is the "IT," the therapeutic relationship and its concomitant endeavor. This relationship is unlike any other kind with its unmasked emotional intimacy, the patient's and the therapist's. This revelatory exchange is not something to be feared when found in trustworthy hands. Instead, the power of the therapist's very being, along with innovative and skilled technique, brings to the patient what s/he needed from the beginning of life, and which now represents new hope for healing unresolved trauma.

CHAPTER NINETEEN

Resolving Trauma

There are two overarching activities in the therapeutic endeavor, which do not occur in a linear manner; rather, they are nonlinear and dynamic, sometimes occurring in a first-then-second-format, other times, interweaving moment-to-moment. They are: *insight* and the *working through* process. Most patients look forward to insight mistakenly thinking that with enough insight, they will change. Patients might also fear insight for the heavy affective load uncovering their inner life could bring. While insight, or self-understanding (autonoesis), certainly supports change, as painful, arduous, and inspiring as it can be, it becomes the easier of the two processes. Working through, or what I find to be the deliberate, purposeful mastery of change, is by far both the higher road and the more precarious. Such effort is inextricably involved with the transformed development of the essential self, an enterprise that requires tremendous courage, delicate dedication to the true experience of the essential self, and the risk to live as that self which has been in necessary hiding for most of one's life.

As we have seen, unresolved trauma consists of acute, repeated acute, cumulative, and vicarious forms or any combination of these. I have also offered what I found to be the six pivotal reasons that trauma remains unresolved. Using both insight and working through within the new interactional relationship of patient and therapist, what are the bedrock opportunities for beginning to resolve such trauma?

In the transformational process of the inter-influence of the seven keystones of development, patient and therapist will also need to embrace a tender and necessary mourning, one whose aim is for unresolved trauma and its consequences to become of the past instead of remaining an activating agent in the present. In this, the patient's life narrative takes its fullest shape. Together, patient and therapist see, even relive, what happened, what was lost, what was necessarily buried. The Developmental Lens opens, ever so carefully, all that needs to be understood and respected, not for *what* happened, but that it *did* happen, and provided with the life-giving ministrations, at last, to heal.

In this exquisite process, unresolved trauma begins to find its resolution in these ways:

First, instead of no responsible and caring adult being available during the originating trauma to comfort, soothe, regulate, or process with the traumatized individual their traumatic experience, or later, its consequences, now, perhaps for the first time, a responsible and caring other is available to offer such comfort and soothing, regulation, and partnering in processing with the individual their traumatic experience and its consequences;

Second, whereas the perpetrator of the trauma was often a significant caregiver or someone who was supposed to be a 'safe island', now, the therapist is truly that safe island and provides the protection and sacred space of the holding environment for the patient to 'face' the perpetrator (especially a previously significant caregiver), either emotionally or actually in real time, with her authorial voice accessible to narrate the impact of the trauma;

Third, originally those to whom the child/adult turned for help either ignored, belittled, or denied the traumatic experience, thus re-traumatizing the individual, now the child or adult's reaching for help is received by someone immensely caring and knowledgeable to validate, authenticate, and help them understand and work through their traumatic experience.

Fourth, no discerning and protective caregiving adult intervened in the trauma's repetition, but now the therapist and patient together forge effective ways to intervene in any traumatic repetition, both in implicit memory reliving and in current time;

Fifth, in the original trauma, the perpetrator was not held accountable nor was required to make reparations and usually was more protected than the victim. Now, through various relational and even perhaps legal means, the perpetrator may come to be held accountable and required to make reparations;

Sixth, alone in managing trauma's consequences, the child/adult formerly became caught in an impossible dilemma, "fright without solution" (Hesse and Main, 2000, p. 1117), facing ongoing triggers and lasting traumatic reactions. Through the therapeutic partnership and its activities of insight and working through, the patient is freed from being caught in the impossible dilemma of "fright without solution" as s/he gains mastery of her new authorial pathways of living.

Within these and other resolution openings, what is fostered ultimately is creativity for the patient and therapist, within the opportunity to live fully in the present, and to have an optimistic sense of the future. In this process of healing, and all that comes alive in its presence, the patient is reunited with her or his originating essential self and finally can become immersed in the transformation of development and maturation of that essential self for his or herself and with others.

Will:

Will and I entered an extended period where at first, with regularity, and then, intermittently, Will said 'purple' if I said 'green'; if I offered 'blue', he moved to 'yellow'. He resisted "going deep" in the sessions, saying he needed to concentrate on practical matters. As we focused our attention on those practical matters, he complained because we were not going deep enough.

He bought new hearing aids, ones he could not only tolerate, but which helped him hear. Then he forgot to wear them or bring them to session. As his financial fortunes flowed briefly, then ebbed, depending on his ability to stay affectively present, he questioned the value of continuing treatment, "the time it takes to come to sessions," "the cost" (which was still at a reduced fee due to his financial compromises).

No sooner did he become ambivalent about treatment, than he re-engaged. After one weekend break, he reported trying to talk to Samantha again, but while their evening "went all right," he was not able to communicate with her the way he was trying to. By the next week, Will told me of putting together several potential projects at his office. When he got home, Samantha had prepared a dinner of catfish, something he liked, but she did not.

"I was really pleased, so I said to her, 'Oh, did you get this for me'?"

"She said, 'No, why do you always think it has to be for you. I got it for the family.' That really stung. Later, as we were cleaning up, I mentioned the residue of corn meal on the floor that I was dabbing up. She thought I was making a barb at her. Maybe I was, retaliating because I had been stung, but I was also noticing and said to her that when she cooked, flour or corn meal kind of flew everywhere, and wasn't that interesting since she likes to keep things so clean, and when I cooked I was very neat and tidy, and I basically like to keep things messy. She was immediately suspicious, and said, 'Are you trying to hurt me?' Instead of becoming confused or defensive, I looked at her and said, 'No, actually I was just noticing that we are different, and that it's okay. In fact, after the flour going everywhere and the wonderful meal, I was thinking I want to go to bed and make love with you."

"That was pretty bold of you," I said.

"Yeah, and, later, you know, it opened up our talking, so that I could finally bring up my dwindling money issue, and talk to her about last weekend and the groceries and her purse, and how I set myself up for being punished and then feeling weak again."

He looked at me, not sideways as he usually did, but with full eye contact, "And then I said to her, 'When you get upset with me, because I messed up, you withdraw, and then there is this cold shoulder all week. Then, because I messed up and you're upset, I zone out. The withdrawal and zoning aren't good for either of us; we might as well be living in separate houses. I don't want to live like that anymore.'"

In the moment, this robust, clear man, with a full self present, was breathtaking. He moved right on.

"The next morning, I went surfing with my friend, no hiding it, no apologies. Samantha got to sleep in, and the kids took care of themselves. Even though my friend was urging me to stay longer because the surf was so beautiful, I said that I'd promised Samantha I'd be home by 10:30. When we got to the house, she had prepared this delicious breakfast for us. Instead of the project day we had planned, we decided to go on a family fun day taking a trip up to the top of Saddleback Mountain, saving our work projects for next weekend.

"I talked with her some more when we got home about what I was learning, about the secondary gains we each get, about how I set up getting punished, and how I didn't want to do that anymore either. You know, I try to write down all this stuff that we talk about in here, so I won't forget. I've been wanting to write about the secondary gains and our system, Samantha's and mine, and I haven't done it, but this time it's okay, because I think I'm getting it in here [pointing to his heart]. Anyway, Samantha took up where I left off, and instead of simply complaining, or belittling me, she said that maybe, since her boss was dismantling his private office and joining the corporate world, instead of going with him and working in a huge corporate setting and working for three, not just one, bosses, she could just quit her job, and go back to school the way she always wanted to, and then begin a new career."

Such a challenge would have collapsed Will just months earlier, but now, while he was afraid of not making the grade, he wanted to try. He began working a structured forty-hour week and stuck to it. Unfortunately, his efforts were not rewarded, with project after project developing difficult problems. Ordinarily, this would have been devastating for Will. This time, he persevered. Samantha, meanwhile, hopefully temporarily, transitioned to the new corporate job.

After weeks of exploration, and with encouragement from me, Will secured a provisional teaching credential, so that if he hit another debilitating interval of managing destabilized projects, he had an alternative. Soon after, he was expressing his frustration and ambivalence once again—he wanted to do something meaningful *and* successful. The potential of his current work could possibly fulfill the successful part, if he succeeded in a big way, but not the meaningful part. He played one possibility against the other. While he argued aloud that the provisional credential could lead to something meaningful if he went back to school and earned a graduate degree, it might not have the same potential for the kind of money he could make if he really succeeded in his current work.

"It would be such a luxury to embark on this new teaching career," he said.

"A luxury? How is that?"

"Well, it would mean that I was successful enough to do something that was meaningful to me. Then the salary wouldn't matter so much."

"You know, Will, if you and Samantha both went after what you wanted, you'd make as much money on a reliable basis as you make now on the roller coaster ride."

"Yeah, you're right."

"So, maybe it's not about that. Maybe it's about how you don't yet have the consistent internal permission to be active in having what you want, and in giving Samantha the opportunity she wants."

"That's the hard part, alright."

Will grew serious, his eyes saddened.

"What's there?" I asked.

"It's kind of strange. I was thinking about when I was four and my little pals and I were in the backyard, kind of interested in seeing how we compared, you know, in a peeing contest, and my mother came out and found us, and I remember how I felt when she reproached me." (Pause).

"How?" I asked.

"Timid."

"Timid." He had found a new way to account for his fear and avoidance. "Will, you've found a perfect way to say what happened to your robust little boy self."

His eyes filled with tears, the corners of his mouth pulling down.

"Yeah, I just did!" his voice choked.

"Maybe it's time for you and Samantha each to have what you consider a luxury."

"I think so."

At our session two days later, Will looked like he'd come from surfing. His eyes were bright, alert. He flushed a bit and then said, "I filled in for someone yesterday. You gave me the push I needed, so I called, and they had an opening. The kids there wanted to know my policy on what to do if they got in trouble. I told them, 'Hey, I remember being that age. You're not little anymore. If you want to go screw up, go ahead. But take responsibility for it.' Then I talked to them about Hamlet, about what Hamlet was wondering about—all the things they worried about—to be or not to be. Same angst."

He was lit from within.

"Will, you're a natural."

"It was really exciting." Another new word for him. Even a new feeling, sustained for hours.

The next day, he was back to the same quandary, project management or his new career, potential money or meaning. Toward the end of the session, he said, "Samantha is so unhappy at her new job, I told her, 'Quit. We've got some savings; we've got some credit. I'm making more money. Do it, we can get by'. Last night, Samantha and I were looking up graduate programs on the Internet, and she asked, 'How long is it going to take you to do something about this'. The usual answer in my mind is something like, '*Uh, I don't know, um three days to six years*'. But I thought, *I'd like to do this in two-week increments*. Do everything I can in two weeks. Then, another two weeks. So I said, 'Two weeks.' I wanted to be bold— enthusiastic, creative. I wanted to plunge in. I can do management at the same time as graduate school. I want it to be okay to make a mistake and fix it. I want to have a flamboyant side to me, to take a chance and know it's not the end of the world."

Samantha quit work and had a several months' holiday, rediscovering leisure, some creative pursuits, and reversing roles with Will. He continued with his work and started graduate school, earning his advanced degree a year and a half later with a near straight-A average. Six months into Will's educational process, Samantha took a far more creative job, but after another six months, missed the income she had previously made, and found a job back in her administrative world, not a perfect fit, but enjoying an advancement of creative responsibilities and increased income. Will took on the task of job hunting, graduate degree in hand, taking one step forward and two steps back, procrastinating putting together his portfolio, then racing to be prepared, while he continued his project management work. He interviewed for a few jobs but was so injured by not being hired, his energy collapsed, and he retreated.

Will continued to struggle over many more sessions with his conflict between making money and creating meaning in his work. One day, he got a call to take on a six-month temporary substitute position. He invested himself heavily in that work, while managing to keep his work projects going. This teaching opportunity required long and regular hours, much planning ahead of time, as well as grading and planning after hours. Will was afraid, dedicated, exhausted, and exhilarated. When the assignment finished and no permanent job was in the offing, Will felt deep disappointment.

His project work stabilized, Will was making a more consistent living, and the marriage to Samantha was going well. We had been working together for five years, and Will decided he wanted to see how he would do without treatment. He wanted to see "if he could fly on his own wings." After several weeks of discussing this, the timing of it, the precipitants of it, we decided on a three-month break, during which time he could contact me if he needed to. We set a future session date and agreed to evaluate at that time whether or not he wanted to return to his analysis. This was a significant step for Will. Even though I did not feel the analysis was finished, I did not want to be the mother who pulled him back as he attempted to step into the world, and I also felt it was very important that I exhibited my belief in him and encourage him.

Three months later, he returned and resumed treatment for two main reasons: one, he could see that he still had trouble in meeting goals he set for himself, and two, he wanted to see if there was something to that long-ago dream I had intuited in our first session. Now, he knew what the dream had involved: his artistic self.

His struggle with conflict was on-going and became more complex as he added a new set of goals for himself, "to make art," while still vacillating between work for money and work for meaning. After applying for a few more jobs in teaching, which did not lead to fruition, he stayed with project management, but enrolled in a new art class. His journal now became a safe place for his drawing rather than only a writing journal, and he considered the various forms his art might take. He "dreamt" about being bold and risk taking, so he set up a studio in his garage for himself and Samantha. Occasionally, he brought in some part of a creative project to share with me, and I could immediately see the "eye" he had, his vision translated onto his medium. His class completed, Will seriously considered whether this could become at least a part-time career, or dedicated avocation. As he pondered the implications of such a decision, fear swept through him, using as an antidote spending his weekend taking care of household projects, helping out his dad, being with the kids.

Six months later, after a string of circumstances, Will was offered a new full-time position being in charge of several large projects that he would oversee and many workers he would supervise. The salary was more than he had ever made, and while it was not related to his desired career or his creativity, he decided to take it, so that Samantha could take the chance she wanted and go to graduate school. He became quickly successful in this new position, no nosebleeds, or headaches. Further, the men he supervised respected him and his skills, Will being able to solve problems as they came up, and deal effectively with vendors and owners.

Soon, he brought up the possibility of taking another break or stopping treatment altogether. As we processed his thinking and the affect that came up around this possibility, Will's old style of ambivalence changed in a fundamental way. Instead of talking about the time it took to come to sessions, the fee, or taking his typical oppositional stance, Will said, "You know, I can feel how much I've changed, and how different I am from when we began. Samantha and I are on the same page, we really enjoy one another, the kids too, and I'm doing well at this job. It's not what I want to do for the rest of my life, but I can do this for a couple of years until I decide what to do next. I also really value coming here, being able to talk to you, and I would miss that. Still, I think I want to take a break, maybe."

On what was to be his last session, at least for another three months, Will began talking about his creativity. "I just don't have the time right now. I try to think about what art I might do at night, after work, or on the weekend, but at night I'm really tired, and on the weekend, there's all the catch-up stuff to do. We're painting the house, inside and out, buying some new furniture, doing some of the things we haven't been able to afford before." He was quiet for a few minutes, then near session's end, he cocked his head, laughed a bit, shaking his head, and said, "I think I shouldn't talk about creating for a while.

I think I should talk about my mother, the car accident, and about why I *don't* create." (Pause). He gathered up his belongings, his keys, his checkbook, his cell phone, and stood, his lanky frame stretched tall. He put an arm around my shoulder and patted it. "Well, I'll see you next week."

And so he did.

Julia:

Over months, Julia and I reached a point where another palpable milestone occurred, with our work shifting in focus from the experiences and repercussions in her life of the relationship with her father to those with her mother. She asked me: "How am I ever going to recover from not having a mother?" She paused then, looked deeply into my eyes, and whispered, "I have you." Another pause. "There is so much inside me about my mother, but I have no way to talk about it; I am mute." After several minutes of silence, she said she wished she could draw—if she could, she could draw all the pictures in her mind.

Many years previously, I attended art school for five years. I thought about what she was saying, considering a concrete avenue. An intuitive sense prodded me forward. In about ten minutes, I taught her three basic principles of drawing and gave her a mini-demonstration.

She arrived for her next session with a small box of colored pencils and some large sheets of drawing paper folded in half. After talking for a few minutes about how she wanted to try to do this, she settled herself on the couch, cross-legged, serious and intent. For several minutes she was quiet and did not move, staring at the paper, pencil poised in her hand. Then slowly, she began to draw. That day, she drew and paused, then drew again, sometimes her brow furrowing, sometimes her eyes squinting. Neither of us spoke a word. I did not move in my chair.

Some twenty or so minutes later, she chose a colored pencil and began to color, then another and another. When she was finished with the coloring, she returned to her black pencil, and I could tell by the way her pencil moved that she was printing. The majority of the session passed in this way, until she put her pencils down and handed me the paper.

The drawings took my breath away. They had the look of a six- or seven-year-old's, except that they captured profound affect. At the top and bottom of each drawing were a couple of simple declarative sentences, much like a six- or seven-year-old's might be, telling about the picture. She asked me to read it aloud to her.

For nearly six months, each of our sessions was spent the same way. In Julia's life, she had been consigned to surviving inside her father's chaotic traumatization and to unremitting aloneness in the 'presence' of her mother's rejection and neglect. For the first time, she was able to be in the involved but unobtrusive presence of a caring analyst/(m)other. In these sessions, I could feel the rewards of my "primary maternal preoccupation" (Winnicott, 1956/1975, pp. 303-304).

Each session, after coloring in her newly drawn picture and printing the few sentences top and bottom, Julia handed me the accumulating sheets. She would ask me to go back to the beginning and read her "story" all the way through. The experience was exquisitely moving for me. I felt a mix of respect and awe. Even the air held a poignant atmosphere.

The feelings in the drawings washed into me in waves. As Julia drew, she was totally concentrated. It did not seem to me that she was feeling what she was drawing as much as she wanted me to feel what she was drawing. And I did. Sometimes, I needed many minutes to look, study, absorb, and be present with what was on the page. We did not even talk very much about what was happening—it seemed far too important for Julia to find her 'voice' than to make mine the one to speak. Months into this process and over twenty drawings rendered, she said one day, "I feel like I am finally getting all of this that I have had to carry inside, outside of me." By now, as I read at the end of our sessions, her story gained momentum and potency. The tragedy of what happened to her permeated me, yet simultaneously, I felt quite peaceful in the unfolding of her innermost narrative.

I considered what was getting outside of her, until one day it occurred to me that it was more than her toxic and painful experiences—it was some of her introjects. She came in another day telling me that she needed more colors and the day following carried in a new set of pencils – a veritable rainbow of choice. She finished the stack of loose pages and arrived with a drawing pad, spiral bound. Her story was evolving in a coherent narrative for the first time in her life.

Finally, a session came when as she drew another picture in the series of being inside a black hole as an infant she said, "I can feel today that maybe this blackness was really my mother's—not mine. I think in the next picture I am going to draw it around her." When the time came for that drawing, she noticed, "No! It was *in her*, then she put it *in me*." I felt such tender feelings for her dedicated communications, even a sense of wonder for her discovery of the representations for her young voice, previously mute.

A year passed without Julia having any direct contact with Oscar. He still called several times a day and heavy breathed or left a brief, menacing message, or just hung up. Some weeks later, as she was drawing, the peaceful energy in the room vanished in an instant, the air charged. I could hardly sit still. Julia's feet were moving, she was restless, tears started streaming down her face. I had never interrupted her, but this time I asked, "What are you drawing?" She showed me. It was an unfinished picture of her father standing in the doorway, watching her. She looked at me with pleading and helplessness. I said, "You don't have to be a hostage all your life." Her brow furrowed, as though the thought had never occurred to her. She was silent the rest of the session as she tried to draw, but she could not finish the drawing.

An hour later I received a voice mail from her. She had called the police annoyance bureau and reported Oscar's phone stalking. By the next day, a trap was put on her line. They traced the calls within the day. That same week, police went to his apartment and gave him a warning, Julia's choice. If the calls continued, she would press charges. She finally disconnected her line and got a new unlisted phone number. Still, she remained watchful and vigilant.

Julia mentioned she had always been interested in mosaics and made some explorations, buying a few supplies and instruction kit. The first completed tile she brought in to show me had one pink shard of glass near a corner, with many shards of different bands of color emanating from that one, all set in black grout. I exclaimed: "It is so beautiful. Now the blackness is a background, but the rays are filled with light and color." She saw then what her unconscious had portrayed: a mosaic so similar to, yet profoundly transformed from, her drawing of the black, bottomless void.

Her platonic friendship with her ex-husband, Greg, was going well under their agreed upon mutual parenting, staying in his house together for this year. Now, they began talking about when and how to sell her home and transition her and the children into a new one. They also used this time to have some couple sessions with another therapist and came to understand what had drawn them together in the first place and why the marriage had come apart, an understanding that proved valuable to each of them, and provided the support necessary for Greg to move into therapy of his own.

Julia felt ready to begin dating but wanted to do so in as protected a way as possible. She also wanted to be sure not to run into Oscar in the local neighborhood, with her date with another man inciting Oscar. She discussed the possibility of some of the matching sites on the Internet, and spent careful time researching them, finally choosing one, then later another, which seemed even more protected. After placing her portfolio on the service, without a photograph, she began several correspondences with a few different men.

But none of them proved to be people with whom she wanted to move into closer contact.

A month later, she began corresponding with one particular man who was a computer expert in medical research —just a couple of years older, also divorced, and who had two college-aged sons. Their communications through the service were extensive and very interesting to Julia. Weeks later, when they felt as though they were each wanting the relationship to move forward, they agreed to send photos. Since both were very pleased by what they saw, they moved to the next step, exchanging actual email addresses. The next step after a few more weeks was to meet for coffee.

Soon after Julia and Thomas began dating, each reported to the other that neither had ever felt this way before, although each had dreamed of such a relationship. They were able to spend long hours together, talking or being silent. He was much taller than she, but trim, so she did not feel threatened by him physically. They were both fit and active, going on hikes and bicycle rides. They discussed how they dreamed of their futures and found commonality in their individual visions. Julia talked about her analysis and some of her now past experiences with Oscar; Thomas shared with her the devastating experience of his father's death when he was in college and the repercussions of that for him. She told me, "I think he's actually brighter than I am, but not in a competitive way. He tracks me; he's actually present." For Thomas, he told Julia that she "is the one," and that he would do whatever it took to make the relationship work. She wanted to move more slowly than he, first, because she did not want to get sexually involved with him until she felt safe and solid in the relationship, a new position for her to hold. But second, she was struggling within herself and in the analysis with believing, taking in, and trusting that someone, other than me, could be protective of her, enjoy her, and want her to be happy. Thomas felt "too good to be true."

After one particular evening out, Julia brought to the session a card he had given her. Obvious to me in reading the card was that Thomas must have spent quite a bit of time to find a card that was as fitting as this one was, one which expressed his desire to be with her in authentic and caring ways. She was dazed in the session, her eyes looking bewildered, yet full of light and pleasure. "I think I am falling in love," she said, "but I hardly know what to do with him, where to put all this inside of me. Nothing to fear? No other shoe to drop? I've never had a man who was both kind and exciting to me." She could not believe that she could let go of the specter of suffering that had ensnared her throughout her life. Once again, we were faced with the struggle of her striving to shift her identification from her trauma to an identification with healing, and ultimately, thriving.

I thought of my deep desires for a sense of peace for Julia that had never had the opportunity to develop in her, and for her happiness. I also realized in this moment that one of the results of her increased capacity to have both peace and happiness would signal an advancement in her capacity for mourning, the mourning for and acceptance of the loss of the kind of mother she originally needed and for the father who so captivated and traumatized her.

In this session, I noticed that Julia's shoulders were drawing up, nearly imperceptibly. I asked her if she was "shrinking away," feeling wary. Blushing, she admitted she was, "a little bit." After stumbling over her tentative words, she confessed that she could not believe that she could have me and a man in her life. Her mother never wanted Julia, but she did not want anyone else to want her either. She was embarrassed that she was "checking me out." Was I going to retaliate if she were happy?

Over the next two weeks, Julia grew increasingly agitated and anxious as her feelings for Thomas expanded and intensified. When a couple of days went by without in person contact with him, her vigilance became acute, and inaccurate. There were small and seemingly large ruptures, yet Thomas was true to his word—acting on his commitment to do what it would take for the relationship to develop. He "got it" that her object constancy with him was shaky, so both increased the time they spent together each week and made increased contact when they were apart. Julia asked him repeatedly and in a variety of ways if she were to jump "into his heart" would he really stay to catch her.

In one session, she could not sit still, her legs bobbing up and down, her fingers bouncing a water bottle against her thigh. She finally confessed to me near session's end that she had been in contact with another man from the Internet matching site, someone who "was quicker in his response to her—exciting." Foreboding squeezed my heart. She said to me, "Don't wince," but before I could actually respond she was already justifying her decision to meet him: "Excitement calms me down. I can't help it! These other feelings are too oceanic." Indeed, as she spoke, I could feel the waters gathering in the room. Walking out the door at session's end, she looked back over her shoulder and said, "I'm having breakfast with Chris in the morning." I thought: *Her 'expansive solution' (Horney, 1950) to gathering self-contempt in the face of her overwhelming need.*

The next day, I was regaled with what a terrific breakfast she had with this new man, handsome, rich, and successful, and so "quick" in his affective presence. Finally, I asked: "How would you feel if you found out that Thomas was dating another woman to cope with his feelings toward you?"

"It would be over," was her immediate response. Several seconds of stunned silence passed. "Oh," was all she could finally muster, "I see." Tears formed in her eyes, her face crumpling as she stammered out her next words, "But I can't bring all this need to him, every day, every minute. It will drive him away. And I go into such a fury inside. There's no way he can meet all that all the time."

I replied, "Perhaps not, but you don't know that yet. He has tapped into a very deep part of you. I can imagine why Chris seems a relief—the problem may be that a relationship with him would leave out the very intimacy and depth you want."

"That's right. What am I going to do?"

"I wonder, do you think you could let all that oceanic need and its consequences just be in the room with me, so that you and Thomas can take the risk of developing an adult and authentic relationship?"

Silence enveloped us once again, Julia's eyes wide, fixed on mine. She nodded, then nodded again. "I feel shy" were all the words she could find.

Julia decided to run/walk in a local marathon with Thomas. She left me a message from her cell phone in the pouring rain: "Here we are, rain ponchos and all. I'm sure I can get to mile fifteen, but do you think if I can't go further, the marathon van will pick me up?"

Yes, Julia.

"Will I be able to find Thomas at the finish line?"

Yes, Julia.

I thought of how often she had said, "Analysis is my hope. Four, five times a week, seven years." According to her timetable, we were nearly two thirds of the way there. She had anguished as many tears as the raindrops that pelted down that day. Another message: "I made it to mile fifteen. And I found Thomas at the finish line. We've had a wonderful day!"

Yes, Julia, yes. And I will see you in the morning.

Catastrophe soon arrived. Julia began receiving a new spate of alternately cajoling and threatening phone calls from Oscar, on her unlisted phone line. Thomas blanched, unable to cope after all, both with Oscar who had found a way back into Julia's life and with the intensity of her fear and angry reaction to these calls. That, combined with Thomas' newly fueled reaction to Julia still living with her ex-husband, raising her children with him, caused him to leave the relationship. Julia was in a fury at Oscar and Thomas, and fantasized retribution, not acting on any of it. She agonized, "How had Oscar located her, and her private line?" She was stunned but had the strength now to do more.

In a flash of good fortune, Julia received a call from a friend about a fund-raiser dinner featuring the man responsible for setting up the police department's anti-stalking team in a major city. Julia went to the dinner, introducing herself to the speaker afterwards who gave her his card. She met with him within days, and they forged a plan. A new phone trap was set and, shortly, Oscar was apprehended. This anti-stalking leader and his deputy accompanied Julia to court to file a restraining order against Oscar. In the process, they discovered that Oscar had managed to get a position in a tele-marketing company that was able to get access to private numbers. They also learned that there were three other restraining orders in place from other women Oscar had harmed and stalked. One of them now filed charges, with proof. Oscar was given substantial jail time, and Julia was free. She moved into a new home with the children, beginning a new life. She told me in a later session, "The knife is no longer in my back. For the first time since I can remember, it's not there."

Julia's youngest child came of age, and with that came contact from the children's grandmother, Julia's mother, expressing to her granddaughter that she wanted to see her and her brother. While they agreed to an occasional dinner or lunch with her, the children also made it clear to their grandmother that she could not see them on a regular basis unless she was also willing to see their mother. By this time, Julia had mourned in our work the loss of that needed original mother and of the costs of the complex love/hate relationship with her father. Her hatred of her mother had mainly resolved and in its place was wisdom. Julia did meet with her mother, and her mother picked up right where she left off, with seemingly no notice of the intervening lost ten years, still with her sing-song little girl voice dismissing significance. While Julia could re-establish whatever contact with her mother that she wished, she was keenly aware of the substantial limitations that existed in her mother's ability to have anything approaching a reciprocal relationship.

A year after their break-up, Julia received a call from Thomas. He wanted to talk. They met for dinner, Julia a chilly and unforgiving presence. He confessed how afraid he had been, but that on a recent vacation he realized that she was the woman he wanted to spend the rest of his life with. Would she give him another chance?

"No."

Thomas worked at regaining her trust. He did not give up and after several months of earnest proof that he meant what he said, Julia opened her heart again, but with caution. Our work was devoted to processing her relationship with Greg, one they had considered reviving in a romantic way, and how the intricacies of her relationship with her father and her mother challenged her in this possible new relationship with Thomas. As Julia and Greg came to the decision again that their relationship would always be only a heartfelt friendship, Julia opened up more and more to Thomas. After intense therapeutic work on both of their parts, Julia and Thomas were married the following summer. Over the next few months, Julia and I came to the decision that she was ready to decrease her sessions.

During our analytic work, there had been times when Julia admitted having trouble hearing me. Despite my encouragement to get her hearing tested, she avoided doing so, believing that she was too young to have a hearing problem and admitting to some vanity about it. A few months into her new marriage, Thomas insisted she get her hearing tested. The specialist found that, indeed, although her hearing was slightly impacted, he noticed in further tests that it was the signal to her brain that was impaired and causing the problem with her hearing. An MRI revealed a benign tumor, and Julia had surgery for its removal. The surgery was a textbook success, but a few days later when she sneezed inadvertently, she heard a 'pop'. Within two days, she was rushed by Thomas to the hospital in an ambulance and nearly died from an infection caused by bacteria moving from her nasal passages to the surgical site. I agonized as she fought for her life. Fortunately, she survived, miraculously so, with no lingering affects other than fatigue for several months. Thomas never wavered.

After processing this near-death experience during her months of recovery, and during the many weeks as she took her first weakened, tentative steps back into her life, she and Thomas considered future possibilities for their life together, where they might live, eventual marriages for each of their children, then grandchildren, and perhaps, a new career direction for her.

One day, near session's end, she said, "I think my analysis is complete. I've been thinking about this for a year, and I think this is the time."

A year?

I should not have been surprised I guess, but I was. After all, she had kept my name and number for a year before initially calling me for a "full analysis, four to five times a week, seven years." We were actually over that time frame by some seven months. As I encouraged her to discuss this ending, and process the experience of finishing with the analysis, she said to me, "If *you* need to process this, I'm happy to do that for you. But, for me, I really feel this is the last session. After all, I got everything I wanted."

Time was up. In a moment's blur, our experience together filled me with awe, and with this parting, grief. I knew I would be processing my own complex feelings for some time to come. She smiled, her long, shiny hair almost dancing in the light. "You breathed life into me, now I have my life. I know if I ever need you, I can come back, and I will. I love you, and I know you will always be there."

Yes, Julia, I will.

Resolved Trauma and Transformed Development

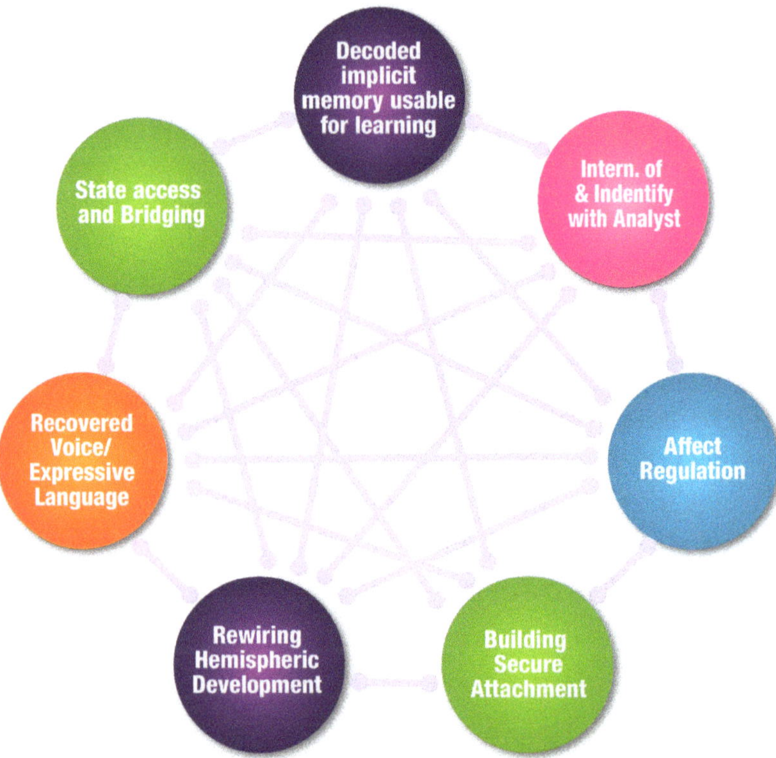

MODEL IV - Renewel of the Essential Self ©Gwyneth Kerr Erwin, 2005

CHAPTER TWENTY

The Seven Keystones of Transformative Development

We have read and seen what is entailed in the deep, challenging, and rewarding work of working with unresolved trauma. Each of the Seven Keystones of Healthy, Wounded, and Traumatized Development have been thoroughly explored, providing us, whether we are clinicians, patients, teachers, students, or parents with a comprehensive lens through which to understand how development proceeds with mastery or is compromised or distorted or arrested by environmental failures and trauma. Now, we turn our attention to see how psychodynamic treatment can be shaped to be compatible with the patient living a life worth living in current time. Model IV of Transformed Development of the Essential Self has as its work and its rewards:

- State Access and bridging
- Decoded Implicit Memory systems making them usable for learning in collaboration with Explicit Memory
- Internalization of and Identification with the therapist's attunement and caring provisions
- Affect regulation
- Secure attachment
- Rewired Hemispheric development
- Recovered personal voice and expressive language

KEYSTONE # 1 – Resolving State Systems

States, "a condition of being" (Putnam, 1997, p. 151), are encompassing, containing memory and mental models as well as perceptual bias, but what is most significant to remember is that they are 'use dependent' (Hebb, 1949), that is, "neurons that fire together, wire together" (p. 70, see also Post & Weiss, 1997).

With healthy development, the individual maintains the sense of essential self even as s/he moves between state experiences. When trauma occurs too early in life, traumatized neuronal pathways are built with looping clusters, and the bridging between life giving states either does not occur or fractures, leaving the child in an internal minefield of reactivity. So, too, for the adults whose state systems are made up of dissociated states imperfectly protecting them from being affectively overwhelmed and physiologically over-or-under aroused. One of the challenges in treatment is accessing these fractured states in ways that are not re-traumatizing and that can build healing bridges between them. On the road to this achievement, though, are the triggering of implicit memory relivings. Decoding and intervening with implicit memory relivings is pivotal to and instrumental in building bridges or links within state architecture since states are use-dependent and implicit memory building encodes state experience. Re-building our state systems is a necessary enterprise for moving toward the health of the self. This re-building takes place within the processing of, gaining insight about, and working through the interactive experience of deep therapy, which establishes new neuronal pathways through new object relating, and helps to de-activate old neuronal systems as implicit memory is decoded and made usable for learning through cross-hemispheric connection to explicit memory.

Julia's mind, for instance, dissociated in an instant her own terror, so as not to be annihilated by it, unconsciously converting it psychoneurobiologically into excitation, which drew her toward danger in an inevitably failing expansive solution, rather than helping her move away or move against it (see Horney, 1945, 1950). Gary Whitmer's (2001) conceptualization of dissociation as an interpersonal defense rather than an intrapsychic one applied to Julia as well. Julia experienced this form of dissociation, too, from her mother's perception and treatment of her, even in earliest infancy, when her mother characterized Julia as "an albatross around her neck."

With repeated injury or neglect, traumatized states can become so engrained that they no longer function only as experience but convert into maladaptive character traits (see Perry et al (1995). In this light, Will 'became' a timid child while Julia 'became' a self-reliant child.

As various patients, including Will and Julia, anguished over their pain and fear provoking states, I have used a particular analogy with my patients. In this analogy, I imagine a bog of quicksand, the equivalent of the implicit memory minefield, or 'bank' of fractured states. No matter how the individual struggles in that quicksand, s/he only sinks deeper. Of course, such a person wants to be rescued from overwhelming experience, even wanting me to "jump in and save her." I know, though, that my task is not to join them in the quicksand, for we would both be lost. But I also know that if I am perched up on a rock on a little hill, at a safe remove, where I can see the quicksand but am not caught in it, I move into a privileged position, not one of empathy or enough of an alignment (Siegel, 1999) either to feel their experience or help them out of it.

Instead, I position myself quite close by, at the very edge of the quicksand, maybe even with my toes in it, where I can see its murky pull, smell its dankness, hear its 'swuup', 'swuup', taste the acrid, thick air around it, but where I can still step back. I am also close enough to throw a rope to my patient and carefully pull her to the edge. Once on safe ground, I carefully wrap her in warmth, care, tenderness, and then move with her to a mossy bank far enough away to be out of the quicksand's lethal grasp, but close enough still to experience it clearly. From this position, we talk together, about what it felt like, what else was in that quicksand, how she stumbled in it or was caught by it unawares, why she was drawn to it, why she could not refuse it. We explore the large and small external factors that played out in the powerful and perhaps irresistible forces of the experience, including anything I might have said or done that inadvertently propelled her into it.

From then on, hopefully, we can come back and sit on that mossy bank near the quicksand at other times, 'visiting' it if necessary, but not needing to be 'in it' again. Of course, this is not a neat and tidy process, especially in the earlier stages of treatment when tests are being made for the patient assessing the analyst's trustworthiness, or when an entrenched implicit memory bank must be relived until it is finally and thoroughly decoded.

Key to the resolution of fractured state systems, as well as implicit memory banks, is affect regulation, ideally within a growing secure attachment. But here again the road is not straight or narrow. The avoidantly attached individual relies almost exclusively upon internal constraints, a system that utterly fails in the face of interpersonal distress. Julia's avoidant attachment to her mother, forged early in life, left her without attunement or comfort, even in her unabated infant crying. Desperate for nourishment that she could incorporate, as Julia fought for her life in the only ways available to her, she was drugged into a submissive state, until she "gave up" (dissociated) that form of communication and her own struggle.

The ambivalently attached person becomes "excessively responsive to inconsistent attachment figures and unable to soothe [her]self... this] approach-withdrawal cycle leaves [the individual] in distress and yet clinging to others in attempts to achieve self-organization" (Siegel, 1999, p. 224). Such was the case for Will, who yearned for a buoyant and vigorous life, but who retreated in the face of life-and-death circumstances and his mother's cocooning, but smothering grasp. Will lived mainly within a confined range of states, a mild zone where he would not move into aroused states of pleasure, of anger, of fear, and of bold living. While a hint of such a state was alluring, it was extinguished quickly in favor of his comfort zone. There, he could feel "fine," be in a state of "mild depression," or a "little anxiety," or much worse, one of failing and being diminished. He could safely experience sexual pleasure with his wife, and the pleasure found in surfing. But what were split off for Will were creatively powered states of strength, of inventiveness, of joy, of discovery.

Likewise, Will found it very "hard" and "difficult" to move into states of terror, grief, even to "feel" the earlier life experiences that carried such significant consequences for him. His mild zoned-out states were contagious for me in the countertransference. This interplay could be thought of rightly as projective identification, perhaps a right-hemisphere-to-right-hemisphere resonance, but mainly I conceptualized my response both as being "given his experience" (and thus being pulled into that bog of quicksand) and being kept at the very privileged remove that would make him feel disconnected from me. Each time I had to work "hard," as he had difficulty doing, to stay alert, to remain focused, in order to help him reach his own dissociated feeling states.

Those individuals with "disorganized attachments are unable to use either internal or external means to regulate their internal states. They live in a chaotic internal world that reflects the external source of terror... which is incompatible with attachment and with a sense of safety" (Seigel, 1999, p. 224-225). For Julia, her early and on-going traumatized states were indeed an internal minefield, set in motion in her childhood by her experiences with her father, in adulthood, with men. Just as Julia was successful at her precocious self-reliance as a baby, toddler, and little girl, so, too, was she successful at cordoning off (dissociating) terror filled states and making choices that would maintain her self-reliant position, as she experienced in her early marriage.

Many times in the treatment, as Julia traversed the chaos inherent in the relationship with Oscar, I was affected by my re-triggered terrors from my own early traumatic experience, fear, of course, for her, but terror within, which I also knew was, at other times, her dissociated state, felt in me when she could not feel it. The paradox was that in order to *feel* safe, Julia had learned implicitly how to split off terrifying feelings; but in order for her to *be* safe, she had to feel the very state she dissociated, a painful enterprise, for her and for me. I both revisited and made productive use of these states and techniques as I learned to use what I was feeling in a surrogate sense as a signal for Julia (and others) until she could tolerate and use this intense state for herself.

For both Will and Julia, the challenge of living inside their own skins, so to speak, was an arduous task, though one not often felt as such by Will. My task, over and over, in assisting them in linking their split off states and learning to make creative use of them was to be willing to stay close to the bog of quicksand, even to have at least one of my very own feet in the lip of it, keeping the other on solid ground, while pulling them to a mossy bank where we could collaborate in deciphering these states, helping them learn to transition states, and use them for protective action and growth.

KEYSTONE # 2 – Decoding Implicit Memory Processes Making Them Usable for Learning

As we have seen throughout this work, implicit (procedural) memory begins to function in the individual in utero in the last trimester, is present at birth, and continues to function throughout the lifespan. Implicit memory formation, in its simplest definition, is the encoding of lived experience, while implicit memory activation is the subsequent retrieval of lived experience, felt as current time experience in the same procedural steps, or order of events, as the originating experience (see Chapter Three), making it both use and state dependent.

Explicit (declarative) memory, on the other hand, begins to function within the individual at approximately three years of age, the same time frame as for left hemispheric 'wiring', and continues throughout the lifespan. This form of memory is cognitive learning, requiring conscious, focal attention for encoding, and as such, represents the encoding and retrieval of factual (or semantic) and autobiographical (or episodic) knowledge and experience.

As I wrote in Chapter Eighteen, when I worked with what I identified as my patients' implicit memory banks, I, like most therapists, used the first two well-known clinical processes of helping patients cope with re-traumatizations, what I determined were 'implicit memory banks': first, bearing witness to their re-traumatizing experience and coming to comprehend the intricacies of how that experience played out and how it impacted them, and second, helping them recover from and re-regulate after such a reliving experience. Third, I worked with my patients in planning how to intervene with subsequent re-traumatizations in the face of likely re-triggerings, planning which was sometimes successful but more often resulted in failed attempts due to the intensity of what was being re-lived.

I discovered the fourth and most effective way of working with these powerful re-livings by turning to the procedural steps of the implicit memory and planning interventions within each transitional shift, so that if one intervention did not succeed, another opportunity was just ahead (see Procedural Steps Planning Pages in the Appendices). These event and affectively laden state transitions were where rich and viable solutions became available. The power of the procedural steps of the implicit memory banks held not only the problem but the solution!

With both Will and Julia, as I was with them in their traumatic relivings and came to understand what was playing out, we utilized the three ways of working with implicit memory. But as we learned, the fourth opportunity of mapping out the procedural steps of an "implicit memory bank" (Erwin, 2005), offered the most innovative and effective path to potent change.

Three examples provide a glimpse into this dynamic decoding and intervention endeavor. In the first, Will and I examined over a long period of time and in several ways, including our work with colored blocks, how he lost track of himself and of his daily activities. Finally, we pieced together his difficulty specifically with morning times and the procedural steps involved with that time of day:

1) When Will was still self-employed, he woke early in the morning, about 5:30 or so.
2) At that point, he experienced an internal barrage of criticism and doubt concerning whatever he was currently worrying about.
3) After perhaps a half an hour of this internal assault, he forced himself to gather up and get out of bed.
4) Then he brought in the newspaper, made lunches for the family, and woke up Samantha and the three children.
5) While they were stirring, he showered and dressed.
6) While they dressed, he prepared breakfast.
7) After the rest of the family was dressed as well, they had breakfast together.
8) At 7:30, Samantha left for work, with Will taking his sons and daughter to school.
9) By 8:30, with fresh-baked donuts he purchased, Will returned home and made a fresh pot of coffee.
10) He sat down, luxuriating in his coffee and doughnuts, opened the newspaper, and began reading.
11) Hours would pass, as he read every word of the newspaper, in every section, back to front.
12) About 11:30 or noon, or sometimes later, he emerged from the newspaper, felt in a fog, noticed the time, but was disoriented, and while thinking he ought to get to work, had difficulty remembering exactly what was on the docket for that day.
13) He struggled to organize enough to work for a few hours.

14) At 3:30, he picked up the kids from school, ran necessary errands, and returned home to collapse on the couch, exhausted.

The first step that changed was the early morning barrage of superego assault that Will usually experienced. In this instance, the change was the result of Will internalizing me and my belief in his potentially robust self. As I became his "light at the end of the tunnel," the barrage diminished. The other steps, returning home to coffee, donuts, and the newspaper, we first understood dynamically as the regressive pull back to his agoraphobic mother and the cocooning she provided, following in his father's retreating footsteps from a vigorous life. Will came to *feel* how every morning was a crisis of choice: would he retreat as had his father, or withdraw to be his mother's version of him, her companion, her timid, retreating-from-the-world, boy? Or would he brave facing the world and engage with it, despite the risks it might pose?

In line with 'working through' procedural and step transition interventions, we tried various strategies, from saving reading the newspaper until the end of a working day as a reward, to planning his work the night before, to shortening the time with the newspaper in decreasing time, initially to two hours, then an hour and a half, then an hour, and to stop reading by a specific time, to using time itself as a transition between the newspaper and going to work, and on and on. Will's many insights as we grappled with this intervention process were rewarding to him, but the working through part was more formidable. He struggled to take notice of how he felt, of what came up for him dynamically as he engaged in this conflict of choice. More than a year passed of one thing working, then not, another strategy working, and then not, before Will finally landed successfully and reliably on a twenty-minute pass at the newspaper, returning to it later in the day after work, or sometimes, not. We also found that the transitional space between steps needed to be only about three to five minutes before he engaged in the next activity required of him, except for lunchtime. By treatment's successful conclusion, he was at work by 7:30, working productively until 5:30. He still struggled with his energy flagging at the end of the day, but that became mainly the result of a hard day's work.

The turning point in Julia's relationship with Oscar and the implicit reliving within that relationship ultimately came after she and I had processed and decoded the sequence of terror and arousal that took place in her relational experiences with her father and played out in the interactions with Oscar. Julia then made the brave move to meet with Oscar to tell him that she would not see him for a month. Over many months we had also processed and struggled with how "hooked" she became with him, and for many weeks, we discussed the typical procedural steps she faced in their meetings and the possible transition points between them:

1) Dinner with Oscar in a quiet, intimate setting on a Saturday night when her children were with their father.
2) At the end of dinner and wine, she tried to leave.
3) Oscar cajoled her, enticing her by touching her arm, or she reached out to feel his 'smooth, hairless' skin
4) At this point, she began to 'melt'.
5) He promised they would have an exciting time together.
6) She resisted
7) He threatened.
8) She felt terror, then excitation.
9) She left with him.
10) He already had several drinks but insisted on driving.
11) She cajoled him into letting her drive.
12) She took him home, but was quickly overpowered by him, either through his threatening her physical harm or forcing himself on her sexually, which she immediately found exciting.

13) After he passed out, before or after their aggressive sexual encounter, she slipped away and drove home.
14) Once she was safely at home, the internal repercussions began.

These steps were procedurally accurate repetitions of what Julia experienced with her father:

1) Young Julia and her father engaged together in a close and interesting activity.
2) At the end of which, Julia grew restless.
3) Her father further enticed her, becoming physically affectionate.
4) She settled in again (beginning 'to melt')
5) He promised her more exciting adventures.
6) She got nervous and resistant.
7) He became threatening, accusing her of 'spoiling' their time together.
8) She felt terror, then excitation.
9) She stayed with her father.
10) He started drinking at this point, if he hadn't already. Then, he ranted and raved if at home, or took her (and perhaps her siblings and mother) driving, drunk.
11) She cajoled him again, trying to calm him down.
12) He overpowered her either by the fact of his age, strength, and/or activity.
13) When he passed out later, she escaped to her own room, her own bed.
14) Once safely there, the internal repercussions of her failure to calm him down, or her shame for joining him, began.

Now, we planned the interventions with Oscar. First, she would arrange to meet him at a busy restaurant near an outdoor mall where there was a good deal of activity on a Saturday night. Next, she would park her car under or near a lighted area. Ahead of time, she found out when a security patrol of the mall would be on duty and scheduled a meeting with the security guard at a specific time to walk her back to her car. Shortly after she arrived, instead of ordering a drink and dinner, she told Oscar that she would not be able to see him 'for a while'. We worked out that the minute he reached for her arm or hand or shoulder, and instead of her reaching out to touch him, she would stand up, be willing to bump into other customers of the restaurant to make a stir, create a bit of a noisy exit if necessary, and start walking to the security guard. The guard would accompany her to the car, wait with her until she locked her door, fastened her seat belt, started the car, and drove off. She had sold her car and purchased a new one the day prior, one Oscar would not recognize. Startled when she left him behind, and seeing her walking with the security guard, he did not follow, and thus did not see the new car she drove away in. She also re-scheduled her hours at the hospital, so that their contact was greatly minimized, and she was protected whenever their paths crossed. Although his phone calls and messages multiplied tenfold or more on a daily basis, in sessions, Julia struggled to come to terms with her kaleidoscopic feelings, mostly not giving in to believing his promises or caving in under his threats.

A very different kind of intervention with Julia's implicit memory banks occurred during the phase of the analysis when Julia began to draw her early experience with her mother and father. During these months of nearly silent work, a profound transformation of implicit memory took place for Julia. Previously, in her young life, the procedural steps of Julia's isolation were:

1) She tried to communicate any distress to her mother.
2) When that invariably brought no results, she played by herself, organizing something in her environment or taking care of her younger sister.
3) She tried to manage her distress, or get on top of whatever reaction she might be having to her traumatic experience.
4) Eventually, she tired, and started spiraling down into depression.
5) She got through the evening pretending to be okay, or dealing with another frightening experience with her father, kissed her parents good-night, tucked herself in, and had screaming nightmares, or startled awake, feeling a terrifying presence in her bedroom.

In adulthood, Julia attempted to calm and re-organize herself in the face of retriggering by:

1) 'Sitting' with herself to find a way to get on top of whatever reaction she was having to a trigger of her traumatic experience by caring for her children or organizing something in her home.
2) While she could not stay with her thoughts for very long without becoming much more distressed, she could organize for hours, finding relief and pride in her efforts.
3) Afterwards, she wanted to share her pleasure at the organizing success with her husband, but he was either still at the office, or not very interested in her activity, even finding it intrusive that she organized 'his mess'.
4) Soon, her depression wound its way around her like smoke, eventually enveloping her.
5) She got the kids off to bed, and went to bed herself, only to have screaming nightmares, or startling awake, feeling a terrifying presence in her bedroom.

Compare these to the steps we co-created and shared in the office:

1) Julia arrived with her drawing materials and settled herself cross-legged on the couch, facing me.
2) Slowly and deliberately, she took out a black pencil and opened a sheet of paper and sat quietly, considering what early experience she wanted to try to capture and process.
3) After maybe three to five minutes or so, she made her choice and began to draw.
4) When she finished the drawing, she chose the pencils that 'fit' and colored in her drawing.
5) Once satisfied, she added a couple of sentences to the drawing, top and bottom.
6) Then, she handed it to me.
7) I took several minutes to study the drawing, allowing the impact of her experience to affect me.
8) I certainly exhibited facial expressions or gestures of what I was feeling, and often, offered a verbal response as well.
9) Finally, I read the sentences silently, allowing myself to fully resonate with her affect in the drawings, then returned to the beginning of her story and read it aloud to her all the way through.

During several of these sessions, I again thought of Winnicott's (1958/1965) paper, "The Capacity To Be Alone." He wrote, "…actually to be alone is not what I am discussing…. Although many types of experience go to the establishment of the capacity to be alone, there is one that is basic, and without a sufficiency of it the capacity to be alone does not come about; *this experience is that of being alone, as an infant and small child, [or patient] in the presence of [m]other*. Thus the basis of the capacity to be alone is a paradox; it is the experience of being alone while someone else is present" (p. 30).

I came to understand this creative, but communicative, silence as a very pivotal part of healing Julia's sheltered wound of isolation and abject aloneness through our shared experience. S. Nacht (1963) asked: "How is this fundamental need for union manifested during the course of analysis? Precisely when the flow of words ceases, giving way to silence, to a silence experienced in serenity, in tranquility. Experience has shown me many times that the patient in the midst of this silence finds an ... internal state of union with the object-analyst, through which he ... reaches ... the innermost depths of his unconscious" (p. 335).

In the presence of this exquisite and most tender of processes, I felt the power and the majesty in this healing, creative act. David Aberbach (1989) wrote of the "struggle for mastery over grief-ridden trauma" (p. 274): Through creativity, the artist [patient] may confront and attempt to master the trauma on his own terms and, in so doing, complete the work of mourning. The unresolved elements of grief may thus themselves be both motive and substance in creativity" (p. 275).

In these decoding endeavors, I found through the "something more than interpretation, those profound 'moments of meeting,' [that] emergent property of the 'moving along' process that alters the intersubjective environment, and thus the *implicit relational knowing*" (D. Stern, 1998, p. 909). As well, the "model scenes" (Lachmann and Lichtenberg, 1992, p. 117) depicted in Julia's drawings, enabled us to "organize previously puzzling information, further integrate previous understanding, and initiate further exploration of the analysand's experience and motivations" (p. 117-118). Julia and I also experienced through "the level of unconscious enactive procedures, the medium is the message; that is, the organization of meaning is implicit in the organization of the enacted relational dialogue" (Lyons-Ruth, 1999, p. 578). Implicit memory banks, traumatized though they may be, hold not only the problem but the solution, where we thought there was none.

KEYSTONE # 3 – Internalization of and Identification with the Therapist

- **Internalization**

Described in Chapter Four was how internalization (Meissner, 1976, 1979) is the *process* by which *who someone started out to be* is built up. This transformational process utilizes external relationships, interactions, and forms of regulation for the purpose of building the *structure* of the internal world, thus setting the tone for the *experience* of the inner world (see Meissner, 1971). Internalization occurs first through incorporation in the earliest months of life, then through primary, and then secondary identifications, ideally in the emotional tie service of growing the developing child's ego, or essential and sense of self.

- **Incorporation**

We have seen that incorporation is the first means by which the infant takes in the m(other), internalizing her into the "inner psychic organization" (Meissner, 1971, p. 287), a parallel to the physical process of oral ingestion. As a mechanism of internalization, incorporation in the oral phase means that, "The union is such that the external object is completely assumed into the inner world of the subject" (p. 287). In Will's experience, his birth trauma not only interrupted even his initial emergency cry for oxygen and the breathing it should foster, but it also stifled the 'emergence' of his true voice, both consequences setting in motion the incorporation of an experience of frailty, before he had the chance to experience an initially robust, searching/finding, self.

For Julia, this incorporation process was abruptly attenuated by her mother's decision to wean her infant from the breast as soon as the mother returned from the hospital when Julia was only five days old. Julia's subsequent battle for the breast can be seen as her early and ferocious attempts to have an object to incorporate, thus to quite literally 'feed' her growing self. Instead, what she was left to incorporate were the introjects of her mother's projections onto Julia as being an "albatross around her [the mother's] neck."

For Will and Julia, the earliest moments of experiencing their essential selves were not only interrupted but traumatized, and their processes of internalization compromised with the introjects (Ferenczi, 1909, Jacobson, 1964) of trauma rather than with objects who each infant could incorporate to help grow their young essential selves. W. W. Meissner (1971) explains in different terms this process that leads to what I call the conversion of trauma into the idealization of the sheltered wound: "Introjections [as] internalizations effectively alter the inner psychic structure in significant ways ... introjects thus become structural components of the psychic system [the superego] but enjoy a certain autonomy that distinguishes them from ego components" (p. 292-293). Introjection is a process of internalization through which objects relations are replaced by an internal modification of the self in the form of an introject" (p. 300).

These powerful introjects become incorporated in the infant by being encoded as a part of implicit memory 'banks', stored as "somatic markers" (Siegel, 1999, p. 143-44) in bodily egos (Freud, 1923/1955, Novick, 1990), or undifferentiated psyche-somas (Winnicott, 1949/1975). When such trauma occurs so early in life, the infant does not even have the opportunity to 'be inside' its essential self. Instead, the trauma is encoded unconsciously into the infant's undifferentiated bodymind through the firing and subsequent wiring of neuronal pathways, converting the essential self into the *wounded self* **felt** as his or her essential self.

This traumatized incorporation process, where the infant/child internalizes introjects rather than affirming objects, sets the stage for the infant/young child moving into the primary identification phase already compromised.

- **Identification**

Whether this identification with trauma came into being through its encoding, without conscious awareness, into an undifferentiated bodymind in infancy, or imprinted through a dissociative response to overwhelming affective experience in young childhood, or as a conscious gathering of testimony to self-experience and as the way to hold onto their integrity of being after the age of three, these individuals suffer from being caught in a terrible bind: their sources of attachment were also their perpetrators.

As a young child, Will had a father with whom he could identify, but in the paradoxical relationship with his mother, a combination of her agoraphobia, her conflict with others, and her overprotective stance with Will, his identification process became far more complicated. The near-fatal car accident, and his prolonged and cocooned recovery, followed by his being overly sheltered, even after recovery, concretized his identification with trauma, putting in place his *sheltered wound* of being vulnerable and weak. Although he tried to strive for an active life, the consequences of his youthful impulsive jump from the carport roof, his inability to compete in team sports, his father's withdrawal from his own vigorous life, followed by Will's uncle's death, eventually solidified Will's conviction that he could not trust himself in a world that seemed unsafe. Any bold striving put him at serious risk.

The greatest challenge in the analytic identificatory process with Will was whether or not he could dare allow himself to internalize me as a support for his own robust self. This challenge was faced over and over again, because while such necessary identification was life saving for Will, it also represented a kind of psychic death to what was familiar. Will's ambivalence, passivity, and timidity were known to him, despite how miserable they also felt to him. Keeping in place his sheltered wound, his vulnerable and weakened self protected him against risk that seemed overwhelming. While action had its fantasy appeal, it seemed mainly dangerous when he was on the threshold of it. At particular choice points—going to his cousin's funeral, confronting the requirements in his marriage, returning for his graduate degree—Will wondered as we have seen if I was encouraging him down a garden path? A number of times, he did not make a choice or act, or even remember the possibility of choice that could lead to a new identification and the healing process, but, instead, relived his early traumas by collapsing in his current life. His terror of the risks in living, and the untrustworthiness of the few impulses he dared to act on earlier in his life (striving to become an architect his first year of college, his teenage marriage, for instance), immobilized him. Even this immobilization was not felt as a consequence of these earlier traumatic experiences, but rather, as a defect within his very being.

In the presence of his immobilization and psychical deadening, I also could become deadened in the sessions. This grogginess threatened to overtake me, just as I was becoming anesthetized by the repetitive 'starting over' of the sessions, I could feel myself fading or 'draining out'. Again and again, I had to marshal my own resilient self, not to overprotect his most tender self, not to become, even countertransferentially, the 'giving up' father or the mother who cocooned him, but to help him build the internal resources he needed to deal with the requirements of life, and especially, even be the analyst who kindly but firmly challenged him to confront a vigorous way of living. I needed to exhibit my belief in him, and courage for him, that he had the fervor, the intelligence, and the creativity to step out into the world and succeed. *That*, at last, despite his doubts and fears, he finally internalized and identified with.

In Julia's case, her premature ego development (see Martin James, 1960) and later precocious self-reliance resulted from her being 'motherless', in the sense that Julia's mother was both physically mal-attuned and psychically absent. James' article also helped me understand the economical and graceful presence I saw in Julia: "The characteristic or fey manneristic qualities are, of course, then not only descriptively but metapsychologically diagnostic of an early narcissistic trauma" (p. 292). Julia did not have a mother who could protect, shelter, and 'hold' her, communicate empathy through her affective attunement and who took Julia's needs seriously. Instead, the one person who could soothe and enliven Julia when she was an infant and child was her charismatic but violent and terrorizing father. Jodie Wigren (1999) wrote, "In a situation of overwhelming threat and anxiety, the child precociously adapts, taking upon the self those protective and defensive functions that should yet remain between self and other. To preserve relationship, perpetrators are misperceived to invent and emphasize positive qualities, while the self takes to itself false identities of power and badness" (p. 257).

Julia's *sheltered wound* (Erwin, 2023) had two branches. One was represented in the dream of herself as a four-year-old who is sent out from the medieval city, disowned, with only a pushcart, one which she could barely manage. She was gotten rid of, sent away to protect the 'inhabitants'. This branch of Julia's sheltered wound was of being the scapegoat, bereft and alone, needing to depend upon herself when she had only the barest of resources with which to cope. The other branch of her wounding was represented by the sensation of the knife plunged into and stuck in her back, the tie to the father who terrorized but excited her. These two branches of wounding then bound her to Oscar, who, though he terrorized her, also excited her and resonated with her wounds, providing her with some sense of 'belonging', and an odd kind of hope.

What the child internalizes, Peter Shabad (1997) explained, is "… the unmourned and, therefore, repeated aspects of the parent's history that have become entrenched in the parent's character and are continually enacted on the child; the helplessness engendered by the traumatic theme derives from the child's continued incapacity to change the parent into a wished-for figure… [the child] must bear the burden of proving the reality of his experiences alone… when the child's experience is that no one is there, he turns inwardly and immediately adapts… by learning stoically how to go it alone and rely on his own resources, a self-reliance that all too often seems to be one of the residual casualties of growing up" (pp. 350-353).

In the analysis, I walked a delicate balance, almost always needing to let Julia lead the way, because had I done otherwise, she would have ended treatment. Yet, she needed so desperately someone to whom she could turn who was attentive and sincerely caring about her, and with whom she could process her trauma filled life, as well as her current daily life experiences. She needed to internalize me for a new kind of calming regulator of affects and states, for a secure attachment, to experience with her the story of her life. But the identification for growing her essential self came only after I proved, again and again, to be the kind of analytic parent who could finally have the emotional authority and authenticity that allowed the relinquishment of the power of her original rejecting and psychically absent mother and her violently terrorizing but exciting father, as well as Julia's own self-reliance, her "Orpha function," (Smith, 2001, p. 5-6), which had helped her survive. More than anything else, especially in the face of my own fears *for* her, it was my learned ability to find and maintain my 'equi-presence' with the playing out of each state aspect of her object world, hand-in-hand with my own states, my genuine affection and respect for, and availability to her, which ultimately allowed her to form an identification with me that initiated the healing of her sheltered wounds.

KEYSTONE # 4 – Affect and Its New Regulation

Affect (see Darwin, 1872/1965, Tompkins, 1962, Stern, 1985, Trevarthen, 1993, for instance), often considered synonymous with emotion, is indivisible from concurrent physiological sensation, and thus has a psychoneurobiological interface. Affective experience is triggered by information coming into the brain through neural pathways from either external or internal stimuli.

Affect, therefore, plays a central role within psychoanalysis, both in theory-making and in the clinical endeavor. Peter Knapp (1987) viewed patients as coming to "psychotherapy because of emotional distress: psychoanalytic technique aims to penetrate defensive mechanisms that ward off full awareness of distress and to expose underlying conflicts, primarily as they emerge in the immediate therapeutic encounter. This strategy is intended to sustain emotional intensity" (p. 227, see also Plutchik, 1962).

Beginning at birth, then overtime into adulthood, Will defaulted to the *hypoaroused* side of the Arousal continuum. While I do not imagine that he would have been that kind of baby had he not experienced his birth trauma, by the time he arrived in adulthood, Will had learned how to 'dampen down' at all costs. His usual presentation was that he was "fine," although he could also feel anxious or "somewhat depressed."

The Arousal Chart (Lillas, 1994, Erwin, 2000) shows the parasympathetic, inhibitory arena of affective life in which Will lived. He fluctuated within a narrow range, from Aware, with in and out processing, to Awake and non-processing, to Distracted, to Shutting Down, and back again. With stimulus, when he moved into the sympathetic range of excitation, he became immediately Anxious and soon Flooded, dampening down quickly to return to *his* homeostasis, the Shutting Down/Hypoaroused mode. In terms of Karen Horney's work and Connie Lillas' formulations, Will's primary interpersonal style was 'moving away' (Horney, 1945), with the physiological correlate in the face of stress a blend of both activated arousal followed by a desire to withdraw, associated with his fright response (see Lillas, 2005). Under the pressure of these conflicting states, Will sought to travel in a 'mild zone', the only one that felt safe to him. Max Stern (1951) captured such a person's dilemma: "Since shock was once experienced as reality, and as even signal anxiety can deteriorate into shock, the anxiety process includes a realistic element progressively gaining strength.... In anxiety we always experience a weak reproduction of the shock, felt as paralysis, and of the defense reaction, as urge to discharge" (p. 193).

In sessions, Will professed the yearning to be bold and robust, and though he felt much more alive when he had an intensity of feeling, he reverted within moments to his safety zone of muted feeling. Harvey Milkman and Stanley Sunderwirth (1987) showed that for those individuals who use *fantasy* as the "preferred way of dealing with the world" (p. 19), they "favor repetitive activation of what some researchers refer to as right-hemisphere thinking. Thoughts become dreamlike, with rapidly shifting imagery and illogical relations between time and space.... People who rely on this style partially overcome their fears by creating fantasies in which they are effective and important" (p. 19). Ironically, in this dampened down, fantasy zone, Will's ability to process his inner world and his outer experience was compromised because he did not have the affective cues he needed for authentic emotion, interaction, and action.

As shown in Chapter Thirteen, Bessel van der Kolk and Alexander McFarlane (1996) explored six issues facing individuals with PTSD dysregulation. Of the six aspects they discussed, Will exhibited five: "1) They experience persistent intrusions of [*implicit*] memories related to the trauma, which interferes with attending to other incoming information ... 3) they actively attempt to avoid specific triggers of trauma-related emotions, and experience a generalized numbing of responsiveness, 4) they lose the inability to modulate their physiological responses to stress in general, which leads to a decreased capacity to utilize bodily signals as guides for action, 5) they suffer from generalized problems with attention, distractibility, and stimulus discrimination, and 6) they have alterations in their psychological defense mechanisms and in personal identity. This changes what new information is selected as relevant" (p. 9). Will's own reaction to his timidity was to feel humiliated and shamed by it: "[subjective] shame as the central emotion in

[his] disordered sense of self" (Malin, 1999, p. 374) and objectively felt, self-aware shame as a "specific and emotional disturbance.... in the disorders of the self" (p. 375, see also Tompkins, 1963, Izard, 1977, Ablon, 1990, Yorke, 1990, Broucek, 1991, Lewis, 1993, Shengold, 1988, Lansky, 1999).

Francis Broucek's (1982) work on shame is pivotal in understanding shame-based experience: "When the already shame-capable child reaches the stage of development when he becomes self-conscious in the objective sense, the shame experience takes on new phenomenological characteristics—a painfully heightened awareness of self as an object of observation for others, with an attendant wish to withdraw or hide one's self" (p. 371, see also Papousek & Papousek, 1975). Through all the research I studied, through my own analytic experience, and in the therapeutic work with Will and Julia, I formulated that when we are traumatically shamed, we can no longer exist as both a subject and an object with a sense of self and other, but instead become *objectified,* leading to a degraded sense of *repudiated self* and *dangerous other* and the failed sense of self-agency and efficacy.

There was never an instance in our seven plus years together where the regulation Will required was for 'calming', soothing and comforting, yes. Rather, the regulation we have engaged in throughout treatment was to enliven him and help him tolerate full, vibrant affect, especially positive affect (Tompkins, 1962). Anger, too, others' anger, but more so, his own, was frightening to Will. Confronted with Samantha's frustration or outrage, Will became quickly conciliatory and compliant, collapsed, or passive aggressive. This immobilization and becoming weak was his dysregulation, but one which had at its heart, a striving for psychical safety. For a long period of time in treatment, he feared his own anger would mean "the end of [his] world," that his anger would destroy everything, so he was safe only when it 'came out' in disguised forms. Ultimately, he was better able to tolerate others' anger and manage his own responses to it, to think about what they might be upset about, feel his own feelings, and work it out. He was also more able to become angry himself and better able to find ways to communicate directly the reasons for his feelings.

What was even more difficult to breathe life into was Will's capacity for 'passion' (see Bion, 1963/1977). Will and his wife were very compatible sexually, and, in fact, their active sexual life was the saving grace in the marriage many times, the way in which they could find connection. But Will struggled with "deep," i.e., intense, feeling. As van der Kolk and Fisler (1994) argued, "the loss of the ability to regulate the intensity of feeling is the most far-reaching effect of early trauma" (p. 187). Will did not lose this capacity so much as he never had the opportunity to develop it. Although he became much more able and willing to tolerate such depth of emotional experience, he found it "hard" to get there, especially when it concerned something that meant so much to him—his own creativity. He yearned to "take [his] creativity seriously," but it always came last, if at all. I think this was the garden path Will feared going down, because he so wanted to embrace art that was edgy, bold, and non-traditional. The work that remained toward the end of treatment for Will and me is what Peter Fonagy (2002) referred to as "mentalized affectivity" (p. 435), the "changing [of] one's relation to one's own affects" (p. 468), of intensity, of creative striving, of passion.

Julia had a much broader range of categorical affects (Darwin, 1872/1965, Tompkins, 1978) available to her at the beginning of treatment than did Will. Defaulting to the *hyperaroused* side of the Arousal continuum made Julia's internal world of vitality affects (Stern, 1985) a landscape of the "naked horror of loneliness" (Fromm-Reichmann, 1990, p. 309), depression, fear, a sense of 'trudging on', 'doing the right thing', and, at times, desperation. Returning to van der Kolk's and McFarland's (1996) six critical issues from which those suffering with PTSD are affected (see under Will, this section), Julia struggled with all six, including, "... 2) they sometimes compulsively expose themselves to situations reminiscent of the trauma"(p. 9). Despite these burdens, Julia had an exquisite sensitivity to the most subtle nuances of others, picking up 'information' from the very air around her. She lived an exemplary life, was an attentive, attuned, yet anxious mother, setting very high standards for herself. But she was also strong-willed, a capacity she forged in her earliest days of life, so she could plant her feet and follow her own counsel exclusively (at times to her detriment), the result of her precocious self-reliance, her 'expansive solution' (see Horney, 1950).

In Virginia Demos' (1986) research model, Demos focused on three aspects of affective complexes: "(a) the triggering event or stimulus, (b) the affective experience per se, and (c) the response of the organism to its own affective experience" (p. 53). Using this model, we can understand Julia's earliest experience with her mother as (a) the triggering event—Julia's mother forceful weaning her from the breast, (b) the affective experience per se—the terror of having a primary need fulfillment withdrawn, and (c) the response to affective experience—Julia's unabated crying (see also Greenacre, 1965, Bick, 1968). But this was just the beginning of years of trauma for Julia. Next, her response to the affective experience of her crying was suppressed by the Phenobarbital. As we saw, Julia was able to capture the experience of this suppression in her drawings. The drawings pictorially represented what Joan Symington (1985) described as: a "catastrophic fear ... of a state of unintegration and spilling out into space and of never being found and held again" (p. 481).

Edward Tronick (1989) recognized that "infants ... evaluate whether they are succeeding or failing and then use that evaluation to guide actions aimed at accomplishing their goal or redirecting their efforts to other goals" (p. 113, see also Trevarthen, 1993).... An evaluation by the infant that the goal is being accomplished results in a positive emotional state ... motivating further engagement ... [when it is] not being accomplished, the infant experiences negative emotions" (p. 113) and may attempt to overcome the obstacle or instead withdraw. Any immediate situation, positive or negative, can have lasting results, if the effects become internally represented.

So it was for Julia, who 'evaluated' early on that her goals of reaching her mother for soothing and processing in feeding, and for comfort in her unabated crying, were not successful. By six months, Julia was feeding herself, with her first words being "Me do." Thus, her precocious self-reliance was established. In all of these ways, Julia fit Greenspan's (1997a) Hypersensitive/Fearful and Hypersensitive/Stubborn, Defiant regulatory disorder types. Looking again at the Arousal Chart (Lillas, 1994, Erwin, 2000), as Julia lived primarily on the sympathetic, excitatory side of the arousal continuum, she was mostly in an Alert and Alert/Anxious position where she was extremely vigilant and finely attuned to her surround and its stimuli. Her interpersonal style of relating was mainly 'moving toward' (Horney, 1945), with the physiological correlate of hyperarousal and its quick swing into acceleration (Lillas, 2005). Despite Julia's almost constant state of hyperalertness, she did not, however, usually withdraw when she experienced activated arousal. Instead, her 'moving toward' increased dramatically and precipitously (see Milkman & Sunderwirth, 1987). Any dampening down in Julia came with the cost of her moving into a Shutting Down/Hypoaroused mode where she became depressed and despairing and experienced a profound sense of futility.

What was unleashed for Julia in being raped the night before she began our full analysis was the wild conversion of terror into excitation, her implicit memory reliving. This overwhelming experience propelled her into a Flooded, Disorganized, and finally Chaotic place (see Arousal Chart) where she then would vacillate between terror and freezing (immobilization), terror and flight, and occasionally rage and fighting back. In this spectrum of dysregulation, Julia's arousal system could not maximize her emotional and physiological states for self-protective action but reinforced her learned maladaptation to her father's chaotic states and her ferocious need for him. Leonard Shengold (1979) helped us understand this ability to "doublethink" (p. 540): "Soul murder involves trauma imposed from the world outside the mind that is so overwhelming that the mental apparatus is flooded with feeling.... The terrifying 'too-muchness' requires massive and mind-distorting defensive operations in order for the child to continue to think and feel" (p. 530). This is precisely why one can love a torturing other.

The lack of availability of recovery processes from Julia's parents consigned her to being a prisoner in her own internal emotional minefield, the disorganizing effects of her own arousal. Sandor Ferenczi (1934) reminded us: "Shock is a destruction of the ability to offer resistance and to think and act in one's own defense" (p. 179). Paraphrasing van der Kolk and McFarlane's (1996) work on how individuals dysregulate and process information in the face of severe trauma, with Oscar, as Julia had with her father, she 1) compulsively exposed herself to situations reminiscent of the trauma with her father, 2) lost her ability to modulate her physiological responses to stress, leading to a decreased capacity to utilize her bodily signals as guides for action, and 3) had alterations in her psychological defense mechanisms and in her personal identity, changing what new information was selected as relevant (see p. 9).

Harvey Milkman and Stanley Sunderwirth (1987) offered me a way of understanding the role Julia's brain chemistry played in her "joy of fear" (p. 93). She could become immersed "in an activity that is incompatible with serious self-evaluation" (p. 15). She could "feel active and potent in the face of an environment that [she] view[ed] as overwhelmingly dehumanizing.... [Her] vast expenditures of mental and physical energy [we]re designed to deny underlying fears of helplessness" (p. 19). Dopamine was increased in her nucleus accumbens, the major reward center of her brain.

Jodie Davies and Mary Frawley's (1994) work was also helpful to me: "...the more sadistic the forms of abuse, the earlier age of the onset, the more central the relationship between victim and perpetrator, the more overwhelmed and disorganized the patient will become... with no self-reflective ego [in those moments] to provide even the rudiments of containment, meaning, and structure to the traumatic events, the child [patient] exists in a timeless, objectless, and selfless nightmare of unending pain, isolation, and ultimately psychic dissolution" (p. 44-45).

Over a three-year period, there was not a single time after an interaction with Oscar that Julia did not feel the repercussions of a superego assault on her very selfhood, the disorders of her self (Kohut and Wolf, 1978). At such moments, she agonized with shame over what I must think of her. She dreaded each day, dreaded the irresistible draw to Oscar, dreaded her own internal consequences of being with him. Ehud Koch (2000) described such dread as, "an extreme form of fear that is induced by terror and horror" (p. 289), which is "manifested in the shapes of a 'dreaded self' and a 'dreaded states of the self'" (p. 289). The common threads running through such dreaded experiences of self and state of the self are: "suddenness and unexpectedness, the potential arousal of intense and overwhelming affect; the loss of one's agency, experiences as acute helplessness or being out of control; and the threat to one's sense of what is 'real', either in one's self or in the external world" (p. 301). Ultimately, such dread is "the experience of *horror* and *terror*... a wary *anticipation of repeating and reexperiencing the awful,* without the aid of an adaptive personal agency" (p. 312).

Julia was mainly in the masochistic position with Oscar being the sadist, yet they could shift roles, especially if Oscar tormented Julia in those moments when she was most 'needing' him. Anna Ornstein (1998) explained such a dichotomy: "Sadistic behavior expresses the rage directly... masochistic behavior also expresses the rage, but [does] so indirectly. Masochistic behavior, in particular, is a powerful accusation directed at the offender for the mental anguish that [the individual] experience[s] as having been carelessly or deliberately inflicted on them" (p. 56). From either position, the individual is "compelled to revenge themselves in order to reestablish self-cohesion and/or a damaged self-esteem.... Narcissistic rage, then... arises from a matrix of a fragmented self or a self that is threatened with fragmentation" (p. 57).

Most often, manipulated by the traumatizing other, such as her father or Oscar, Julia experienced "a catastrophic breakdown of potential space [the location for self-development] ... the disruption of basic beliefs and internalization of malevolent objects ... the destruction of fundamental relationship and the consequent ability of the self to perceive itself as human ... wreak[ing] havoc on the psyche of [this] developing child" (Wigren, 1999, p. 256). But in the next time of being with Oscar, Julia's affective signals of fear/terror, shame, dread and judgment evaporated in an instant, replaced with a driving craving to touch him and his smooth, hairless skin, accompanied by an overpowering excitation in being with him. Milkman and Sunderwirth (1987) explained such a dynamic: "The repeated pairing of opposite emotional experiences, and their underlying physiological counterparts, may be the sustaining force behind all forms of human compulsion" (p. 104). Julia also did not have an "empathic wall" (Nathanson, 1986, p. 175) that would allow her "to monitor [her] affective experience and determine whether the affect of the moment [wa]s generated from within or without, thus defining the difference between self and other" (pp. 175-176).

In the transference, I could variously seem and become to Julia the ineffective mother who was helpless to intervene, or who 'passed her over' to the malevolent other; I could be the spoiler of her exciting pleasure, an unwelcome conscience, or fearful about her well-being, as she herself was after each incident. Most times, I was the containing and soothing other, the new involved and caring object who worked with her to process, decode, and comprehend her experience.

We worked in ways that I learned later were quite similar to Fonagy's (2002) three elements of mentalized affectivity. We spent much time *identifying* the emotions Julia felt under everyday experiences versus times with Oscar. We used The Arousal Chart (Lillas, 1994, Erwin, 2000) to help her track her arousal process and her affective response to various kinds of stimulation. As I pointed out earlier, one of the most difficult and paradoxical challenges in the treatment was to help Julia, and myself, stay with her terror rather than move into its conversion (excitation for Julia, numbing or the threat of internal fatigue for me). I discovered that this was resonant with Fonagy's notion of *modulating* the affect "in intensity or duration or refining the affect by sustaining it, or by its moving upward, toward the positive, or downward, toward the negative," (p. 440).

I was regularly reminded of what Gabor Maté (2003/2011) called "emotional competence" (p. 263), my own hard-won and that capacity I was helping Julia establish within herself. Maté described emotional competence as "... the capacity that enables us to stand in a responsible, non-victimized, and non-self-harming relationship with our environment. It is the required internal ground for facing life's inevitable stresses, for avoiding the creation of unnecessary ones and for furthering the healing process.... Pursuing the seven A's [acceptance, awareness, anger, autonomy, attachment, assertion, affirmation] of healing will help us grow into emotional competence" (p. 263).

As I regulated myself in staying affectively present, and as Julia internalized me and the regulation I offered her, I became fairly certain that the terror would diminish into a usable fear state for her, since terror can only be maintained in a state of being abjectly alone. Experiencing me 'with' her, she might then be able to tolerate enough the fear when away from me that she could begin to use it as a signal for protective, rather than exposing, action. Staying in this very painful affect was a great deal to ask of her, as was the necessary recovery and attempt to try again after repeated failures.

Eventually, we succeeded, but it was a slow and arduous process for both of us. At this last stage, when Julia was able to cut off contact with Oscar, we were working in what Fonagy called *expressing*, that is, "the outward manifestation of the affect in the world, and the inward expression of affects as a strategy in situations where the expression of one's affects outwardly is undesirable. This inward expression of affects is consistent with self-reflexivity, reflecting on one's affects while one remains with the affective state, rather than from a position of distance" (p. 440). We were, in Allan Schore's (2003b) terms, "within an interactive, growth-facilitating environment, working toward the establishment of a self-system that is capable of effectively modulating a broad range of affects, integrating these into a variety of adaptive motivational states, utilizing affects as signals, and linking coherent behavioral states to social contexts" (pp. 279-281).

KEYSTONE # 5 – Building Secure Attachment

As we saw in Chapter Five, attachment is universally described as proximity-seeking behavior on the part of the infant/child in order to find safety, comfort, and protection with the adult caregiver (Bowlby, 1951, 1958, 1959, 1960, 1969). As the dyad establishes their *secure* interpersonal relationship, the infant/child's immature brain uses the mature regulating functions of the adult's brain to organize its own processes, to experience amplification of its positive emotional states and modulation of its negative states (see Siegel, 1999). Such successfully repeated interactional experiences then become encoded in the infant/child brain as implicit memory, serving as templates and expectations for future relating. Attachment thus provides the core foundation from which the body/affective mind develops and is key to the resolution of fractured state systems.

Once again, the crucial interrelationship among the Seven Keystones of Development is clear. Internalization via identification leads to affect regulation (and vice versa), fostering secure attachment, healthy hemispheric development, memory functions that enable processing and learning, a flow of self states, and the development of personal voice, expressed in affective language. Primary to emotional growth, and to each of the seven foundational aspects of development, is the authenticity of the realness embedded within the therapeutic relationship.

Will had a secure attachment to his father, although he certainly also felt disappointment in this relationship with his father's work required absences and when his father retreated from a much more vigorous life. Will's attachment to his mother was mainly Insecure, Ambivalent. Although he did not exhibit clinginess or upset upon separation, he also could not easily separate or even begin to individuate until he was well into his twenties, when he could utilize emotional withdrawal in his efforts to move away from her smothering of him. The ambivalent flavor was certainly present in our analytic relationship. While Will was dedicated to his treatment and revealing of very vulnerable parts of himself (representing the secure attachment with his father), he also vacillated regularly and persistently with his attachment to me, especially in those areas where he felt his dependence on me or when what he perceived as the garden path loomed. For instance, during the 'break' he took late in treatment, he did not call or seem to miss his analytic work. But upon his return he was eager to re-engage, admitting that he missed me and the work we did. As he re-invested himself in treatment, he seemed to have developed a secure attachment to me at last, based, I think, on a combination of my trustworthiness and my ability to 'let him go' when needed, within the modeling provided by my on-going authentic emotional presence.

Julia clearly exhibited an Insecure, Avoidant Attachment and Reactive Attachment to her mother, never really having had an opportunity to attach to a caring, comforting, and responsive (m)other. Her attachment to her charismatic but violent father (and Oscar) followed the lines of the Insecure, Disorganized/ Disoriented Attachment and Traumatized Attachment, the result for Julia of being "markedly frightened by [her] primary haven of safety" (Hesse and Main, 2000, p. 1102).

In each of the forms of insecure attachment, there is a failure in both connection and the necessary repair after rupture. Julia did not have a mother who could offer her baby her maternal preoccupation (see Winnicott, 1956/1975). For Julia, her psychical connection did not exist, and there was no recognition on her mother's part that repair was ever needed. While the interactions with her father could be enlivening for Julia, as these interactions turned threatening, they soon propelled her into terrifying states, eventually leading Julia into despair, in which, again, there was no repair. In fact, Julia was held responsible for any repair with either parent, compliance with her mother, soothing for her father, and when she failed, she was castigated.

In my opinion, because Julia was born with a sturdy self and was so bright, and of necessity had to become prematurely precocious, she could reconstitute herself to live 'a normal and responsible life' in early adulthood, albeit one peppered with depression and anxiety. In regards to this, Novick and Novick (1991) made a point that seems relevant to Julia: the injured child uses "the experience of helpless rage and pain magically to predict and control their chaotic experiences [by entering] an imaginary world where safety, attachment, and omnipotent control [are] magically associated with pain" (p. 313).

One of my assertions is that the building of a secure attachment for the patient with the therapist is requisite for the necessary identification with that clinician in the service of healing trauma and the sheltered wound. T. Berry Brazelton and Bertrand Cramer's (1990) six environmental activities were pivotal guides for me in building that attachment with both Will and Julia, activities which "make possible the … unfolding of attachment:

- synchrony between parent and infant in terms of responding to arousal,
- symmetry of infant's capacities and parent's respects for infant's thresholds in response to stimuli,
- contingency of parent's signals based upon baby's states and capacity for signaling,

- entrainment in anticipating each other's responses and setting up a rhythm, which establishes expectancy carrying the dyad along,
- play that builds upon entrainment in order to continue to learn about each other and their interactions, and
- autonomy developing in the baby in the flexibility within a stable dyadic and family system (p. 121-127).

My 'equi-presence' with all aspects of Julia's inner life and the tumult of her external experience with Oscar, as well as in my quiet and attentive presence during the phase of therapy where she built her narrative through 'drawing' her early life story, were each essential to her attachment to me becoming secured. In this, also pivotal to this unfolding attachment were our synchrony, symmetry, contingency, entrainment, play, and the establishment of a new kind of autonomy for her within the stable but flexible analytic environment. Even our on-going processing voice mails helped in this endeavor, allowing me to be available to her on a consistent basis that had never been available to her before. Underscoring these aspects of our experience together was my genuine caring and concern for her that stood all the tests (see Weiss and Sampson, 1986) and challenges mounted in the treatment, for me, staying affectively present with all aspects of her terrorizing three-year long experience with Oscar, so viscerally brought into the analytic work.

KEYSTONE # 6 – Rewiring Hemispheric Development

In Chapter Six, we found that originally in an infant's development, what was needed for healthy hemispheric development was "the psychobiologically attuned caregiver interactively regulat[ing] the infant's positive and negative states, thereby co-constructing a growth-facilitating environment for the experience-dependent maturation of a control system in the infant's right brain" (Schore, 2003b, p. 179). Conversely in Chapter Thirteen, we learned that with traumatized development, "the abusive caregiver not only shows less play with her infant, she also induces traumatic states of enduring negative affect.... Instead of modulating she induces extreme levels of stimulation and arousal, either too high in abuse or too low in neglect.... Such states are accompanied by *severe alterations in the biochemistry of the immature brain,* especially in areas associated with the development of the child's coping capacities" (Schore, 1996, 1997, 2003a, p. 181, italics added). These consequences are upon "the critical period organization of limbic cortical and subcortical connections that mediate homeostatic self-regulatory and attachment systems ... [which] lead to a regulatory failure ..." (pp. 252-253).

In drawing our attention to how the brain constructs perception, Louis Sander (2002) wrote about how "the brain first deconstructs its sensory input into the bits and pieces that make up the perception. It places each sensory component of the input into a category—line, color, depth, contour, movement—which the brain then processes, each category in a different brain area. The map of this widely distributed process is then brought back together to construct the whole of the percept, including relevant affective, or emotional, categories ... and from these, the meaning of the percept is constructed for the perceiver ..." (p. 27).

This inherent function of the brain becomes concretized and rigidified in the right hemisphere when unresolved trauma becomes encoded in fractured state systems. Then, the taking apart of perception does not automatically come back together to form whole percepts. Rather than the brain's being able to use its integrative functions, it 'organizes' distorted and split apart perceptions from repeated intense traumatic experience into implicit memory neuronal pathways, usable only for being re-triggered in the current moment.

Fortunately, we know now that long-term and effective psychotherapy and psychoanalytic treatment 'rewires' those neuronal pathways. As Allan Schore (2003b) says, when we, the analytic dyad, are successful in using interactive repair, "… that disconfirm[s] the patient's perceptual biases, and allows for the emergence of a right brain system that effectively regulates the intensity, frequency, and duration of negative and positive affects…" (pp. 279-281), healing can occur. This healing takes place on the hemispheric level because the "dyadic affective transactions within the working alliance cocreate an intersubjective context that allows for the structural expansion of the patient's orbitofrontal system and its cortical and subcortical connections. Orbitofrontal function is essential not only to affect regulation but also to the processing of cognitive-emotional interactions and affect-related meanings" (p. 264). The hope in analytic treatment is the rewiring of previously maladaptive hemispheric development, "the creation of new neuronal linkages, then, allows the internal constraints of the dynamical system of the brain to change" (Siegel, 1999, p. 306).

Will not only learned implicitly to dampen down his affect when it threatened to over-excite or overwhelm him, but his brain had long ago learned unconsciously to dampen him down, with the slightest provocation from the external world and from his own internal signals. With such trauma-based dampening came his dysregulation and disorganization, to the point that he could not keep track of himself across transitions or even within his daily activities. Through the course of treatment, his hemispheric rewiring was demonstrated in his ability to remain engaged in emotional contact much of the time, including when he and his wife were negotiating a conflict, when he needed to stay on task, even to multi-task, and when he was supervising multiple projects overseeing a number of individuals at work. When Will finally chose to pursue his creative interests, what still needed to link up was the power of his pleasurable affects, his passion, with his ability to take his own creative pursuits seriously, and devote the commitment of time and energy to them that they required.

Julia's measured way of adult living was compromised severely in the rape by Oscar and its aftermath, revealing a hemispheric mis-wiring system that she had managed to live 'on top of' throughout her life, due to choosing a subdued marriage that would not trigger her. Being disowned by her family of origin had the inadvertent 'benefit' of removing her from the kind of stimuli that ordinarily would have rekindled her distress. In our exacting work together, we strove to understand how her psychoneurobiological system functioned. Harvey Milkman and Stanley Sunderwirth's (1987) work was invaluable to me:

> The soma [cell body] acts as a small computer. It must decide from a 'discussion' with a multitude of surrounding neurons whether to 'fire' and send the impulse to the axon, or to remain dormant. Since this is the soma's only decision, and it is made very quickly, we may think of the soma as a 'fast idiot'.... The intensity of feeling determined by frequency of neuronal firing rather than by the strength of the electrochemical jolt... the receptors are tailor-made to receive only neurotransmitters that have a shape that complements that of the receptor. This relationship between neurotransmitter and receptor is very much like a lock and key.... People may repeat certain behaviors to bring about alterations in neurotransmission consistent with their characteristic ways of coping with stress. That is, the person who actively confronts fear or tension seeks out risk-taking activities... in order to increase neurotransmission (p. 8-12).

Julia was primed in her hemispheric responses to Oscar through the enlivening, but violent, relationship with her father, along with the extreme deprivation she experienced with her maternal figure. Oscar's skin was a powerful enticement to Julia, skin into which she wanted to melt in symbiotic merger. No sooner was that need met successfully by Oscar, than he would drink like her father, become taunting and sexually charged like her father, and finally violent and terrifying, which Julia could not feel as her soma cell bodies fired, putting the key into the lock of her receptors. Only when the contact was shaming and over, could she regain any sense of herself, and then, it was a degraded sense that had made her "inhuman."

Ultimately, we were successful in transforming these responses: Julia was able to relinquish her mother, even as a 'hated' figure; Julia was able to move out of the enflamed and torturing relationship with Oscar as her "manic defence" (Winnicott, 1935, p. 132) resolved; and she was able to create a new life for herself and her children, including a solid friendship with her ex-husband. At last, Julia had solved her "problem with men." She then was able to form an enduring romantic relationship with a new husband who was exciting to her as well as caring, respectful, protective, and safe. While I write of the various dynamics that played out in the analytic relationship, I think Bessel van der Kolk's (1996) comments are germane: "Much of the treatment of victims of trauma is intuitive; it depends on both a sensitive understanding of the unique issues that make every individual different from all others, and clinical knowledge about the accurate timing of appropriate interventions. What occurs between a patient and therapist is a function not only of a particular diagnosis of the patient, but also of the unique and personal relationship between patient and therapist" (p. 539).

KEYSTONE # 7 – Recovering Personal Voice and Expressive Language

Personal voice. The vocal and written expression of our unique, fundamental, and indispensable essential self. As well, this personal voice communicates using affective, elaborative language comprised of words that arise out of mental and emotional imagery, which represent one's experience using all six senses—sight, hearing, taste, touch, smell, and intuition, and which builds within communication with the other. But, patients with unresolved trauma do not have a voice to express the "wordless thought process" (Damasio, 1999, p. 108) of their essential selves, or words with which to represent their experience, until they experience the therapeutic relationship as one of safety and ultimately, secure attachment.

Then, there are the words. Stanley Greenspan (1997b) provided two pivotal notions that help us understand the development of language for emotional experience. The first is what he called representational elaboration: "representational capacities, the ability to form mental images... permit individuals to move from merely acting out experiences to mentally representing them.... The therapeutic challenge is to help an older child or adult move from a behavioral discharge mode to a representational one. A particular patient's representational mode may not be developed at all, while another patient's is constricted and exists only in relationship to selected emotions or affects" (p. 225).

Greenspan developed a chart called the Hierarchy of Affects showing how language develops in concert with the mastery of each of his six functional emotional milestones, language beginning at the prebehavioral level (looking, listening, relating nonverbally) and then moving to the behavioral (discharge) level (hitting, kicking, biting, hugging, holding, smiling, frowning, etc) , the somatic, earliest representational ("I hit him," to "I want to kick him," to "My heart aches," to "I feel awful") into the full and symbolic representational, where words have "a combined affective/cognitive meaning and refer to specific differentiated feeling states" (p. 230). In this, the therapist helps the patient 'move up' the developmental ladder in terms of learning to describe their experience at whatever developmental level they are at (behavioral, somatic). This may be the first time a patient has had anyone to even listen to her words. Ultimately, after many, many sessions of circles of communication and elaborative languaging, the patient herself will begin to build bridges between her experience and the 'right' words with which to capture it.

Greenspan's second notion is what he called representational differentiation: "when an individual can represent experience in the form of a multisensory image and categorize it. This ability to categorize experience is the first step in the differentiation process. The second step involves building bridges between various categories of experience… including] organiz[ing] experience according to what's 'me' and what's 'not me', or the self and nonself, or object… what is subjective and what is objective, what is fantasy or make-believe and what is reality… and experience can also be categorized in terms of the dimensions of time and space" (p. 313). In this, the therapist helps the patient "form connections between different affects, themes, and areas of representation… dealing with conflicts between different representational dramas and tries to help the person find connecting bridges" (p. 314).

One of the therapist's most significant contributions then is to decipher within the patient's implicit memory relivings the nature of their wounded self, and, encapsulated within the trauma, the personal voice of the patient's essential self. Once this personal voice is tapped, the collaborative task then becomes assisting the patient in finding the elaborative expressive language that might represent their traumatic history, perhaps for the first time in his or her life. As Peter Shabad (1997) so poignantly captured, "the traumatic theme causes the child to transform his strangled communications into the belated effects of posttraumatic symptomatology. A person's unique constellation of psychological symptoms reflects the lonely, nonverbal journey of the repetition compulsion to bring out proof of his sufferings" (p. 355). Not until such patients find safety within the therapeutic relationship over time, and, ultimately, in a secure attachment to the analyst, can their personal voice and elaborative language be found, let alone risked, again.

Will's personal voice was severely compromised from birth. Rather than a hearty cry, he was strangled by the umbilical cord, finally able to emit but a hiccup two minutes after birth. I think that his hearing loss following the car accident contributed even to the way his own voice sounded to him, as well as how he experienced, and at times struggled to hear, vocal interactions with others. As an adult, he possessed a rich and expansive vocabulary, could teach well anything he knew to others, but from our first session he stammered and repeated the same few words whenever he struggled to put into semantic language his personal voice and his affective experience. "I—uh—uh—well—I—I—um—yes—well—no—I—uh—" was commonplace in many years of working together. As Will gained insight into his life experience and became able to tolerate more of an affective range, his voice came alive, and he was much more affectively coherent. But even after this fluidity of self-expression was available to him, when he came in contact with deeper and more disturbing affect, his uncertainty and stammer could return.

Julia was a talented and creative, natural storyteller. Her use of language was vivid, sensory based, and engrossing. She had the most wonderful way of tying together in a representational elaboration (Greenspan, 1997b) the people of her world and their stories, creating metaphors to communicate an understanding of their culture, their experience, including her own. But when it came to the traumatic moments of her life and the overwhelming affect encapsulated in those experiences, Julia was mute. Not only did she have no words for such experiences, she had no voice within them. Rather than having a mother who could track and decipher what her baby's noises, gestures, and various cries meant, so that she could tend to and regulate her infant's somatic and emotional life (Edgcumbe, 1981, Greenspan, 1999), Julia had a mother who desperately needed to stifle those cries, drugging her until, at three months of age, she "learned to stop crying." As Selma Fraiberg (1982) discovered through her research with severely compromised babies, when the babies learned that their cries, screams, and frantic gesturing were ineffective in drawing mother to them in ameliorating ways, their crying ceased.

Most babies, at these same three months of age, can communicate distress and pleasure, and begin to express outward directed looks and gestures, both as response to various sensory stimulation and to initiate contact. The baby uses her communicative skills to make things happen. Roy Schafer (1980) pointed out, "In considering the psychology of the self, one wants to know who or what esteems or does not esteem the self. It seems that some sort of superself or superordinate self is implied, in which case one does implicitly get back to some central and unitary agency as a point of reference.... The self, then, is not what one *has* but what one *does*; and it is what one tells about what one does" (p. 91).

In healthy development, as early as toddlerhood and into the twos and threes and fours (see Brown & Hernnstein, 1975, Chomsky, 1980, Vgotsky, 1986, Carter, 1998, Crain, 2000) when a child begins to use semantic language, his or her personal voice is fully established. But patients with unresolved trauma have had their personal, authorial voices preempted or silenced by neglect or abuse. Within the first two years of life, as their traumatic experiences are encoded implicitly within the right hemisphere, there may be few or no words attached (see van der Kolk, 1996). Unable to express or prevented from expressing the reality of their essential selves, "silence... [becomes] an attempt to protect a precious core of authentic experience from destruction" (Kurtz, 1984, p. 232, see also K. K. Novick, 1990). Even when semantic language becomes available to whatever degree, the implicit environmental threat may be such that the child is inhibited from placing the veneer of words onto his/her affective experience (see Whitmer, 2001).

In the resolution of trauma and the recovery of personal voice and elaborative expressive language, the therapist's voice and language play indispensable roles and functions. Tone matters, and its soft comfort, its steadiness in confrontation, its lilt for encouragement. Words matter, their sensory valence, their imagery, the stories they weave. Stories matter, delivered with empathy, or humor, or for inspiration. Metaphor, simile, analogy. All of these are the therapist's verbal tools of processing, clarification, and interpretation to be used in meaning-making ways to couch the patient's experience in vivid resonance, often offering fresh words where there have been none before. In pivotal moments, the therapist's unique personal voice reaches the patient's heart and mind on the wings of language to give breath and life to the patient's courage of risking the use of his or her own voice.

Of the many ideas presented in Leo Kovar's (1994) paper, one was particularly pertinent in resonance to my work with Will and Julia:

> There can be no talk without our remembering others and their remembering us, in words. Talking, that which makes a human community possible, both enables and requires us to exist in history (555).... The psychoanalytic situation, through its design if not by its intent, satisfies this requirement for being remembered. The minimum frequency, the regularity, the provision of a respectable duration for each visit, guarantees a listener as oral historian (p. 557).... The analyst here joins his ancestors, the priests, as the repository of the community's secrets (p. 558).... We are in the hands of someone who is taking some pains to pay careful attention to what we have to tell him of matters crucial to our well-being (p. 558)... *that* the patient comes to talk is more overriding than *what* he talks about (559)... The good therapist must invent the therapy as it goes along, must strive to hold no presuppositions other than the essentiality of talk for sanity, just as in everyday conversation we must hold no presuppositions if we are to respond fully to the entirety of what is said to us (p. 560).... Careful listening must attempt to grasp the enormous range of meanings of what is said, from the most literal denotation to the endless connotative and metaphoric complexities

> that provide the texts for a psychoanalysis (p. 565).... [the analyst does] not simply hear or remember words... nor is [her] listening sufficient if simply add[ing] word meanings to the words spoken. [The analyst] must *en-vision* the words spoken. Bare by themselves, they must be clothed pictorially, not with stills but with movies, to correspond to the flow of talk (p. 566).... The therapist of the word, at his best, gives his patient a gift that cannot be purchased.... True concern entails the attending to highly detailed complexities of what is listened to and equally careful judgments as to what ought to be said in response.... The talking therapist must have the desire and the aptitude to talk to his patient in such a way that this intangible gift-giving becomes almost palpable (p. 569).

W. W. Meissner (2000) considered the multiple levels of communication and meaning in analytic listening: "Communication would falter completely if we did not accept... the patient's discourse at face value. But we know that this level is but the tip of the iceberg of reference and implication. This is one facet that distinguishes analytic listening from ordinary listening.... The problem, of course, is how the listening analyst gains access to and understanding of these hidden dimensions of meaning. If the patient does not have direct or immediate access, how can the analyst have any purchase on the patient's inner world?" (p. 320-321). The answer lies in the fact that, "The analyst listens not merely to the words and the meanings they express, but also to the tone, pace, affective coloring, nuances of expression, and any other behavioral factors contributing to the overall impression—gestures, agitation, restful or disruptive movements, facial expression, tears, sobs, sighs, groans, chuckles, laughter, etc. All these observations become integrated into the listening process and may convey shades of meaning and reverberations, particularly affectively" (p. 322).

Mixed in with these multiple levels and aspects of listening, Meissner added three components operating within the analytic interaction:

"transference (with its corresponding countertransference), the therapeutic alliance, and, finally, the real relationship ... they are all present and active at any point in the analytic process" (p. 333). Therapeutic listening is a particular kind of capacity, capacity in the sense that while active listening is something we are trained to do as absorption, even when non-verbal, culling for layers of latent content within the manifest, it is truly about presence. The therapist 'showing up', fully engaged in whatever the patient offers, respecting that, regardless of the form such presentations take, the story is the message, and the therapist's receiving of that story in its nuances, intricacies, or even reckless boldness, is of inestimable value. When Will feared my leading him down a garden path, he was simultaneously wanting to be led, fearing any possible loss of agency, and tentatively striving to find hope within courage. When Julia needed an "abominable snowperson," she could 'dream' me as that source of fierceness to stop her father and yet be 'furry" enough to scoop her up and carry her to safety. My months and years of multi-layered listening presence created the holding environment in which their most personal narratives could unfold.

- **The Narrative Process**

In the resolution of trauma and the recovery of personal voice and expressive elaborative language, the narrative process becomes an indispensable activity of re-claiming the patient's agency, efficacy, and "authorial self" (Wolf, 1990, p. 185). As Daniel Siegel (1999) wrote, "Children begin as biographers and emerge into autobiographers" (p. 323).

Narrative making requires both right and left hemisphere involvement: the right hemisphere makes sense of what is perceived, processing "the overall gist of a scene and creat[ing] a context-rich representational 'understanding' ... to perceive the mental states of others and to represent others' minds" (Siegel, 1999, p. 326-327); the left hemisphere is the 'interpreter', the understanding of cause and effect relationships. Siegel has suggested that "Coherent narratives are created through inter-hemispheric integration" (p. 331).

Together, as Will and I wove his narrative, Will recovered his personal voice word by word. Finally procuring hearing aids that he could tolerate and that were useful to him also contributed to Will's ability to take risks when it concerned the expression of his most personal voice. Eventually, when he felt not only safe, but the safety was real, he could speak eloquently about his most intimate experiences. Where Will found his most emboldened and passionate voice was through his creativity. This was what he resisted and experienced as so fear producing, yet the hope that his essential self could be expressed and, therefore, revealed, beckoned him until his resistance was replaced with budding passion.

Julia's affective narrative and her personal voice came into being through the pictures she drew over many months of treatment, pictures that captured the story of her infancy and young childhood, her ruptured relationship with her mother, her terrifying and captivating relationship with her father. While the one or two sentences she wrote to accompany each picture were not the articulation of her natural story telling ability, the voice of her child self was plain, simple, and true. No need to hide anymore.

As in the beginning of life, with the birth cry of personal voice, so, too, do we return to a rebirth in the analysis, which breathes respiratory life into that personal voice emerging through the wounding our patients carry. In the doing, as the elements of each of these seven keystones of human development (resolved states, decoded memory processes, internalization of and identification with the analyst, the establishment of affect regulation, secure attachment, rewired hemispheric development, and found personal voice and affective language), integrate and influence one another, the patient becomes able to hold his or her originating wounding with the respect it deserves while moving toward healing and the transformed development of his or her essential self. Yet, in the process of reclaiming one's essential self, there is a necessary mourning, for all that has been lost, for all that had to be endured, the years spent in turmoil, and for all that otherwise might have been.

- **Mourning**

Mourning can occur spontaneously or deliberately at any point within the treatment, even appearing as an active dynamic from the very beginning. This necessary and profound struggle of the patient's may wish to be avoided or ended, but it is an inevitable part of treatment, one to be met with the therapist's empathy, respect, and partnership. While mourning is not consigned to any particular period in the therapeutic endeavor, there is often a season towards the end of treatment when the patient's new connection to transformed development brings with it a deep sadness for the years lost without having been able to live an expressive life as his/her essential self.

Mourning occurs in the era of resolution and integration because it is a healthy response to loss—the loss of time, of the misapprehension of sense of self, of opportunity. Even change can signal mourning, for the letting go of the familiar in the face of embracing the unknown can be formidable. This is especially true in the shift from wounding to healing and the concomitant shift in identity that the individual undergoes.

Peter Shabad (1997), in examining incomplete mourning found in the "backward-looking yearnings" (p. 351) of patients who suffer from the psychic loss of physically present parent(s), addressed how the child must "bear the burden of proving the reality of his experiences alone" (p. 351). He explained, "Unlike the acute and overt trauma of physical loss, the experience of psychic loss derives from a relatively intangible trauma that evolves over many years, the residual effects of which are felt only after the fact ... (such as, "a parent's exploitation of the child for narcissistic purposes, giving the 'silent' treatment when angry, offering harsh criticisms, being excessively intrusive ... a mother's extreme martyrdom, a father's explosive drunken rages, the breaking of small promises consistently, being called stupid ...)" (p. 350).

While this mourning process can be gut-wrenching or temporarily heartbreaking, it is ultimately freeing, not because of the myth of closure, but because in all these ministrations of healing, the previously unresolved trauma is resolving, healing is taking place, and the past can finally become of the past, not of the present. What is now ushered in is the vast potential and inspiring experience of creativity.

- **Creativity**

The creative process as a healing agent lies within and emerges from the heart of the resolution of trauma, the attachment nature of the analytic relationship, and the narrative process in which analyst and patient engage to weave together for the first time the patient's lived experience. I think of creativity as the manifestation in tangible expression of invisible and ineffable dreams, imaginings, and inspirations. For the traumatized, dreams have been nightmares, imaginings had to be used to plan for catastrophe, and inspiration was quickly dashed by belittlement or denial of inept or harmful caregivers. For both Will and Julia, the nature, challenges, and risks inherent in the creative endeavor were central to their recovery. I long ago embraced, through my own creative yearnings and struggles, the visceral knowledge that I did possess a creative nature, one of which I could be proud. Throughout my earlier years I desperately tried to find sources of expression for that nature, often being told I was a "flibberty-jibbit"or was at risk for becoming a "jack of all trades, master of none." These supposedly well-meaning cautions were attempts to get me to focus, to stay on task, and not be "so sensitive" as I would "become too hurt by life." Unfurled in my marriage and raising our family was my husband's undying respect for and tender care of my creativity. After years of editing (the midwife to others' creativity), I found in my own writing and in the privilege of partnering healing journeys with many patients, that certain provisions are absolute necessities for the creative process:

- A holding environment fashioned of protection, beauty, and the deep care of reliability, attunement, and support for the courage of discovery
- Relationships that are non-competitive and empathetic toward each partner's aspirations—soothing in the face of failed attempts and celebratory of renewed strivings leading to fulfillment
- The ability to be alone or together with the respectful awareness of internal and external space and timing
- Free, even wild, thinking at the beginning of the creative process, so that leaps of imagination can take us to safe but innovative places we never used to embrace
- Showing up—again and again—even when that feels impossible

The Seven Keystones of Transformed Development are alive as well in the creative living of our essential selves:

- Having learned the nature of states and state architecture and resolving our state system traumata, we practice our state transitions, learning ever more effective ways to shift into Creative states
- Our implicit memory is the vital potency for encoding the power of our creativity, so that we can link it to explicit memory functions, guaranteeing that we can depend on the retrieval of such encoding in ever more artistic expression
- We internalize the richness of the creative world around us, ordinary as well as extraordinary, whether found in nature, art, books, the sharing of a delicious meal, music, walking with a grandchild, tending someone who is ill or suffering and use familiar and new emotional ties to identify with aspects of others in those ties that help us grow our essential selves

- We learn ever more reliable and productive ways to self-regulate, repeatedly bringing ourselves into an open, processing space from the too muchness of excitation or dampening down.
- We work relationally to foster secure attachments between ourselves and those most significant to us
- We recognize that our brain maintains elasticity throughout our lifespans and nourish it with healthy lifestyle, novelty, and dedicated, responsible use of its vast resources
- We embrace the courage of our personal voice of our essential selves, using it with expressive elaborative language within shared dialogues, meaningful and delightful, kind and playful, serious and bold with others.

In the healing progression provided by *The Development Lens* and all that comes to fruition in the deep and challenging work of such psychodynamic treatment, the patient is re-united with his or her original essential self. By welcoming the responsibility of caring for our recovered essential self, we can move forward into transformed development of that essential self, living fully relationally in the present with an optimistic sense of the future.

But this transformed development of, and the living out of, the essential self is not free from fear, from a sense of exposure, from potential threat, leading to the temporary grasping for a return to the paradoxical comfort of wounds in spite of the therapeutic spirit of recovery, of freedom, and of possibility. Even creative transformation can take one's breath away, giving the patient 'second thoughts'. Here, again, the personal presence of the therapist provides decisive strengths. S/he remains someone with whom the patient can identity, as the regulator of these dizzying possibilities within their secure attachment. The therapist's personal voice and creativity make safe enough the patient's brave new steps, the patient knowing s/he can return 'home' as necessary for comfort, soothing, and for the seasoned encouragement and partnership to try again. And so, this exacting and exquisite journey continues on…

Appendices

Healthy Development of the Essential Self

MODEL I - the Essential Self ©Gwyneth Kerr Erwin, 2001

Development of the Wounded Self

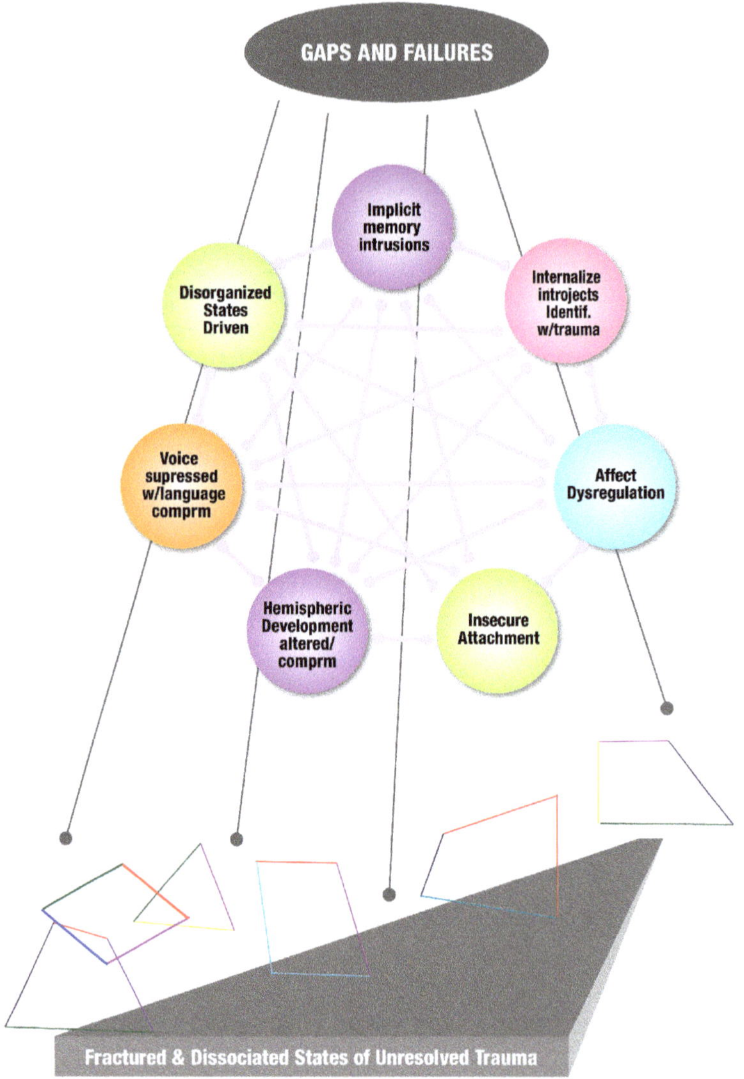

MODEL II - the Wounded Self ©Gwyneth Kerr Erwin, 2001

Development of the Traumatized Self

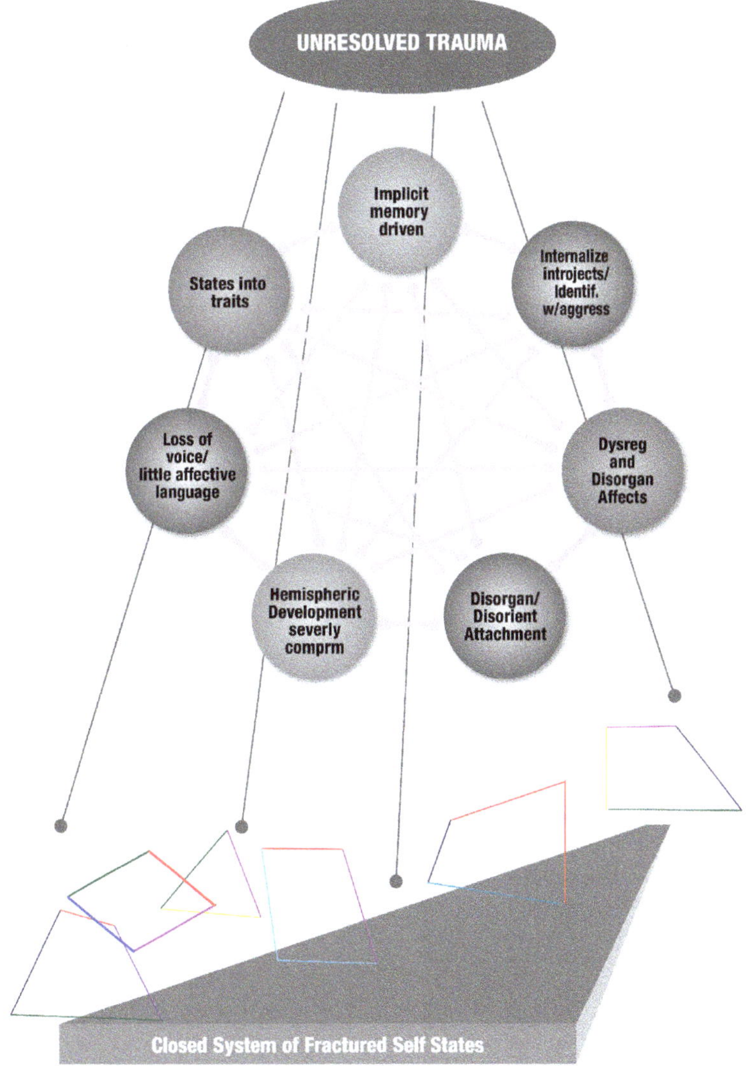

MODEL III - the Traumatized Self ©Gwyneth Kerr Erwin, 2001

Resolved Trauma and Transformed Development

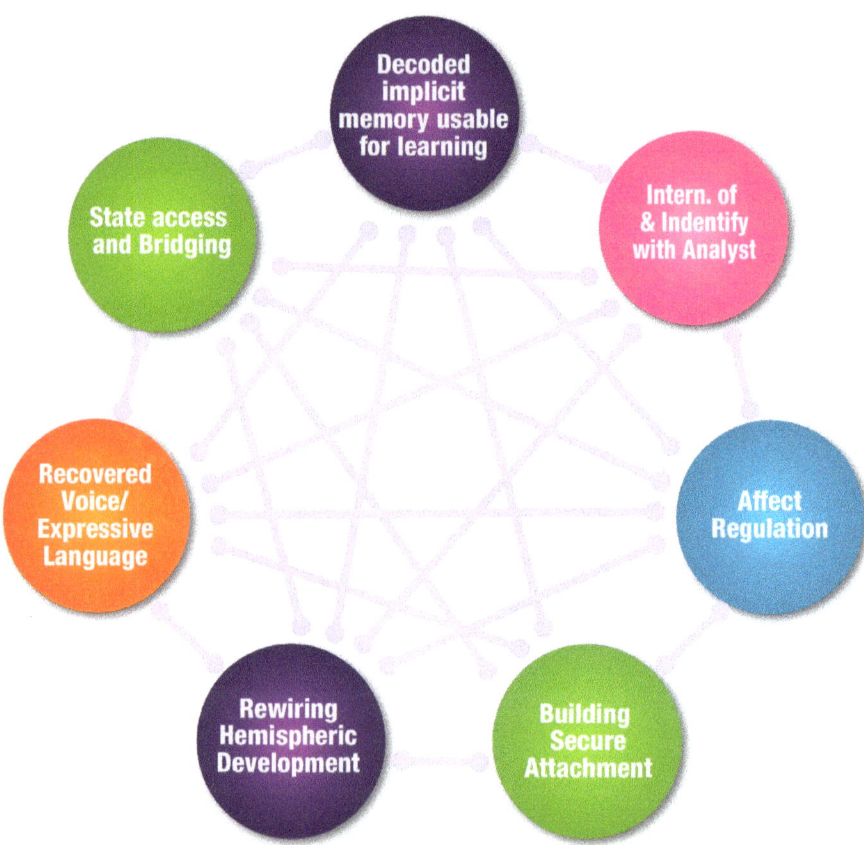

MODEL IV - Renewel of the Essential Self ©Gwyneth Kerr Erwin, 2005

MEMORY COMPARISON CHART

by Gwyneth Kerr Erwin,Ph.D., Psy.D.

IMPLICIT MEMORY	EXPLICIT MEMORY
Present at birth and functions throughout the lifespan	Functions from 3 years of age throughout the lifespan
The encoding and retrieval of lived experience	The encoding and retrieval of factual (semantic) and autobiographical (episodic) information and experience
Does *not* require conscious attention for encoding	Requires focal attention for encoding or retrieval
Encoded and retrieved in the *procedural steps* of the originating experience	Cortical processing selects events to forma part of permanent storage
To e*ncode*, mind needs intensity, duration, and repetition, to be *triggered* only needs a whiff of original experience	To learn, mind needs conscious repetition and practice
When triggered, the past becomes current time experience	Recall of the past
Accurate and stable over time	Alters over time as influenced by further experience, people, context
Use and state dependent	Cognitive learning
No subjective sense of recalling self or time	Sense of recall includes the self and time frame
Made up of emotional, sensory, perceptual, and body experience, in emotional language'	Made up of facts, mind operations, verbal behavioral (linear, semantic) language
Establishes mental models, and therefore, "perceptual bias"	Establishes order, sequence, spatial locations time, and dimensional sense of self,
Amygdala is the mediating limbic structure, which is *activated* during traumatic retrieval	Hippocampus is the mediating limbic structure, which is *suppressed* during traumatic encoding and retrieval
When cocooned in the right hemisphere, implicit memory cannot be used for learning, only for reliving	Must be integrated with implicit memory so that implicit memory can become usable for learning

References: Schore, A. (2003a). *Affect dysregulation and disorders of the self*. New York: W. W. Norton & Company. and Siegel, D. J. (1999). The developing mind: Toward a neurobiology of interpersonal experience. New York: The Guilford Press.

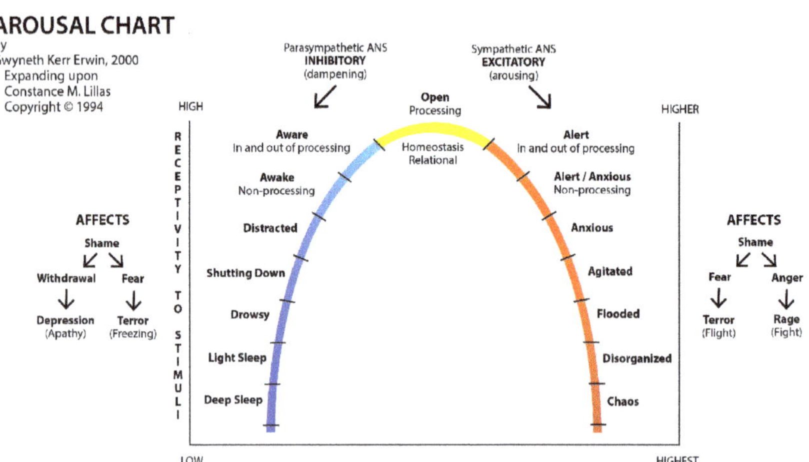
AROUSAL CHART
by
Gwyneth Kerr Erwin, 2000
Expanding upon
Constance M. Lillas
Copyright © 1994
Parasympathetic ANS
INHIBITORY
(dampening)
Sympathetic ANS
EXCITATORY
(arousing)
HIGH
Open
Processing
HIGHER
RECEPTIVITY TO STIMULI
Aware
In and out of processing
Homeostasis
Relational
Alert
In and out of processing
Awake
Non-processing
Alert / Anxious
Non-processing
AFFECTS
Shame
Withdrawal
Fear
Depression
(Apathy)
Terror
(Freezing)
Distracted
Shutting Down
Drowsy
Light Sleep
Deep Sleep
Anxious
Agitated
Flooded
Disorganized
Chaos
AFFECTS
Shame
Fear
Anger
Terror
(Flight)
Rage
(Fight)
LOW
HIGHEST

The Seven Keystones of Development Assessment Map

by Gwyneth Kerr Erwin, Ph.D., Psy.D.

CLINICIAN'S NAME:	CLINICIAN'S SIGNATURE:
PATIENT'S NAME (OR INITIALS):	DATE (AND/OR RANGE):

HEALTHY DEVELOPMENT

STATES	MEMORY SYSTEMS	INTERNALIZATION IDENTIFICATIONS	AFFECTS	ATTACHMENT	HEMISPHERIC DEVELOPMENT	VOICE & LANGUAGE
	☐ Implicit	☐ Mother	☐ Flow	☐ Secure	☐ Right	☐ Personal Voice
☐ Bridging		☐ Father		☐ Mother		
	☐ Explicit				☐ Left	☐ Expressive Language
☐ Transitions		☐ Sibling	Temperament Type: ☐ HF ☐ HD ☐ AC	☐ Father		
						☐ Circles of Communication Ave #
		☐ Grandparent	☐ Hypo	☐ Other	☐ Cross-Hemispheric	
	☐ Cross-Hemispheric					
		☐ Other	☐ Inattentive			

WOUNDED DEVELOPMENT

STATES	MEMORY SYSTEMS	INTERNALIZATION IDENTIFICATIONS	AFFECTS	ATTACHMENT	HEMISPHERIC DEVELOPMENT	VOICE & LANGUAGE
☐ Transitions	☐ Implicit Memory Intrusions	☐ Introjects	☐ Dysregulation	☐ Insecure	☐ Adaptive	☐ Personal Voice
			☐ Hyperarousal			☐ Altered
			☐ Hypoarousal	☐ Ambivalent	☐ Right	☐ Compromised
☐ Dissociated		☐ Mother	☐ Mild			☐ Suppressed
	☐ Types of Memory Banks		☐ Moderate	☐ Avoidant	☐ Left	
			☐ Severe			☐ Expressive Language
☐ Depersonalized			☐ PTSD	☐ Disorganized	☐ Split	☐ Absent
		☐ Father	☐ CPTSD			☐ Halting
			Types of:	Mother's: ☐ Am ☐ Av ☐ Dis	☐ Primarily One-Sided (emotional)	☐ Stilted
			☐ Shame			
☐ Derealized			☐ Fear			☐ Lack of Coherence
		☐ Sibling	☐ Anger	Father's: ☐ Am ☐ Av ☐ Dis	☐ Primarily One-Sided (cognitive)	☐ Minimizing
	☐ PTSD		☐ Depressive			☐ Verbose
			☐ Immobilization			☐ Behavioral
	☐ CPTSD	☐ Other	☐ Fleeing & Hiding		☐ Cross-Hemispheric	☐ Symbolic
			☐ Fighting Back			☐ C of C #

TRAUMATIZED DEVELOPMENT

STATES	MEMORY SYSTEMS	INTERNALIZATION IDENTIFICATIONS	AFFECTS	ATTACHMENT	HEMISPHERIC DEVELOPMENT	VOICE & LANGUAGE
☐ States into Traits	☐ Implicit Memory Driven	☐ Identifications with trauma	☐ Disorganized Affects	☐ Disorganized/ Disoriented Attachment	☐ Severely Compromised	☐ Loss of Voice
			☐ PTSD		☐ Right	
Characteristics	☐ PTSD			☐ Mother		
☐ Fear based					☐ Left	☐ Little Expressive Language
☐ Shame based	☐ CPTSD	☐ Aggression Against Others		☐ Father		
☐ Anger based			☐ CPTSD		☐ Split	
☐ Other						☐ C of C #
		☐ Aggression Against the Self		☐ Reactive Attach	☐ Cross-Hemispheric	
				☐ Traumatized Attach		

THE AFFECTIVE QUESTIONNAIRE

What Soothes You?
What Enlivens You?

by

Gwyneth Kerr Erwin, Ph.D., Psy.D.

SO = Mark those items (and any you would add) with an **SO** for those activities that help you become soothed when you've become distressed (anxious, worried, angry, afraid) or "hyperaroused" (THE RED ZONE).

EN = Mark those items (and any you would add) with an **EN** for those activities that help you become enlivened when you've become depressed (or tired, cynical, fearful, giving up) or "hypoaroused" (THE BLUE ZONE).

REMEMBER YOU ARE TRYING TO COME BACK TO AN **OPEN, PROCESSING SPACE** (THE GOLD ZONE!)

VISUAL (sensory modality #1)					
	watching a fire in the fireplace		fluorescent lighting		order
	watching fish swim		lamp light		clutter
	watching the sunrise/sunset		candlelight		something far away
	being near trees		sunlight		something close up
	bright light		twilight		something busy
	dim light		darkness		something still

Add yours					

AUDITORY (sensory modality #2)					
	the sound of water		soft voices		shouts
	the sound of music (name instrument/s)		loud voices		clutter
	the sound of humming		crying		poetry
	the sound of breathing		laughing		stories
	heartbeat		whispers		

Add yours					

ORAL (sensory modality #3)			
	Taking slow, easy breaths		"Chewing" on (gum, hair, strings, buttons, coins, pencil, pens)
	Sucking on hard candy		"Crunching" on (pickle, olives, pretzels, chips, ice, hard candy, nuts)
	Sucking on something cold (ice chips, popsicles, frozen edibles)		Eating something sweet
	Sucking or licking (lips, tongue, inside of cheeks)		Eating something salty
	Whistling or other noises with your mouth		Eating something tangy/sweet-sour
	Biting nails, cuticles		Eating something bitter
	Sipping something hot (cocoa, tea, coffee, warm milk)		Alternating flavors (sweet to salty, for example)
	Drinking something cold (milkshake, ice water, carbonated sodas, milk)		Eating alone
	Drinking something hot (cocoa, coffee, tea)		Eating with others

Add yours			

SMELL (sensory modality #4)			
	something sweet		something crisp, like fall air
	something woodsy		something fresh
	something floral		something sour
	something pungent		something tart
	fire in a fireplace		something like baked bread

Add yours			

TOUCH/KINESTHETIC (sensory modality #5)			
	twisting/stroking your hair		rubbing skin/clothing
	moving objects in your pocket		fidgeting (with a straw, paper clips, fingers/nails, etc)
	cool shower/bath		feeling a breeze
	warm shower/bath		sitting near someone
	having a massage		sitting alone
	petting a dog/cat/other animal		feeling something itchy
	drumming fingers		feeling something soft
	jiggling foot		feeling something smooth
	jerking muscles		

Add yours			

MOVEMENT/VESTIBULAR (sensory modality #6)			
	rocking		running
	shifting/squirming		riding a bike/horse
	pushing back chair on two legs		tapping toes
	exercise		dancing
	lifting weights		tapping an object
	scrubbing/cleaning		yard work
	rolling neck and head		stretching/shaking
	cracking knuckles		walking/hiking
	bouncing or jiggling		sports

Add yours			

PROCEDURAL STEPS OF IMPLICIT MEMORY BANK

by

Gwyneth Kerr Erwin, Ph.D., Psy.D.

TRIGGER IN CURRENT TIME:

ORIGINATING TRAUMA:

HOW IT IS PLAYING OUT IN CURRENT TIME:

HOW IT IS PLAYING OUT IN THERAPEUTIC RELATIONSHIP:

PROCEDURAL STEP #1	CATEGORICAL AFFECT	VITALITY AFFECT	STATE
PROCEDURAL STEP #2	CATEGORICAL AFFECT	VITALITY AFFECT	STATE
PROCEDURAL STEP #3	CATEGORICAL AFFECT	VITALITY AFFECT	STATE
PROCEDURAL STEP #4	CATEGORICAL AFFECT	VITALITY AFFECT	STATE
PROCEDURAL STEP #5	CATEGORICAL AFFECT	VITALITY AFFECT	STATE
PROCEDURAL STEP #6	CATEGORICAL AFFECT	VITALITY AFFECT	STATE
PROCEDURAL STEP #7	CATEGORICAL AFFECT	VITALITY AFFECT	STATE
PROCEDURAL STEP #8	CATEGORICAL AFFECT	VITALITY AFFECT	STATE
PROCEDURAL STEP #9	CATEGORICAL AFFECT	VITALITY AFFECT	STATE
PROCEDURAL STEP #10	CATEGORICAL AFFECT	VITALITY AFFECT	STATE
PROCEDURAL STEP #11	CATEGORICAL AFFECT	VITALITY AFFECT	STATE
PROCEDURAL STEP #12	CATEGORICAL AFFECT	VITALITY AFFECT	STATE

ADDITIONAL NOTES:

PROCEDURAL STEPS INTERVENTIONS
for
IMPLICIT MEMORY BANKS

by
Gwyneth Kerr Erwin, Ph.D., Ph.D.

There are four overarching opportunities for working and intervening with Implicit Memory relivings, thus making the implicit memory (right hemisphere) usable for learning as it is linked up with Explicit Memory (left hemisphere)—what I call "bending the river." Years ago, as I learned about explicit memory and the power of implicit memory to understand what was playing out with various traumatized patients, I found, not uncommonly, that the first of two intuitive opportunities most therapists, including myself, utilized in working with any re-traumatization, whether or not they had any knowledge of implicit memory, was the benefit of viscerally feeling what that experience was like for patient. As such experience was invariably repeated, I understood it in ever more complex ways and was able either to help them find, or bring to them, the emotional language to narrate that experience. For the first time in their lives, patients were able to share with another what had happened to them and to have that other be a bearing witness for the previously unbearable. This, in and of itself, promoted healing.

The second opportunity was in the processing of patients' traumatic experiences that we engaged in together (not just once but repeatedly), usually as therapeutic 'Monday morning quarterbacking,' but valuable enough since this after-the-fact processing had been so absent in their originating experience, which contributed to the trauma remaining unresolved. In such new processing, I was able to help them recover from the reliving through soothing and regulating, bringing my affective *presence* to our relationship, which provided some healing to the psychical *absence* they had lived with for decades. But, as I fostered recovery from their implicit memory relivings, I realized these were often the only opportunities most therapists and patients found to understand and recuperate from what I came to call the reliving of implicit memory banks "till the next time."

The third opportunity built upon the first two: together, patients and I planned *how* to intervene with their relivings before they occurred at the very point that they anticipated a possible trigger. Comprehending the triggers was not a perfect science, since there was a broad variety of possible triggers that could catch them unawares. We worked to establish intervening strategies that could be effective, physiologically, and emotionally, in helping the patient regulate, as well as behavioral strategies for intervening in the acting out that often accompanied the driven nature of the implicit memory.

There was a great deal of trial and error, success and failure in these interventions, because what seemed workable in the safety of my office and within the calm of our moments together did not necessarily transition into triggered experience. In these failing instances, I needed to function as an empathic and regulating other, withstanding their dismay, and modeling and teaching for their identificatory purposes how to become soothed and make another attempt. Despite the successes we did have, and the obvious rewards of understanding, recovery, and future planning, a tremendous amount of anguish existed for patients when they were unable to prevent their implicit memory response from activating the next time it was triggered. I needed to find additional ways of decoding these 'banks' and create substantial opportunities for intervention.

One day as I was struggling with how to help a patient, I thought of how useful it was for me personally in various circumstances to break large tasks or challenges into much smaller steps. I realized in that moment that while there were times when pre-planning with a patient how to intervene before such a 'bank' was triggered had been somewhat successful, it basically was 'too large' a task. I also was acutely aware of how demoralizing it was for patients when they became swept up again in a reliving despite their best efforts. So, I turned to the actual procedural steps of the implicit memory bank.

I discovered this fourth opportunity within these procedural steps (Erwin, 2005). With my then patient's eager collaboration, we played psychic detective, taking an implicit memory bank and breaking it down into its smallest steps (see and use the Procedural Steps Chart). Once we were fairly sure we had unearthed all the steps and then sequenced them in order, we looked for where transitions occurred between the steps, paying particular attention to the affective/state shifts occurring within that reliving. I came to appreciate why it was so nearly impossible for someone to intervene once they were in the throes of any one of the steps/states, since those state experiences were ripe with overwhelming affect. But in the moments of shift (like a breath), between the steps, where one affect or state shifted into another, there often existed a subtle but noticeable 'exhale' of one affective state before an 'inhale' of another.

I discovered that these were where rich opportunities existed. I realized that if one intervention failed earlier on in a reliving, another transition was just ahead, with its own opportunity for intervention. Subsequently, careful planning for each of these transitions led me and various patients to find that once even one small intervention worked, such success helped them regulate within the transition as well as finding that they could intervene in any acting out that often accompanied their relivings. The success of the following transition opportunities then became exponentially possible.

In the presence of this exquisite and most tender of therapeutic processes, I found the power and the majesty in this creative and healing discovery. Implicit memory banks, traumatized and traumatizing though they may be, hold not only the problem but the *solution* where we thought there was none.

Decoding and intervening with implicit memory 'banks' is the new 'royal road' where previously there have been only problems without solutions. Patients experienced for the first time in their lives both profound relief at how they made what I called "emotional sense" and a renewed belief in themselves (and an eagerness) that they could actually *intervene with* and *change* these internal minefields. Not that this was an easy endeavor. But such new autonoesis (self-knowing) gave my patients the courage to try and try again with me until they were successful.

PLANNING IMPLICIT MEMORY INTERVENTIONS

by

Gwyneth Kerr Erwin, Ph.D., Psy.D.

TRIGGER IN CURRENT TIME:

ORIGINATING TRAUMA:

HOW IT PLAYS OUT IN CURRENT TIME:

HOW IT PLAYS OUT IN THERAPEUTIC RELATIONSHIP:

PROCEDURAL STEP #1	TRANSITIONAL SPACE INTERVENTION	RESULT
PROCEDURAL STEP #2	TRANSITIONAL SPACE INTERVENTION	RESULT
PROCEDURAL STEP #3	TRANSITIONAL SPACE INTERVENTION	RESULT
PROCEDURAL STEP #4	TRANSITIONAL SPACE INTERVENTION	RESULT
PROCEDURAL STEP #5	TRANSITIONAL SPACE INTERVENTION	RESULT
PROCEDURAL STEP #6	TRANSITIONAL SPACE INTERVENTION	RESULT
PROCEDURAL STEP #7	TRANSITIONAL SPACE INTERVENTION	RESULT
PROCEDURAL STEP #8	TRANSITIONAL SPACE INTERVENTION	RESULT
PROCEDURAL STEP #9	TRANSITIONAL SPACE INTERVENTION	RESULT
PROCEDURAL STEP #10	TRANSITIONAL SPACE INTERVENTION	RESULT
PROCEDURAL STEP #11	TRANSITIONAL SPACE INTERVENTION	RESULT
PROCEDURAL STEP #12	TRANSITIONAL SPACE INTERVENTION	RESULT

RECOVERY, FUTURE INTERVENTION PLANNING, NOTES:

References

Aberbach, D. (1989). Creativity and the survivor: The struggle for mastery. *International Review of Psychoanalysis, 16,* 273–285.

Ablon, S.L. (1990). Developmental aspects of self-esteem in the analysis of an 11-year-old boy. *Psychoanalytic Study of the Child, 45,* 337–356.

Ainsworth, M., Blehar, M.C., Waters, E., & Wall, S. (1978). *Patterns of attachment: Assessed in the strange situation and at home.* Hillsdale, NJ: Lawrence Erlbaum.

Amini, F., Lewis, T., Lannon, R., Louie, A., Baumbacher, G., McGuinness, T. & Schiff, E.Z. (1996). Affect, attachment, and memory: Contributions toward psychobiologic integration. *Psychiatry, 59,* 213–239.

Armstrong-Perlman, E.M. (1989). *The allure of the bad object.* Paper presented at The W.R.D. Fairbairn Centennial Conference.

Aron, L. (1991). Working through the past—Working toward the future. *Contemporary Psychoanalysis, 27,* 81–108.

Atwood, G.E., Stolorow, R.D. & Trop, J.L. (1989). Impasses in psychoanalytic therapy—A royal road. *Contemporary Psychoanalysis, 25,* 554–574.

Atwood, G. & Stolorow, R. (1997). Defects in the self: Liberating concept or imprisoning metaphor? *Psychoanalytic Dialogues, 7,* 517–522.

Balint, M. (1936). The final goal of psycho-analytic treatment. *International Journal of Psychoanalysis, 17,* 206–216.

——— (1968). *The basic fault: Therapeutic aspects of regression.* New York: Brunner/Mazel.

——— (1969). Trauma and object relationship. *International Journal of Psychoanalysis, 50*, 429–435.

Beebe, B. & Lachmann, F.M. (2002). *Infant research and adult treatment: Co-constructing interactions.* Hillsdale, NJ; The Analytic Press.

Bergmann, M.V. (1992). An infantile trauma, a trauma during analysis, and their psychic connection. *International Journal of Psychoanalysis, 73*, 447–454.

Bick, E. (1968). The experience of skin in early objects-relations. *International Journal of Psychoanalysis*, 49, 484–486.

Bion, W.R. (1959) Attacks on linking. *International Journal of Psychoanalysis, 40*, 308–315.

——— (1963/1977). Elements of psychoanalysis. In *Seven servants: Four works by Wilfred R. Bion.* New York: Jason Aronson.

Blatt, S. &. Levy, K. (2003). Attachment theory. Psychoanalysis, personality development, and psychopathology. *Psychoanalytic Inquiry, 23*(1), 102150.

Blum, H. (1986). On identification and its vicissitudes. *International Journal of Psychoanalysis, 67*, 267–275.

Bollas, C. (1989). *Forces of Destiny: Psychoanalysis and human idiom.* Northvale, NJ: Jason Aronson, Inc.

Bowlby, J. (1951). *Maternal care and mental health.* Geneva: WHO; London: HMSO; New York: Columbia University Press.

——— (1958). The nature of the child's tie to his mother. *International Journal of Psychoanalysis, 39*, 350–373.

——— (1959). Separation anxiety. *International Journal of Psychoanalysis, 41*, 89–113.

——— (1960). Grief and mourning in infancy and early childhood. *Psychoanalytic Study of the Child, 15*, 9–52.

——— (1969). *Attachment and loss, Vol. 1.* London: Hogarth Press.

Brazelton, T.B. & Cramer, B. (1990). *The earliest relationship.* New York: Addison Wesley.

Breuer, J. & Freud, S. (1889/1955). On the psychical mechanism of hysterical phenomena: Preliminary communication. In J. Strachey (Ed. and Trans.), *Standard edition of the complete psychological works of Sigmund Freud* (Vol. II). London: The Hogarth Press.

Brierley, M. (1937). Affects in theory and practice. *International Journal of Psychoanalysis, 18,* 256–268.

Bromberg, P. (1991). On knowing one's patient inside and out: The aesthetics of unconscious communication. *Psychoanalytic Dialogues, 1,* 399–422.

——— (1994). Speak! That I may see you: Some reflections on dissociation, reality, and psychoanalytic listening. *Psychoanalytic Dialogues, 4,* 517–547.

——— (1995). Resistance, object-usage, and human relatedness. *Contemporary Psychoanalysis, 31*(2), 173–191.

——— (1996/1998). Standing in the spaces: The multiplicity of self and the psychoanalytic relationship. *Standing in the spaces: Essays on clinical process, trauma & dissociation.* Hillsdale, NJ: The Analytic Press.

——— (1998). Staying the same while changing: Reflections on critical judgment. *Psychoanalytic Dialogues, 8,* 225–236.

Broucek, F.J. (1982). Shame and its relationship to early narcissistic development. *International Journal of Psychoanalysis, 63,* 369–378.

——— (1991). *Shame and the self.* New York: The Guilford Press.

Brown, R. & Herrnstein, R.J. (1975). *Psychology.* Boston, Massachusetts: Little, Brown.

Carter, R. (1998). *Mapping the mind.* Berkeley, CA: University of California Press.

Chomsky, N. (1980). *Rules and representations.* New York: Columbia University Press.

Chu, J.A. (1998). *Rebuilding shattered lives: The responsible treatment of complex post-traumatic and dissociative disorders.* New York: John Wiley & Sons, Inc.

Cicchetti, D. & Toth, S. (1995). Child maltreatment and attachment organization: Implications for intervention. In S. Goldberg, R. Muir, & J. Kerr (Eds.), *Attachment theory: Social, developmental, and clinical perspectives* (pp. 279–308). Hillsdale, NJ: The Analytic Press.

Cleveland Clinic. (2018). *Reactive attachment disorder (RAD)*. Cleveland, OH: Cleveland Clinic Foundation.

Coates, S.W. & Moore, M.S. (1997). The complexity of early trauma: Representation and transformation. *Psychoanalytic Inquiry, 17*, 286–311.

Crain, W. (2000). *Theories of development: Concepts and applications* (4th ed.). NJ: Prentice-Hall.

Damasio, A. (1999). *The feeling of what happens: Body and emotion in the making of consciousness*. New York: Harcourt Brace & Company.

——— (2021). *Feeling & knowing: Making minds conscious*. New York: Pantheon.

Darwin, C. (1872/1965). *The expression of the emotions in man and animals*. Chicago: University of Chicago Press.

Davies, J.M. & Frawley, M.G. (1994). *Treating the adult survivor of childhood sexual Abuse: A psychoanalytic perspective*. New York: Basic Books.

Demos, V. (1986). Crying in early infancy: An illustration of the motivational function of affect. In T. B. Brazelton & M.W. Yogman (Eds.). *Affective development in infancy* (pp. 39–73). Norwood, NJ: Ablex Publication Corporation.

Diagnostic and Statistical Manual of Mental Disorders (DSM-5). (2013). Arlington, VA: American Psychiatric Association.

Edgcrumbe, R.M. (1981). Toward a developmental line for the acquisition of language. *Psychoanalytic Study of the Child, 36*, 71–103.

Emde, R. (1983). The prerepresentational self and its affective core. *Psychoanalytic Study of the Child, 38*, 165–192.

Erwin, G.K. (2000). *The Cherished wound: Theoretical and treatment implications for identification with unresolved trauma.* [Certification paper]. Tustin, CA: Newport Psychoanalytic Institute.

——— (2001). Instructor of developmental theories. Newport Psychoanalytic Institute. Tustin, California.

——— (2003). Instructor of developmental theories. Newport Psychoanalytic Institute. Tustin, California.

——— (2005). *The cherished wound: Theoretical and treatment implications for identification with unresolved trauma.* [Doctoral dissertation, Newport Psychoanalytic Institute at Tustin, CA].

——— (2011). Weather: A poetic psychoanalytic essay. *Psychoanalytic Perspectives 8*, 117–120.

Fairbairn, W.R D. (1954). Observations on the nature of hysterical states. *British Journal of Medical Psychology*, 27, 105–125.

Ferenczi, S. (1909/1952). Introjection and transference. In E. Jones (Trans.), *First contributions to psychoanalysis* (pp. 35–93). New York: Brunner/ Mazel, Publishers.

——— (1932). Confusion of tongues between adults and the child. In M. Balint (Ed.), *Final contributions to the problems and methods of psychoanalysis* (pp. 156–167). New York: Brunner/Mazel, Publishers.

Fiscalini, J. (1988). Curative experience in the analytic relationship. *Contemporary Psychoanalysis, 24*, 125–142.

Fisher, J. (2021). *Transforming the living legacy of trauma: A workbook for survivors and therapists.* Eau Claire, WI: PESI Publishing & Media.

Fonagy, P. (1999). Points of contact and divergence between psychoanalytic and attachment theories. *Psychoanalytic Inquiry, 19*, 448–480.

———, Gergely, G., Jurist, E.L., & Target, M. (2002). *Affect regulation, mentalization, and the development of the self.* New York: Other Press.

Fraiberg, S. (1982). Pathological defenses in infancy. *Psychoanalytic Quarterly*, 51, 612–635.

Frankel, S. (2000). *Hidden faults: Recognizing and resolving therapeutic disjunctions.* Madison, Connecticut: Psychosocial Press (International Universities Press).

——— (2001). New and creative development through psychoanalysis. *Contemporary Psychoanalysis, 37*(4), 523–550.

——— (2005). *Making psychotherapy work: Collaborating effectively with your patient.* Madison, Connecticut: Psychosocial Press (International Universities Press).

Freud, A. (1936/1966). *The ego and the mechanisms of defense* (rev. ed.). Madison, CT: International Universities Press.

Freud, S. (1892–1899/1955). Extracts from the Fleiss papers 1950. In J. Strachey (Ed. and Trans.). *Standard edition of the complete psychological works of Sigmund Freud.* Vol. I. London: The Hogarth Press.

——— (1895/1955). The psychotherapy of hysteria. In J. Strachey (Ed. and Trans.). *Standard edition of the complete psychological works of Sigmund Freud.* Vol. II. London: The Hogarth Press.

——— (1896/1955). Further remarks on the neuro-psychoses of defence. In J. Strachey (Ed. and Trans.). *The complete psychological works of Sigmund Freud.* Vol III. London: The Hogarth Press.

——— (1897/1954). Letter 58. In M. Bonaparte, A. Freud, & E. Kris (Eds.), *The Origins of Psycho-Analysis. Letters to William Fleiss, Drafts and Notes: 1887–1902.* New York: Basic Books.

——— (1898/1955). Sexuality in the aetiology of the neuroses. In J. Strachey (Ed. and Trans.). *Standard edition of the complete psychological works of Sigmund Freud.* Vol. III. London: The Hogarth Press.

——— (1900/1955). The interpretation of dreams. In J. Strachey (Ed. and Trans.). *Standard edition of the complete psychological works of Sigmund Freud.* Vol. IV–V. London: The Hogarth Press.

——— (1905/1955). Three essays on the theory of sexuality. In J. Strachey (Ed. and Trans.). *Standard edition of the complete psychological works of Sigmund Freud.* Vol. VII. London: The Hogarth Press.

——— (1910/1955). The future prospects of psychoanalytic theory. In J. Strachey (Ed. and Trans.). *Standard edition of the complete psychological works of Sigmund Freud.* Vol. XI. London: The Hogarth Press.

——— (1914/1955). Remembering, repeating, and working through. In J. Strachey (Ed. and Trans.). *Standard edition of the complete psychological works of Sigmund Freud.* Vol. XII. London: The Hogarth Press.

——— (1915/1955). Instincts and their vicissitudes. In J. Strachey (Ed. and Trans.). *Standard edition of the complete psychological works of Sigmund Freud.* Vol. XIV. London: The Hogarth Press.

——— (1921/1955). Group psychology and the analysis of the ego. In J. Strachey (Ed. and Trans.). *Standard edition of the complete psychological works of Sigmund Freud.* Vol. XVIII. London: The Hogarth Press.

——— (1923/1955). The ego and the id. In J. Strachey (Ed. and Trans.). *Standard edition of the complete psychological works of Sigmund Freud.* Vol. XIX. London: The Hogarth Press.

——— (1926/1936). *The problem of anxiety.* New York: W.W. Norton & Company. Fromm-Reichmann, F. (1990). Loneliness. *Contemporary Psychoanalysis, 26,* 305–330.

——— & Breuer, J. (1893/1955). On the psychical mechanism of hysterical phenomena: Preliminary communication from studies on hysteria. In J. Strachey (Ed. And Trans.). *Standard edition of the complete psychological works of Sigmund Freud.* Vol. II. London: The Hogarth Press.

Gaensbauer, T.J. (1995). Trauma in the preverbal period. *Psychoanalytic Study of the Child, 50,* 122–149.

Greenacre, P. (1965). Infantile Trauma. *Psychoanalytic Quarterly,* 34, 168–149.

Greenspan, S. (1995). The challenging child: Understanding, raising, and enjoying the five 'difficult' types of children. Reading, MA: A Merloyd Lawrence Book/Addison-Wesley Publishing Company, Inc.

——— (1997a). *The infancy and early childhood training course.* Children's Hospital, Los Angeles, California.

——— (1997b). *Developmentally based psychotherapy.* Madison, Connecticut: International Universities Press.

——— (1999). *Building healthy minds: The six experiences that create intelligence and emotional growth in babies and young children.* Cambridge, Massachusetts: Perseus Books.

Hacker, D. & Sommers, N. (2021). *A writer's reference: Tenth edition.* Boston, Massachusetts: Bedford/St. Martin's Press.

Hebb, D.O. (1949). *The organization of behavior: A neuropsychological theory.* New York: Wiley.

Heimann, P. (1950). On counter-transference. *International Journal of Psycho-analysis,31,* 81–85.

Herman, J. (1992). *Trauma and recovery.* New York: Basic Books.

Hesse, E. (1996). Discourse, memory, and the Adult Attachment Interview: A note with emphasis on the emerging cannot classify category. *Infant Mental Health Journal, 17,* 4–11.

——— & Main, M. (2000). Disorganized infant, child, and adult attachment: Collapse in behavioral and attentional strategies. *Journal of the American Psychoanalytic Association, 48,* 1097–1127.

Holmes, J. (2001). *The search for the secure base: Attachment theory and psychotherapy.* New York: Brunner-Routledge.

Hopper, E. (1991). Encapsulation as a defence against the fear of annihilation. *International Journal of Psychoanalysis, 72,* 607–624.

Horney, K. (1945). *Our inner conflicts: A constructive theory of neurosis.* New York: W.W. Norton & Company.

——— (1950). *Neurosis and human growth: The struggle toward self-realization*. New York: W.W. Norton & Company.

Inderbitzin, L.B. & Levy, S.T. (1998). Repetition compulsion revisited: Implications for technique. *Psychoanalytic Quarterly, 67*, 32–53.

International Classification of Diseases.9.CM. (2005). Los Angeles, CA: Practice Management Information.

Izard, C. (1977). *Human emotions*. New York: Plenum Press.

Jacobson, E. (1964). *The self and the object world*. New York: International Universities Press.

James, M. (1960). Premature ego development. Some observations on disturbances in the first three months of life. *International Journal of Psychoanalysis, 41*, 288–294.

James, B. (1989). *Treating traumatized children: New insights and creative interventions*. New York: The Free Press.

Khan, M.M. (1963). The concept of cumulative trauma. *Psychoanalytic Study of the Child, 18*, 286–306.

Klein, M. (1932). The technique of early analysis. *The Psychoanalysis of Children, 22*:40–64.

Knapp, P.H. (1987). Some contemporary contributions to the study of emotions. *Journal of the American Psychoanalytic Association*, 35, 205–248.

Koch, E. (2000). Representations of dread: The dreaded self and the dreaded state of the self. *Psychoanalytic Quarterly, LXIX(2)*, 289–316.

Kohut, H. (1972). Thoughts on narcissism and narcissistic rage. *Psychoanalytic Study of the Child, 27*, 360–400.

——— (1977). *The restoration of the self*. New York: International Universities Press.

——— & Wolf, E. (1978). The disorders of the self and their treatment: An outline. *International Journal of Psychoanalysis*, 59, 413–425.

Kotulak, R. (1996). *Inside the brain: Revolutionary discoveries of how the mind works.* Kansas City: Andrews and McMeel/A Universal Press Syndicate Company.

Kovar, L. (1994). Freud's legacy—The laying on of words. *Contemporary Psychoanalysis, 30,* 522–575.

Krupp, G. R. (1965). Identification as a defence against anxiety in coping with loss. *International Journal of Psychoanalysis, 46,* 303–314.

Kumin, I. (1989). The incorrect interpretation. *International Journal of Psychoanalysis, 70,* 141–152.

Kurtz, S. A. (1984). On silence. *Psychoanalytic Review,* 71:227–245.

Lachmann, F.M. (1996). How many selves make a person? *Contemporary Psychoanalysis,* 32, 595–614.

Lachmann, F.M. & Lichtenberg, J. (1992). Model scenes: Implications for psychoanalytic treatment. *Journal of the American Psychoanalytic Association, 40,* 117–137.

Lansky, M. (1999). Shame and the idea of a central affect. *Psychoanalytic Inquiry, 19*(3), 347–361.

LaPlanche, J. & Pontalis, J.B. (1973). *The language of psycho-analysis.* New York: W.W. Norton & Company, Inc.

LeDoux, J. (1996). *The emotional brain.* New York: Simon and Schuster.

Levine, P. (2015). *Trauma and memory: Brain and body in a search for the living past.* Berkeley, CA: North Atlantic Books.

Lewis, M. (1992, 1995). *Shame: The exposed self.* New York: The Free Press.

Lichtenberg, J. (1975). The development of the sense of self. *Journal of the American Psychoanalytic Association,* 23, 459–490.

Lichtenstein, H. (1961). Identity and sexuality—A study of their interrelationship in man. *Journal of the American Psychoanalytic Association,* 9, 179–260.

——— (1963). The dilemma of human identity—Notes on self-transformation, self-objectivation, and metamorphosis. *Journal of the American Psychoanalytic Association, 11*, 173–223.

Lillas, C. (1994/1996). *The arousal chart*. Instructor, Infant Observation. Newport Psychoanalytic Institute. Orange, California.

——— (1996). Personal communication.

——— (2005). Personal communication.

——— & Turnbull, J. (2009). *Infant/child mental health, early intervention, and relationship-based therapies: A neurorelational framework for interdisciplinary practice*. New York: W.W. Norton & Company.

Lindy, J. (1996). Psychoanalytic psychotherapy of posttraumatic stress disorder: The nature of the therapeutic relationship. In B. A. van der Kolk, A. C. McFarlane, & L. Weisaeth (Eds.), *Traumatic stress: The effects of overwhelming experience on mind, body, and society*. New York: The Guilford Press.

Lingardi, V. & McWilliams, N. (Eds.). (2017). P*sychodynamic diagnostic manual*. Second Edition. New York: The Guilford Press.

Lyons-Ruth, K. (1998). Implicit relational knowing: Its role in development and psychoanalytic treatment. *Infant Mental Health Journal, 19*, 282–289.

——— (1999). The two-person unconscious. *Psychoanalytic Inquiry, 19*, 576–617.

——— (2001). The two-person construction of defenses: Disorganized attachment strategies. Unintegrated mental states and hostile/helpless relational processes. *Psychologist Psychoanalyst, XXI*, 40–45.

Main, M. See under Hesse & Main (2000).

Malin, B. (1999). The role of affect integration and regulation in disorders of the self. *Psychoanalytic Inquiry, 19*(3), 373 –387).

Maté, G. (2003). *When the body says no*. Canada: Alfred A. Knopf and (2011) Hoboken, NJ: John Wiley & Sons, Inc.

Mayo Clinic. (2022). *Reactive attachment disorder.* Rochester, MN: Mayo Foundation for Medical Education and Research (MFMER).

McDougall, J. (1978). Primitive communication and the use of countertransference—Reflections on early psychic trauma and its transference effects. *Contemporary Psychoanalysis, 14,* 173–210.

McWilliams, N. (1994/2020). *Psychoanalytic diagnosis: Understanding personality structure in the clinical process.* Second Edition. New York: The Guilford Press.

Meissner, W.W. (1970). Notes on identification i: Origins in Freud. *Psychoanalytic Quarterly, 39,* 563–589.

——— (1971). Notes on identification ii: Clarification of related concepts. *Psychoanalytic Quarterly, 40,* 277–302.

——— (1972). Notes on identification iii: The concept of identification. *Psychoanalytic Quarterly, 41,* 224–260.

——— (1976). A note on internalization as process. *Psychoanalytic Quarterly, 45,* 374–392.

——— (1979). Internalization and object relations. *Journal of the American Psychoanalytic Association, 27,* 345–360.

——— (1992). The concept of the therapeutic alliance. *Journal of the American Psychoanalytic Association, 40,* 1059–1087.

——— (2000). On analytic listening. *Psychoanalytic Quarterly, LXIX*(2), 317–367.

Milkman, H. & Sunderwirth, S. (1987). *Craving for ecstasy: How our passions become addictions and what we can do about them.* San Francisco: Jossey-Bass Publishers/John Wiley & Sons.

Mitchell, S. (1991). Contemporary perspectives on self: Toward an integration. *Psychoanalytic Dialogues, 1,* 121–147.

——— (1993). *Hope and dread in psychoanalysis.* New York: Basic Books.

Modell, A.H. (1991). Resistance to the exposure of the private self. *Contemporary Psychoanalysis, 27,* 731–737.

Nacht, S. (1963). The non-verbal relationship in psychoanalytic treatment. *International Journal of Psychoanalysis, 44*, 334–339.

Nathanson, D.L. (1986). The empathic wall and the ecology of affect. *Psychoanalytic Study of the Child, 41*, 171–187.

New Oxford American College Dictionary. (2002). New York: G.P. Putnam & Sons.

Nilsson, L. & Hamburger, L. (1990). *A child is born*. New York: Delacorte Press/Seymour Lawrence.

Novick, J. & Novick, K.K. (1991). Some comments on masochism and the delusion of omnipotence from a developmental perspective. *Journal of the American Psychoanalytic Association, 39*, 307–331.

Novick, K.K. (1990). Access to infancy: Different ways of remembering. *International Journal of Psychoanalysis, 71*, 335–348.

Ornstein, A. (1985). Survival and recovery. *Psychoanalytic Inquiry, 5*, 99–130. Ornstein, A. (1998). The fate of narcissistic rage in psychotherapy. *Psychoanalytic Inquiry, 18*, 55–70.

Paolino, T.J. (1982). The therapeutic relationship in psychoanalysis. *Contemporary Psychoanalysis, 18*, 218–235.

Papousek, H. & Papousek, M. (1975). Cognitive aspects of preverbal social interaction between human infants and adults. *Ciba Foundation Symposium Parent-Infant Interaction*. New York: Association of Scientific Publications.

Parish, M. & Eagle, M.N. (2003). Attachment to the therapist. *Psychoanalytic Psychology, 20*(2), 271–286.

Perry, B.D., Pollard, R. A., Blakley, T.L., Baker, W.L., & Vigilante, D. (1995). Childhood Trauma, the neurobiology of adaptation, and "use-dependent" development of the brain: How states become traits. *Infant Mental Health Journal, 16*, 271–291.

Plutchik, R. (1962). *The emotions: Facts, theory, and a new model*. New York: Random House.

Poland, W. (1986). The analyst's words. *Psychoanalytic Quarterly, 55*, 244–272.

——— (2000). The analyst's witnessing and otherness. *Journal of the American Psychoanalytic Association, 48*(1), 17–34.

Pollack, G.H. (1977). The mourning process and creative organizational change. *Journal of the American Psychoanalytic Association, 25*, 3–34.

Porges, S.W., Doussard-Roosevelt, J.A., & Maiti, A.K. (1994). Vagal tone and the physiological regulation of emotion. In N.A. Fox (Ed.). The development of emotion regulation: Biological and behavioral considerations. *Monographs of the Society for Research in Child Development, 59*(2–3, Serial No. 240), 167–188.

Post, R.M. & Weiss, S.R.B. (1997). Emergent properties of neural systems: How focal molecular neurobiological alterations can affect behavior. *Development and Psychopathology, 9*, 907–930.

Putnam, F. (1997). *Dissociation in children and adolescents: A developmental perspective*. New York: The Guilford Press.

Renik, O. (1999). Playing one's cards face up: An approach to the problem of self-disclosure. *Psychoanalytic Quarterly 68*: 521–539.

Ribble, M. (1943). *The rights of infants*. New York: Columbia University Press.

Richards, A. (2018). Some thoughts on self-disclosure. *Psychoanalytic Review, 105*(2); 137–156.

Riess, A. (1988). The power of the eye in nature, nurture, and culture—A developmental view of mutual gaze (1). *Psychoanalytic Study of the Child, 43*, 399–418.

Rose, G.J. (1996). *Trauma and mastery in life and art*. Madison, Connecticut: International Universities Press.

Rubens, R. (1994). Fairbairn's structural theory. In J.S. Grotstein & D.B. Rinsley (Eds.), *Fairbairn and the origin of object relations*. New York: The Guilford Press.

Sander, L.W. (2002). Thinking differently: Principles of process in living systems and the specificity of being known. *Psychoanalytic Dialogues, 12*(1), 11–42.

Schafer, R. (1980). Action language and the psychology of the self. *Annual of Psychoanalysis, 8,* 83–92.

Schore, A. (1994). *Affect regulation and the origin of the self: The neurobiology of emotional development.* Hillsdale, NJ: Lawrence Erlbaum Associates.

——— (1996). The experience-dependent maturation of a regulatory system in the orbital prefrontal cortex and the origin of developmental psychopathology. *Development and Psychopathology, 8,* 59–87.

——— (1997). Spring Conference. Newport Psychoanalytic Institute. March, 1997. Newport Beach, CA.

——— (2003a). *Affect dysregulation and disorders of the self.* New York: W.W. Norton & Company.

——— (2003b). *Affect regulation and the repair of the self.* New York: W.W. Norton & Company.

Schwaber, E.A. (1992). Countertransference: The analyst's retreat from the patient's vantage point. *International Journal of Psychoanalysis, 73,* 349361.

Schwartz, A. (2020). *A practical guide to complex PTSD: Compassionate strategies to begin healing from childhood trauma.* Emeryville, CA: Rockridge Press.

Schwartz, H.L. (1994). From dissociation to negotiation: A relational psychoanalytic perspective on multiple personality disorder. *Psychoanalytic Psychology, 11*(2), 189–231.

Schwartz, R. (2021). *No bad parts: Healing trauma and restoring wholeness with the internal family systems model.* Boulder, CO: Sounds True Publishing.

Seligman, S. (1999). Integrating Kleinian theory and intersubjective infant research. Observing projective identification. *Psychoanalytic Dialogues,* 9(2), 129–159.

Shabad, P. (1987). Fixation and the road not taken. *Psychoanalytic Psychology, 4*(3), 187–205.

——— (1993). Repetition and incomplete mourning: The intergenerational transmission of traumatic themes. *Psychoanalytic Psychology, 10*(1), 61–75.

——— (1997). Trauma and innocence. *Contemporary Psychoanalysis, 33,* 345–366.

Shaw, D. (2003). On the therapeutic action of analytic love. *Contemporary Psychoanalysis, 39*(2), 251–278).

Shengold, L. (1978). Assault on a child's individuality: A kind of soul murder. *Psychoanalytic Quarterly,* 47, 419–424.

——— (1979). Child abuse and deprivation soul murder. *Journal of the American Psychoanalytic Association, 27,* 533–559.

Siegel, D.J. (1999). *The developing mind: Toward a neurobiology of interpersonal experience.* New York: The Guilford Press.

——— (2003). An interpersonal neurobiology of psychotherapy: The developing mind and the resolution of trauma. In M.F. Solomon & D.J. Siegel (Eds.), *Healing trauma: Attachment, mind, body, and brain.* New York: W.W. Norton & Company.

Silverman, M. (1986). Identification in healthy and pathological character formation. *International Journal of Psychoanalysis, 67,* 181–190.

Slavin, M.O. & Kriegman, D. (1998). Why the analyst needs to change: Toward a theory of conflict, negotiation, and mutual influence in the therapeutic process. *Psychoanalytic Dialogues, 8,* 247–284.

Smith, N.A. (2001). Angels in the architecture: A contemporary case of orphic functioning. *Journal of the American Academy of Psychoanalysis, 29*(4), 575–583.

Stechler, G. (1982). The dawn of awareness. *Psychoanalytic Inquiry, 1,* 503532.

Stechler, G. & Kaplan, S. (1980). The development of the self — A psychoanalytic perspective. *Psychoanalytic Study of the Child, 35,* 85–105.

Stern, D. (1985). *The interpersonal world of the infant: A View from Psychoanalysis and Developmental Psychology.* New York: Basic Books.

Stern, D.N., Sander, L.W., Nahum, J.P., Harrison, A.M., Lyons-Ruth, K., Morgan, A.C., Bruschweilerstern, N., & Tronick, E. (1998). Non-interpretive mechanisms in psychoanalytic therapy: The 'something more' than interpretation. *International Journal of Psychoanalysis, 79,* 903–921.

Stern, M.M. (1951). Anxiety, trauma, and shock. *Psychoanalytic Quarterly, 20,* 179–203.

Symington, J. (1985). The survival function of primitive omnipotence. *International Journal of Psychoanalysis, 66,* 481–486.

Symington, N. (1986). *The analytic experience.* New York: St. Martin's Press.

——— (1996). The patient makes the analyst. *Psychoanalytic Inquiry, 16,* 362–375.

Tompkins, S. (1962). *Affect, imagery, consciousness: Vol. 1. The positive affects.* New York: Springer.

——— (1978). Script theory: Differential magnification of affects. *Nebraska Symposium on Motivation, 26,* 201–236.

Trevarthen, C. (1993). The function of emotions in early infant communication and development. In J. Nadel and L. Camioni (Eds.), *New perspectives in early infant communicative development.* London: Routledge.

Tronick, E. (1989). Emotions and emotional communication in infants. *American Psychologist, 44*(2), 112–119.

Valenstein, A.F. (1973). On attachment to painful feelings and the negative therapeutic reaction. *Psychoanalytic Study of the Child, 28,* 365–392.

van der Kolk, B. (1987). *Psychological trauma.* Washington, DC: American Psychiatric Press, Inc.

——— (1996). Trauma and memory. In B.A. van der Kolk, A.C. McFarlane, & L. Weisaeth (Eds.). *Traumatic stress: The effects of overwhelming experience on mind, body, and society.* (pp. 279–302). New York: The Guilford Press.

——— (2002). Posttraumatic therapy in the age of neuroscience. *Psychoanalytic Dialogues, 12*, 381–392.

——— (2014). *The body keeps the score: Brain, mind, and body in the healing of trauma*. New York: Penguin Books.

——— (2019). *Developmental trauma disorder: Towards a rational diagnosis for children with complex trauma histories*. Pre-publication.

——— & Fisler, R.E. (1994). Childhood abuse and neglect and loss of self-regulation. *Bulletin of the Menninger Clinic, 58*, 145–168.

——— & McFarlane, A. (1996). The black hole of trauma. In B. A. van der Kolk, A.C. McFarlane, & L. Weisaeth, L. (Eds.), *Traumatic stress: The effects of overwhelming experience on mind, body, and society*. (pp. 3–23). New York: The Guilford Press.

Viederman, M. (1991). The real person of the analyst and his role in the process of psychoanalytic cure. *Journal of the American Psychoanalytic Association, 39*, 451–489.

Wagner, J.C. (1992). Personal communication.

——— (2001). Personal communication.

Weiss, J. & Sampson, H., & the Mount Zion Psychotherapy Research Group. (1986). *The psychoanalytic process: Theory, clinical observations, and empirical research*. New York: The Guilford Press.

Whitmer, G. (2001). On the nature of dissociation. *Psychoanalytic Quarterly, LXX*(4), 807–837.

Wigren, J. (1999). As hardly killed, as easily wounded: Posttraumatic challenges to the working alliance. *Contemporary Psychoanalysis, 35*(2), 253–269.

Winnicott, D.W. (1935/1975). The manic defence. *Through paediatrics to psycho-analysis*. New York: Basic Books.

——— (1949/1975). The mind and its relation to the psyche-soma. *Through paediatrics to psycho-analysis*. New York: Basic Books.

——— (1955–6/1975). The clinical varieties of transference. *Through paediatrics to psycho-analysis*. New York: Basic Books.

——— (1958/1965). The capacity to be alone. *The maturational processes and the facilitating environment*. Madison, Connecticut: International Universities Press, Inc.

——— (1960a/1965). Ego distortion in terms of true and false self. *The maturational processes and the facilitating environment*. Madison, Connecticut: International Universities Press, Inc.

——— (1960b/1965). The theory of the parent-infant relationship. *The maturational processes and the facilitating environment*. Madison, Connecticut: International Universities Press, Inc.

——— (1974). Fear of breakdown. *The International Review of Psychoanalysis, 1*, 103–107.

Wolf, D.P. (1990). Being of several minds: Voices and versions of the self in early childhood. In D. Cicchetti & M. Beeghly (Eds.), *The self in transition: Infancy to childhood* (pp. 183–212). Chicago: University of Chicago Press.

Yorke, C. et al. (1990). The development and functioning of the sense of shame. *Psychoanalytic Study of the Child, 45*, 377–400.

Acknowledgements

For me, life is about *showing up*: with one's own presence and within one's community. Showing up involves paradox: the paradox of individuality and of belonging, the paradox of prudence and of generosity, the paradox of respect for others and of standing upon one's own values, the paradox of sacrifice and of love. I thank all those in my community, close up and far flung, for showing up for me.

I find the practice of contemporary psychoanalysis to be a profound privilege, so I thank my patients for inviting me into that most intimate experience of their psychological worlds and sharing with me their struggles, yearnings, and strivings. I am especially indebted to Will and Julia each of whom influenced me and changed me, as much as I may have them.

My heartfelt appreciation: to the faculty of Newport Psychoanalytic Institute who fed my enquiring mind to the brim during my analytic training and to the many outstanding theoretical thinkers who shared their knowledge and hard-won experience; to my supervisors for guiding my nascent uncertain steps into those of confidence, modeling for me the willingness always to learn from my patients; to my colleagues and students, thank you for opening your minds and hearts to me. To Ray Calabrese, dear friend and my personal CFO, thank you for helping me navigate the financial shoals of life. Dr. Steven Frankel and I shared weekly conversations for five years, discussing clinical formulations and written work, his and mine. He gave me the courage *not* to know and to discover. He has inspired me on the path to co-creation between patient and analyst that produces the most profound creative development for both. Steve, thank you for your many ways of collaborating and for being such a wonderful friend. Dr. Connie Lillas, mentor, your warm heart and knowledge gave direction and authority to my life-long interest in early human development. Noel Riley Fitch, my most instrumental writing guide, thank you for being my champion at a most significant time in my creative career. Dr. Jane Clifton Wagner, who encouraged me, challenged me, and cared for me over and around all the rocks in the road of my most personal journey.

To the family of my beginning:

To my mother, Laura Nowak Kerr, who, while fulfilling the hefty mid-1900s' requirements of wife and mother of four, managed between our school hours of 9-3 to author into publication ten books, most of which are still available on Amazon. To one of my mother's closest friends, Jene Barr, children's book author, who recognized something in me as a young child and named it "creative," offering me an early hint of cherishing it. To my beloved grandmother, Anna Fortiner Nowak, who is still one of the greatest influences in my life, for bringing me into the magical world of nature, books, and words. To my father, William Dodge Kerr, who modeled his creative nature and care as an eminently successful financial expert, paving the way for the prosperity of many, while consistently reminding me I could achieve whatever I put my mind to. To my brother, Dr. Bill Kerr, who literally saved my life twice, for showing me what it takes in the toughest of times and that there can be happy endings to such times. To my sister, Jackie Dye, who loved me from the beginning and who was a significant support in my childhood. To my sister, Nancy Carroll, for her friendship. To my niece, Lisa Carroll, who I first held in my arms when I was fifteen years old and discovered what it was like to fall into 'mommy-love'. We share the rare delight of growing together ever since in a deep and abiding bond.

I am most fortunate indeed to have treasured friends who never fail to show up.

Jeanie Ardell, my writing buddy, thank you for helping to keep alive my writer's self, even when there were stretches of time when I spent our time together lamenting being unable to write because of other compelling life requirements. With your helpful and honest feedback, you are a great playmate in our writing sandbox!

Minette and Ken Carter have been wonderful friends for forty-five years. We have shared in life's worst tragedies and greatest joys and found grace and hope together. Thank you for sharing rollicking good humor, intelligence, companionship, and all that life brings.

Alitta Kullman, you have always taken my mind seriously and challenged me to do the same. Even better is the friendship we have forged. For all the reasons we both know, my true gratitude.

Jen Shakti, artist and Shaman. Without your skills and encouragement, my YouTube Channel would not have come into being. Even more than contributing to my internet presence, thank you for your artistic and sublime energy, schooling me in nuanced healing arts while restoring me through the challenging and final stages of my husband's illness.

Jane Schichi, fine artist, came into my life as an illustrator for the children's books we create. We became the most precious of friends. We are alternately each other's Lucy and Ethel, Grace and Frankie, yin and yang. Every day, Jane, whether we are talking about anything that springs to mind, spirit, and soul, or celebrating and creating art, you are an artist of enduring support and friendship, gracing me with their boundless rewards.

To two particularly special men without whom this book would not exist: Dr. Jay Martin, thank you for opening a new door to my creativity and gently but resolutely nudging me across the threshold; and Rabbi K'vod Wieder, thank you for inspiring my hands in writing black fire and beckoning and protecting the spirit of my white fire.

To my creative champions: Dr. Arnold Richards, Editor-in-Chief of International Psychoanalytic Books, who captured my vision and embraced it. Dr. Lawrence Schwartz and Tamar Schwartz, who shared in that vision and brought it into such beautiful realization. You have been fundamentally instrumental in helping my dream come true. Noel Morado, who brought elegance, accessibility, and ease of reading onto every page. Lyn Walker and Linda Lyman of Graphic Productions, who gathered my ideas and my words into the design and fulfillment of my brand, my website, and online courses, and this book's covers. You are wizards of the highest order! Heather Stephens, and her Wise Owl Marketing, for her (endless) patience and encouragement in taking me into the deep dive of a formidable world, and my cohorts in the GMM and GLAC groups for providing me with "floaties!"

To my created family:

I will refrain from embarrassing my now adult children with my sentimental nature and relieve them and these pages of streams of tears. Kudos, kids, for surviving being the children of two psychoanalysts and for doing homework side by side with me all those years. Brit, Dawn, Autumn, and Jeremy, you are my joy and inspiration. Being your mother is the gift of my lifetime.

To my sprouted family: Adam, Dawn's husband, a son-in-law who is really a son, and their children, my grandson Liam and his Cypris, soon-to-be new granddaughter (in law), my granddaughter Bella, and grandsons Eli and Ozi; Tyson, Autumn's husband, also a son (in law), and their daughter, my granddaughter Olivia, all of whom teach me continuously the richness and magic of creativity, theirs and mine. You each captured my heart and moved right in to stay forever; and Royden, dear one, who became a treasured member of our family.

And then, there is Bill. Many knew him as Co-Founder and Dean of Newport Psychoanalytic Institute, Psychoanalyst, Supervisor, Teacher, and Friend. To us, he was Husband, Dad and Grandfather (Deda) and the kindest, and perhaps, quirkiest man we have ever had grace our lives. I came to know him on one date and married him ten days later. In the forty-four years of our never-ending love, we built a strong and lively village together, rich in creativity and collegiality, enduring friendships, with our beautiful children and grandchildren. Pretty good, huh. I love you.

Thank you, all.

About the Author

Dr. Gwyn Erwin, contemporary developmental psychoanalyst, dedicates her professional life to healing through psychodynamic and creative processes. An expert in human development and working with trauma, Gwyn works with individuals, couples, families, children, and adolescents, serving as a therapeutic and creative partner in measurably improving patients' quality of life.

Dr. Erwin is Past President of the Newport Center for Psychoanalytic Studies and its Training Division, the Newport Psychoanalytic Institute. As a faculty member at NPI, she has taught a variety of didactic courses and Case Conferences, including the Developmental Courses, which she designed, in addition to the clinical writing and dissertation classes. She has also served as an adjunct Faculty member at ICP and LAISPS in Los Angeles.

Born in Chicago, Illinois, she earned her Master in Professional Writing from the University of Southern California (double major in non-fiction and fiction). As a professional writer, book doctor, and editor of twenty-five years, she conducts private professional writing groups and is a dissertation consultant at a number of graduate schools and psychoanalytic training institutes. An articulate and vibrant speaker, Gwyn Erwin is often a contributing presenter at both analytic and writing conferences.

She is a Member of Division 39 of the American Psychological Association, the Newport Center for Psychoanalytic Studies, the Association for Autonomous Psychoanalytic Institutes, and the American Counseling Association.

www.ingramcontent.com/pod-product-compliance
Lightning Source LLC
Chambersburg PA
CBHW052107030426
42335CB00025B/2878

* 9 7 8 1 9 5 6 8 6 4 2 7 4 *